THE COMPETITIVE CONSULTANT

The Competitive Consultant

A Client-Oriented Approach for Achieving Superior Performance

Allan P.O. Williams
Professor of Organisational and Occupational Psychology
and Head of the Department of Business Studies
City University Business School
and Director of the Centre for Personnel Research and Enterprise Development

and

Sally Woodward
Research Fellow, Centre for Personnel Research and Enterprise Development
City University Business School

First published 1994 by
THE MACMILLAN PRESS LTD
Houndmills, Basingstoke, Hampshire RG21 2XS
and London
Companies and representatives
throughout the world

ISBN 0-333-60729-5

A catalogue record for this book is available
from the British Library.

Printed in Great Britain by
Antony Rowe Ltd
Chippenham, Wiltshire

Contents

List of Figures

List of Tables

List of Boxes

List of Case Histories

Acknowledgements

The nucleus of this book is a major piece of research. The research was made possible because a number of individuals, institutions and firms were prepared to help us; we are grateful to them all. An initial literature survey was financed by a grant from the T. Ritchie Rodger Research Fund, and the findings encouraged us to further research. The British Consultants Bureau and the Institute of Management Consultants were generous in the publicity they gave to the project when we were trying to gain access to consultancies. We are clearly indebted to the consultancies who provided us with the raw material for our research, and even more so to those who also made a financial contribution to the costs of the research.

We have had valuable discussions with a number of consultants in the process of developing our ideas, and we should particularly like to thank Calvert Markham in this context. We are also grateful to Professor Peter Herriot for the useful observations and suggestions he made on reading the manuscript. In addition we must acknowledge the part played by those students who attended the Consultancy Skills Elective on our MBA programme over the last four years; they were constructive critics of our ideas and learning materials.

A good deal of clerical work goes into the preparation of a book. As secretary to the Centre for Personnel Research and Enterprise Development, Margaret Busgith has done a splendid job with patience and good humour. The Library staff of the Business School and the University have also been most helpful in the process of obtaining references.

Above all we must thank Alan Elliot, a Visiting Research Fellow at the Business School. He freely gave us his time at the data collection stage, has been a continuous source of stimulating ideas and made many valuable comments in reading an early draft of the book.

ALLAN P.O. WILLIAMS
SALLY WOODWARD

Part 1
The Context

1 Introduction

There are three related reasons for writing this book. They are:

- the economic importance of the consultancy industry;
- the competitive imperative; and
- the need to train consultants in superior client-oriented skills.

We shall discuss each of these in turn. But first, what do we mean by 'consultancy'?

CONSULTANCY DEFINED

Within the context of work most people think of the term as being synonymous with management consultancy. This is far too limiting, for it takes no account of those who consult in many other sectors: accountancy and finance, architecture, design, engineering, health, the legal profession, to name but a few. It may also be too limiting to think of consultancy as involving an outsider as conveyed in the following definition: 'Consultancy is a relationship in which an outsider makes his knowledge and experience available to an organisation' (Markham, 1991, p.1). Many large organisations incorporate implicit or explicit consultancy resources within their structure.

We shall view consultancy as a process in which a consultant provides a service to a client (i.e. an organisation or an individual acting on behalf of an organisation or a unit within that organisation) for the purpose of meeting the client's need. Implicit in the idea of service is the notion that the consultant is making his or her expertise available to the client. This definition is sufficiently broad to go beyond management consultancy, and to include internal consultancy. It is also sufficiently narrow to exclude consultants who are primarily involved in providing a service to individual clients in their personal capacity, such as doctors to their patients or solicitors to their private clients. These are the boundaries to the territory we propose exploring.

IMPORTANCE OF THE INDUSTRY

It is common to read of consultancy as a large and growing industry. But it is very difficult to give a reliable picture as to how large it is, or how fast it has grown in the last few years, because it is not an officially recognised entity. But we can gauge some idea of its potential for overseas earnings. Take the case of the United Kingdom(UK). British Invisibles (previously The British Invisible Export Council) obtains statistics about the overseas earnings of consultants. The consultancy profession contributed net overseas earnings of around £1.5 billion in 1992. One contributor to this figure is the Management Consultancies Association, which has several of the larger consultancies as its members. It states that 14 per cent of the income of their members came from international services in 1992 (MCA, 1993).

Financial returns are one way of gauging the importance of the consultancy industry to the economy of a country. There are others, particularly in the dissemination and utilisation of knowledge and in the effective use of highly skilled human resources. As James Quinn (1992) and others have pointed out, companies start small and it is ideas and intellect – not physical assets – that build them into great companies. The know-how gained by one company is eventually disseminated and applied elsewhere through a variety of media, including: movement of key individuals from one company to another, publications and formal courses, and through 'expert' individuals moving into consultancy to serve a larger constituency.

The role of consultants in generating and facilitating the application of new ideas cannot be overestimated. In the process of adapting to a changing environment, particularly at times of financial crises, organisations are open to new ideas and to the influence of consultants. This no doubt partly explains the waves of fashion which go through sectors of industry at given times; for example, management by objectives in the 1960s and total quality management in the 80s and 90s.

Consultancy can also be seen to be the beneficiary when highly skilled human resources are released from employment. During periods of recession, organisations shed large numbers of employees. They also shed employees when developing flatter organisations to cope more effectively with changing markets – a process often referred to as downsizing or de-layering. Some redundant specialists and professionals become self-employed as consultants. While their employer may lose their services, potential clients gain their expertise! To minimise overheads, and to increase flexibility in the face of rapid change, organisations are drawing on the service of experts as the need arises rather than on a continuing basis. In recent years this has been particularly noticeable in the growth of IT (information technology) related consultancy.

Forced and unforced changes such as these have had a considerable impact on the number of individuals entering consultancy and the number of firms in the industry. This growth trend is likely to continue in the light of increasing business environment complexity, competition, internationalisation and technological change (Keeble *et al.*, 1991). Accompanying this growth there have been established various organised groups aimed at promoting and protecting the interests and professionalism of their members. Thus in the UK there is the Management Consultancies Association to which many of the larger firms in the industry belong, the British Consultants Bureau which caters for the interests of firms keen on expanding their overseas clientele and the Institute of Management Consultants which is geared to individual rather than corporate membership. In addition there are a host of other bodies attached to professional or semi-professional organisations which cater for the needs of consultants, such as the Division of Occupational Psychology in the British Psychological Society, the Association for Management Education and Development, and so on.

All these bodies recognise that enduring profitability is brought about through the setting, achievement and maintenance of standards in the service given to clients. It is only when satisfactory introduction of structures and processes for setting, achieving and maintaining these standards are in place that consultancy will formally emerge as a profession with chartered status. This has been attained in certain pockets of consultancy (e.g. chartered accountants, engineers, surveyors, and psychologists), but not as yet in the general area of management consultancy. Appropriate training and the monitoring of standards are critical ingredients in achieving professional status. Consultants will attract adverse criticism if these are not sufficiently visible in their case; in turn this will have unfavourable effects on the demand for their services, and alternative means of meeting the adaptive needs of organisations will evolve.

The interactive or reciprocal relationships we have been discussing between environmental changes, the growth or decline of consultancy, and consultancy as a profession are shown in Figure 1.1. More light will be thrown on these relationships and their implications in the next chapter. The aim here is to draw attention to the significance of the industry today, and some of the factors which will affect its future impact.

THE COMPETITIVE IMPERATIVE

In the task of remaining competitive, there is one unusual feature that marks out consultancy: it is very difficult to monitor the products or services of your competitors. In manufacturing industry and

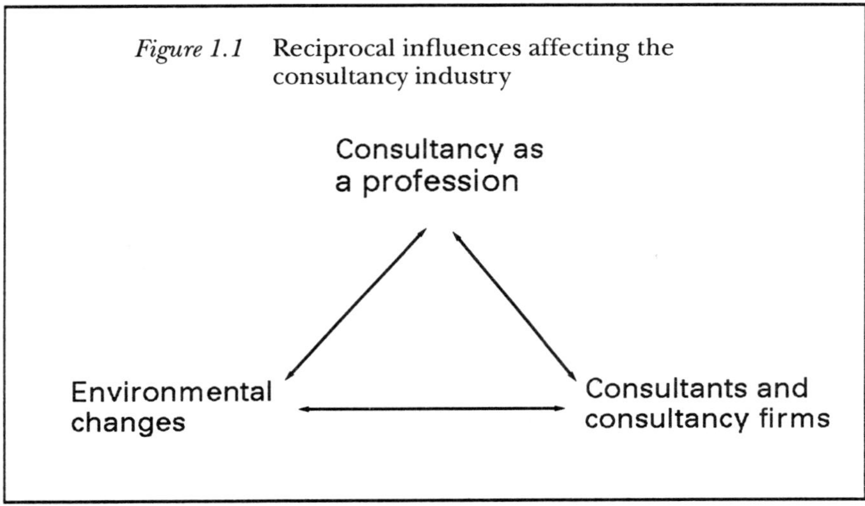

Figure 1.1   Reciprocal influences affecting the
consultancy industry

in most of the service industries, it is quite easy to take a very close look at what your competitors are offering. And you can usually survey customers and find out why they bought.

Consultancy is necessarily a confidential profession. Clients' secrets must be preserved. Articles and brochures may carry examples of assignments undertaken, but in outline only; the details of the paddling that the swan does to maintain a smooth flow over the surface are missing. It is very hard to find out the credible realities of why you lost a job.

All in all, it is not easy in consultancy to find out exactly what your competitors are successfully selling, or exactly why clients are buying the particular services that they do buy. This makes it that much more difficult to adapt to the marketplace.

There are a host of textbooks and courses designed to help managers learn how a service organisation such as a consultancy can go about increasing its competitiveness. The conventional response to a competitive environment is to review and to reinforce or change the organisation's business strategy, structure and culture. As a result, changes may occur in the policies and practices relating to marketing, finance, operations, information technology, organisational design and human resources.

All these ingredients are important for continued survival and growth. Our thesis is that these conventional responses are nothing new to the major players in the consultancy industry, indeed they are in the business of advising clients in these areas! But there is an area falling under the personal competence umbrella where consultancies can still achieve a competitive advantage. Consultancies whose staff can quickly learn to cope with the unexpected and unclear needs of clients are more likely to achieve new and repeat business. The speedy acquisition of the necessary skills requires that planned learning replaces trial-and-error learning, and scientifically based theory and knowledge replaces 'that-is-how-we-have-always-done-it' theory and knowledge.

TRAINING FOR SUPERIOR CLIENT-ORIENTED SKILLS

A story, but a true story. The place, a recently commissioned power station in a Third World country. The consultant was Tony. At that time Tony probably knew more about the design and construction of turbine-houses for coal-fired power stations than any but a handful of people in the Western world.

For the past year or two, his firm had had a team working on the power station. At the start of the project, before they were involved, things had not gone well. Another organisation had originally been engaged by the client and somehow the relationship had not gone as smoothly as it should. The people in the other organisation had wanted to press on; the client's people had wanted to take things step by step, to gather advice and make the key decisions rather than follow prescriptive recommendations. Their natural national pride did not take easily to the expertise proffered by the outsiders. The project slowed and fell behind.

Tony's firm was asked to put in a team to help get it back on track. Led by a man of quite unusual insight and humanity, they had seen that the solution lay not so much in the expertise that was provided but in the way it was provided. It was vital that the clients should feel and know that the ultimate achievement was their own. This, then, became the basis on which the new team structured the working relationship. It succeeded.

Tony was talking about a visit that had recently been made by a delegation from the Far East to the new operative power station. He had been invited to accompany the visitors when they went round the turbine-house and he had listened with growing delight and surprise as the client's leader talked. 'Everything he told them', said Tony,

> was about what they had achieved. We were scarcely mentioned, yet they could never have done it all without us. It wasn't the kind of thing I ever expected to hear when I came out here, and I'll admit that a big part of me did long for recognition of all we had done. But then, consultancy is not always what you expect, is it?

From our experience of consultancy, and in talking to others, it seems to us that consultants are having to undertake an increasing variety of roles in order to see their assignments through to a successful conclusion. Success in consultancy, it appears, is no longer always to be measured in terms of fulfilling the contract as it was originally conceived. It is not just extending the contract, with new and enlarged terms of reference. It is rather that there turns out to be an important element in the core of the job that has not been specified at the contracting stage, has not even been mentioned. But fulfilling it is part of the criteria on which success will ultimately be judged.

To make it more difficult, it is usually up to the consultant to find out not merely what this element is but that it exists at all – that the client has from the start, or has developed as the assignment proceeds, unspoken expectations relating to how consultant and client will interact.

To digress for a moment. When an employee is taken on by a firm he or she is given a formal contract of employment stating salary, job title and other conditions. Superimposed on this contract is an unwritten 'psychological contract' consisting of additional expectations which the employee has of the employer, and the employer of the employee. These expectations develop as a result of the interactions which take place between the two parties during recruitment, selection, training and job experience. From the point of view of the employee these expectations may relate to one's career (e.g. 'You have potential, and given appropriate training and experience there is no reason why you should not make top management sometime in the future'), working conditions ('You will have your own office in a month or two'; 'We are proposing to provide company cars to staff at your level in the future'), and so on.

By their very nature expectations are changeable, and the changes taking place may have behavioural consequences. In the employment situation, if the employee feels that the psychological contract is not being honoured, he or she is likely to become dissatisfied, to develop low commitment to the organisation and to leave when something better appears on the horizon.

The concept of the psychological contract is applicable to the consultancy situation and, from the point of view of the participants, it is as important as the formal contract in determining their behaviour toward one another.

Our discussions with others in the consultancy world confirmed that the 'project-with-a-twist' was not a figment of our imagination. The twist was also nearly always related to the roles which the client expected the consultant to undertake. Failure to fulfil these roles successfully may result in failure to obtain follow-up work which had been confidently expected by the consultant. What are these roles? What can be done to ensure that consultants respond appropriately when these unexpected twists occur? Two things are certain: consultants are not born with the skills which enable them to perform well in these roles; and consultants who have acquired them will be in short supply.

THE KNOWLEDGE GAP

Systematic training based on valid theory is the answer to the second question posed in the last paragraph. Unfortunately there is a dearth of published *scientific* studies relating to the roles which consultants may be required to undertake, and their associated skills. Reasons for this include:

- The confidential nature of much of the work, and the high level of competition within the industry, militate against co-operating in a research programme.
- The industry is not sufficiently organised or professionalised to invest in research which will be of common benefit.
- It is only relatively recently that consultancy has come to be seen as a discipline worthy of serious academic study, since in the past consultancy was not regarded as a high-status area for research by academics.
- Much of the relevant literature has been written by practitioners who have developed, and promote, a particular approach to consultancy.

This book is offered as a contribution to the task of meeting a need for an empirically based theoretical framework, and an accompanying methodology, for use in the training of consultants in a set of generic skills. In order to ensure that the reader approaches the contents of this book with realistic expectations, it may be helpful to position the book relative to the two main categories of texts in the consultancy field which are intended to promote the effectiveness of consultancy.

First, there are the books on management consultancy which aim to be general and comprehensive. They cover the business side of consultancy (e.g. product development, marketing, finance), the technical (e.g. project management, data collection), the professional (e.g. ethics), and also discuss the roles which consultants adopt on assignments. A classic example of this category is Milan Kubr's *Management Consulting*, first published in 1976 and now in its second edition (1986). Another more practical and skills-related example is Calvert Markham's *The Top Consultant* (1993).

Second, there is a vast array of books which promote particular theoretical approaches to consultancy as a process of procuring change. Examples are Edwin Nevis's *Organisational Consulting* (1987), which is written from an orthodox Gestalt perspective; and Edgar Schein's seminal *Process Consultation* (1969), which is identified with a social psychological approach to consultancy. The majority of texts in this category are ones which we associate with 'organisation development' or OD, for example, Robert Golembiewski's *Handbook of Organisational Consultation* (1992).

The Competitive Consultant clearly does not belong to the first category, since it focuses primarily on one aspect of the consultancy process, i.e. the roles which consultants may have to adopt when on assignments. This is the aspect which we have identified as needing more attention if consultants are to gain a competitive edge for their firms by acquiring what we are labelling as superior client-oriented' skills.

Although closer to the second category of texts, the book does not sit comfortably here. We develop a general model of consultancy roles for training purposes, based on what a heterogeneous group of consultants actually do on assignments. As such we are concerned with the consultancy process, a common interest with OD consultants. But *The Competitive Consultant* is not restricted to OD-type change assignments, nor is it embedded in the OD value system (see French and Bell, 1984, for an authoritative account of OD). Accordingly it adds something new to the literature, and at the same time enriches the supply of case histories for learning purposes.

The title conveys the underlying theme of the book – success in a competitive market will be achieved by developing consultants with superior client-oriented skills. These are the skills that will enable consultants to meet those client needs which are often unclear and unexpected, but nevertheless important from the point of view of the client and the success of the assignment. They are also the skills that are most likely to make the client feel that they have been helped – surely the criterion *par excellence* of a successful consultancy assignment!

STRUCTURE OF BOOK

This book should be of interest to several groups of readers, each one having their own particular agenda. First, experienced consultants who are interested in discovering whether there is anything new to learn that may improve the performance of themselves or their subordinates as consultants. Second, trainee consultants or MBA students who are motivated to learn some of the latest thinking about the roles consultants adopt in interacting with clients. Third, trainers and educators who are looking for new theories and learning methods to facilitate their task of laying the foundations for superior consultancy performance. Fourth, commentators and opinion leaders who are concerned with the development of consultancy as a profession and as a competitive force. Fifth, fellow academics who recognise the role of business schools in stimulating and promoting a sound academic base for consultancy through scientific research that is useful and usable. Such a relatively diverse readership indicates the need for brief guidelines to enable individual readers to identify those aspects of the book most likely to cater for their needs.

The book is logically structured. Part I focusses on the context of consultancy. Chapter 2 describes how the role of the consultant has developed. The growth and economic importance of the industry is discussed, as is the need for a sound knowledge base for use in the training of consultants. The limitations of current training are touched upon and the need for training beyond one's area of expertise is highlighted. This additional training is determined by the actual roles that consultants find themselves adopting. Chapter 3 therefore analyses the concept of roles within the context of the consultancy process and examines typical models of roles that appear in the literature. The limitations of these models are identified, particularly when used in training, and the need for more scientific research emphasised. The 'commentator' readership is likely to be interested in Chapter 2. Those not already familiar with the concept of roles in consultancy should read Chapter 3.

Part II deals with a new scientifically-based model of consultancy roles – the 1+7 model. The findings of the pilot and main studies are discussed in Chapter 4 and presented in terms of a model encompassing eight roles. While due prominence is given to the role of 'expert', the model emphasises that the execution of this role is dependant upon the consultant's performance in seven other roles. Chapter 5 looks at each role in more depth so as to alert the reader to some of the competences underlying effective role performance. A critical review of the model in the light of current knowledge follows in Chapter 6. Part II is the core of the book and should be of interest to all readers.

Part III is concerned with the application of the 1+7 model in the process of developing superior client-oriented skills. In order to understand the potential value of the model as an aid to learning, and how it can be incorporated into a training programme, Chapter 7 looks at learning theories and the insights that they give us into the development of expertise. Chapters 7 and 8 are concerned with the case study approach to learning about consultancy roles, a method that is suitable for both trainee and experienced consultants. The case studies in Chapter 9 are a selection of those leading to the formulation of the 1+7 model. Chapters 7, 8, and 9 are likely to interest the 'trainer/educator' readership.

The concluding Chapter 10 is relevant to all readers. It reminds the reader: (a) of the increasing importance of consultancy and the changed environment in which its operating, and the consequent need for training that is based on a new model of consultancy roles; (b) that the potentially powerful 1+7 model differs from others in the literature in being scientifically rather than experientially based, and in successfully integrating the content expertise and the process skills of the consultant; (c) of the value of certain learning principles, and exercises based on case studies, in helping trainee and experienced consultants to assimilate the 1+7 model into their mental sets and thence into their behaviour. The model represents a novel client-oriented approach for achieving superior performance.

2 Consultancy: A Developing Profession

In this chapter we shall explore further the concept of consultancy, the range of purposes to which it is applied, the strategies or styles of application, and particularly its relationship with the recognised professions. Since consultancy has become a growth industry there are good reasons for arguing for the need for increased 'professionalisation' and this will be briefly explored. One of the conclusions we shall draw from this chapter is that consultancy is an embryonic profession and will remain so until a firmer scientific base has evolved. Central to this development are the generic knowledge and skills that consultants should be able to display in the process of meeting the needs of their clients.

CONSULTANCY IS MORE THAN GIVING ADVICE

In Chapter 1 we gave a definition of consultancy that we are adopting for the purposes of this book. Let us elaborate consultancy further. Chambers' dictionary defines a consultant as 'one who gives professional advice'. Yet some people who use the term 'consultant' in their occupational title do not give advice that might be regarded as 'professional'. Others who may not see themselves as consultants give professional advice as part of their role. For example, doctors, social workers, teachers, lawyers, architects, bank managers, accountants, town planners and engineers all offer advice. Each profession has its own particular expertise and its practising members prove their competence to advise through success in difficult examinations, many years of practical experience involving apprenticeship (training on-the-job) and adherence to a code of conduct.

Professional advisers can help individuals, groups or larger systems. For example, doctors and social workers may advise and work with the client (patient) or may choose to work with a client system (family). Lawyers, bankers and accountants may advise and work with an individual such as the company secretary or finance director, or may work with the Board. In a complex project an interdisciplinary team of professionals may work with people from international aid agencies, a government and the nation's state industries. It all depends on the purpose of the assignment/engagement.

Arthur Turner (1982) produced a hierarchy of purposes of consultancy in the area of management consulting. These were:

1. Providing information to a client;
2. Providing a solution to a client's problem;
3. Making a diagnosis, which may necessitate a redefinition of the problem;
4. Making recommendations based on the diagnosis;
5. Assisting with the implementation of recommended solutions;
6. Building consensus and commitment around corrective action;
7. Helping clients learn how to resolve similar problems in the future;
8. Permanently improving organisational effectiveness.

Excepting the final purpose, they can refer to consulting in general. The American Institute of Certified Public Accountants (AICPA) has also produced a functional classification for business advisers. This includes, in addition to advisory services, transaction services (these relate to a specific client transaction and generally involve a third party; examples include insolvency services and analysis of a potential merger or acquisition) and executive leasing services. Executive leasing involves companies hiring experienced managers for a period of, usually, less than a year, to help with a variety of activities, including turning around an ailing subsidiary or filling the position of a senior manager who has left suddenly. A number of leasing companies exist in the UK to hire out executives. During their time with the hiring company the consultants carry full executive authority and, in many cases, report to the Board (cf Muns *et al.*, 1991; Summers and Knight, 1975; Zitelli and Tucker, 1991).

Both of these classifications demonstrate that, in reality, consultancy involves many other activities in addition to giving advice. Hence our definition of consultancy in Chapter 1 as 'a process in which a consultant provides a *service* to a client' based on expertise.

Turner suggests that the lower-numbered purposes in his list are those generally requested by clients and are more easily understood and practised. He also proposes that many consultants aspire to the higher levels and such intentions are essential to effective consultancy. But moving up requires increasing competence in process consulting skills, including managing the consultant–client relationship. We now move on to consider some of the strategies that consultants might adopt in their relationships with clients.

STRATEGIC CONSIDERATIONS IN CLIENT–CONSULTANT RELATIONSHIPS

Clients and consultants relate in several ways. For example, there are contractual relations (both spoken/written and unspoken) and there are problem-solving relations. The types of relationship adopted affect the consultancy process.

Contractual Relations

We can describe a client as a person (or persons) who chooses to avail themselves of a consultant's service in order to meet some need that they have identified (the need may simply be a feeling of something needing to be done rather than a fully intelligible situation). A client system may be a functional or product group, a private sector firm, a public sector body or larger systems such as industry/sector and even nation.

Between a consultant and client there is, usually, a mutually agreed:

- *voluntary* contract implicit in the relationship; that is the client chooses the consultant (either an internal or external body) and the consultant chooses to accept the client,
- *formal* contract explicit to the situation relating to purposes, approach, resources, costings and timing,
- a formal differentiation of roles.

In the initial meetings between client and consultant (terms which may refer to individuals or to groups) there is an attempt to 'enact' the situation, in Karl Weick's terms (1979), i.e. to develop an appreciation of problems and/or opportunities within the framework of structures, norms and values which lead to a tacit contract. A varying degree of understanding exists between client and consultant regarding the extent of the consultant's remit resulting from this implicit, unspoken contract. The importance of this stage has been demonstrated in a recent empirical study (Fullerton and West, 1993). However, as many of the case histories to be described later in this book will show, it is difficult if not impossible to accurately identify in advance what is going to be needed of the consultant. The corporate client is a social system, and the individual clients not only represent that system but often have their own private agendas. This means that client needs or problems may arise that were not apparent when the project first started. To operate effectively in such a context a consultant is required to be flexible and to be skilled in a wide range of roles (this theme is developed further in subsequent chapters).

Problem-Solving Relationships

There are a number of ways in which consultants can give help and advice, and this affects the client–consultant relationship. In certain problem-solving situations consultants may focus on the *problem* to the exclusion of the client, in others they may include the client. Alternatively, they can focus on the *client* rather than the problem – a process rather than content approach.

This produces four possible helping strategies.

1. A problem-centred approach that excludes the client; exemplified in the 'technical expert' role in traditional medical and teaching models and in some information-technology-system design situations.
2. A problem-centred approach that includes the client; evidenced in the 'learning model' where consultants create situations/events through which clients can actively learn.
3. A client-focused approach including the client; the 'tutoring model' where the consultant assists the client's thinking processes in identifying a problem or determining a solution.
4. A client-focused approach that excludes the client is where the consultant covertly guides the client.

This last approach, while having negative connotations of manipulation, does occur in cases where espoused theory and theory-in-use, unbeknown to some consultants, conflict. For example, Adrian McLean and colleagues (1982) highlighted discrepancies between the role of the organisational development (OD) consultant as portrayed in the literature, and the activities they found in a research study investigating the reality of OD as it is practised.

John Heron (1990), in a development of Blake and Mouton's work (1972), suggests that, at the individual level, there are six types of intervention. The first three are similar to (1) and (4) above. They are helping strategies excluding the client, in a major way, from the problem-solving process. The consultant seeks to influence the client either overtly or covertly. Heron terms these approaches 'authoritative'. They are:

● Prescriptive interventions, where the consultant seeks to influence and direct the client's behaviour,

- Informative interventions, where the consultant seeks to impart knowledge, information and meaning, and
- Confronting interventions, where the consultant seeks to bring into awareness something the client was not conscious of.

In these three strategies the consultant assumes greater responsibility for change and direction and thus the relationship is unequal and hierarchical.

Heron's second form of helping strategies relate to (2) and (3) above. They are aimed at including the client in the problem-solving process and are termed 'facilitative'. They are:

- Cathartic interventions, where the consultant enables the client to discharge painful emotion such as grief, fear and anger,
- Catalytic interventions, where the consultant elicits in the client self-discovery, self-directed living, learning and problem solving,
- Supportive interventions, where the consultant affirms the worth and value of the client.

In these three strategies the client and consultant work together in a partnership, with the consultant encouraging the client to take equal responsibility for the success of the assignment.

The experience of the participants and the immediate context determine consultant–client relationships, which then determine what sort of intervention is appropriate at any point in time. Without formal training individual consultants are unlikely to be able to exhibit all of the behaviours encompassed by these helping strategies since they cover such a disparate grouping.

The general climate in consulting has changed over this century and most people nowadays seek to be active participants in their use of consultants. While consultants are expected to be knowledgeable in their area(s) of expertise, clients also expect that their views will be considered. In consequence, and as Charles Margerison, in his book, *Managerial Consulting Skills* (1988) observes, consultant's expertise must support client needs rather than dominate them. This means that in addition to specialist and technical knowledge, consultants today need good process and interpersonal skills. Successful consulting means the client feeling helped; this results, in part, from clients and consultants monitoring the unspoken contract which develops during interactions with each other.

Rolf Torstendahl (1990) draws our attention to the fact that around 400 years ago clients in Europe were 'most often aristocrats who asked for submissiveness rather than advice from their preachers, orators, master builders and scribes'. Nowadays the individual client is less common and 'is often at best an equal in status to the professional whose services he will engage'. In addition, over the last 100 years or more, collective clients (i.e. people operating on behalf of organisations) have become more numerous in all types of professional activity, and they have also become more demanding in their relationship to the practitioner in the professional field. Because of these factors, differences between the private practitioner and the employed professional have been reduced.

WHO IS A CONSULTANT?

Whereas in the past it was considered that only persons employed in private practice could act in a consulting role (the 'stereotype' in our terminology of roles), there is now a wider use of the term. This includes professionals employed within organisations as 'internal' consultants (here the term is a functional one and can refer to consulting activities undertaken as part of another stereotypic role). This has come about in spite of concerns that the individual may not give an 'independent' view, since he or she may be pressurised to adopt the employer's values rather than those enshrined in a given professional code of ethics.

Margerison (1988) points out that consulting activities can be undertaken either as an internal or as an external consultant and from either an advisory or an executive position. This produces four consultant types:

- External consultant: the first type encapsulates the traditional view of an external consultant who provides professional advice – on contract, for a time – to clients. Most professionals will be able to adopt this role and undertake assignments at the lower levels of Turner's hierarchy, using their specialist knowledge. However, with increases in the scope of assignments, in the 'fuzziness' of a problem area and in the involvement of clients, additional competences are needed. These are invariably acquired through experience in practice, via 'reflection-in-action' (Schön, 1983). An adjunct to experience is the use of experiential methods in formal learning situations as for example case studies. The pedagogic justification for this is covered in Chapter 8.
- External project manager: the second type of consultant is often found in the information/communications technology and construction industries, where a project manager (often an engin-

eer or architect) from an outside organisation has responsibility for delivering an assignment but acts as a consultant to the clients and as a line manager in his or her own organisation.

- Internal consultant: the third type has grown rapidly in many organisations over the last 40 years or so. We can find a multitude of internal professional advisers in organisations, all providing information and guidance to executives (Steele, 1982). Titles of such people include business development advisers, internal auditors, management development staff, corporate lawyers, public relations managers and work production engineers – indicating the wide variety of specialist areas covered. These internal advisers (like their external counterparts) can provide a number of services either on their own or in liaison with external advisers.

- Internal manager: a fourth type of consultant occurs when a full-time executive/manager acts as a consultant to his or her subordinates or colleagues in a coaching, supporting and facilitating manner. If predictions about the changing nature of management come about this is a role that managers will need to adopt with their empowered employees. Staff at the customer interface will take decisions and executives higher up will have the role of enabling that decision-making process, in much the same way as the role of the supervisor changed with the introduction of new technology and autonomous work groups in manufacturing.

SUMMARY

Consultancy and consultants are terms which have broadened in range and scope. The traditional distinctions of the expert providing knowledge and the client/executive taking action have broken down. Turner, among others, illustrates the ever widening scope of consultancy services. As a consequence there has been an expansion in the range of roles that external consultants are asked to perform. Margerison illustrates the fact that, in addition to the traditional role of the external consultant, a large number of other people are now in roles with relationships which require consultancy skills and expertise. As well as providing advice, the internal consultant seeks to achieve change by or through the executive via a variety of intervention strategies. Additionally, managers in line or staff functions provide advice and support to their staff and counsel them to encourage development. As Milan Kubr (1986) pointed out, consultancy can be viewed both as a profession and a method which is applied by competent persons whose main occupation is

not consultancy. To be effective this latter group need to master
consulting tools and skills and follow the ethics of consulting.

TRENDS IN CONSULTANCY

Growth and Economic Significance

We mentioned in the previous chapter that consultancy as an
industry or sector grouping is extremely difficult to quantify since
it encompasses diverse areas such as management consultancy,
information-technology consultancy and consulting engineering –
all of which can overlap. This means that a number of figures for
consultancy exist, many of them varying by considerable amounts.
For example, figures for management consultancy suggest it was
one of the fastest-growing industries in the world during the
1980s. Whereas around fifty years ago the management consulting
industry was almost unknown in Europe, during the mid to late
1980s it was seen to increase by about 25 per cent a year (Payne,
1987). The market in Western Europe was thought to be worth
about \$5 billion in 1990, and in the United States it was estimated
as exceeding \$8 billion. Robert Metzger (1989) suggested that
worldwide it amounted to around \$20 billion. These figures are
usually based on consultancy firm fee-income for consultancies
who are members of a recognised association. However, the base
of firms comprising these associations changes over the years. It is
agreed that growth occurred in the 1980s – the industry is pres-
ently being affected by the recession – but no one can give, with
certainty, exact figures.

The Management Consultancies Association (MCA) in the UK,
a body which represents a high proportion of the industry (estimates range between 45 and 65 per cent), shows the annual revenue of members for 1992 to be £810 million. If we accept the
world market size to be \$20–25 billion, the British share approxi-
mates 7 per cent. This is less than that suggested by other writers
(cf Schlegelmilch *et al.*, 1992), and reflects the disagreement created by definitional difficulties and to the frequent omission of
small consultancy firms.

The MCA is a member of the Federation Européenne des
Associations de Conseils en Organisation (FEACO), and European
Community (EC) statistics for the management consultancy sector
in 1990 reveal that nearly six in ten of EC-registered management
consultants work for firms in the UK or Germany. While Germany
has a lot of small enterprises (310 firm members), a majority of UK

consultants work in large registered firms (227 persons per firm in the UK, compared with 23 persons per firm in Germany). In terms of ranking by turnover (in thousand ECUs (European Currency Units) per consultant) Germany, France and Denmark are ahead of the UK (221, 216, 183, 161 respectively). In terms of turnover, the UK produced around 20 per cent of the FEACO membership's turnover, which is estimated as slightly less than half the total market turnover of the EC.

However, in the UK these figures do not include activity of small firms that are not members of the MCA. Recent work by the Small Business Research Centre, based in Cambridge University, has highlighted the importance of small consultancy firms to the industry. The researchers' findings suggest that firms with less than 10 consultants or a turnover of less than £1 million in 1989–90 account for three-quarters of all firms in management consultancy, with only 10 per cent of firms employ more than 50 consultants. Indeed, they say that by 1990 small management consultancy firms 'probably accounted for more consultancy turnover than either medium firms or large companies' (42, 22 and 36 per cent respectively) (Keeble *et al.*, 1991).

The Association of Consulting Engineers (ACE) was founded in 1912 and is the body representing the consulting engineering profession in the UK. ACE is also a member of the European Federation of Engineering Consultancy Associations (EFCA). 1990 European statistics for the consulting engineering sector reveal the UK, at 49 000, to have the largest number of persons employed of any European member, while Germany, France and Italy have about half that number each. Turnover for consultancy engineering firms in these four countries ranges between around 2 and 2.5 billion ECUs for each country. EFCA represents 25 national associations of consultancy firms, from all EEC countries, employing over 200 000 qualified engineers (Commission of the European Communities, 1992).

Factors Contributing to Growth

We have already alluded to some of the factors which have stimulated the growth in consultancy. There are several interlinking factors:

- Increased business complexity resulting from globalisation, new legislation, intense competition, need to re-structure organisations (e.g. more flat structures), mergers and acquisitions, the impact of new technology, and so on. Because managers are operating in uncertain, unpredictable and complex settings, they have a constant need for professional or expert people who are likely to understand their problems and can help in resolving them.

- As we mentioned in Chapter 1, one of the reasons why consultancy is a growth industry in the United Kingdom is that during the last 10 years or so, many organisations have been reducing staff and head offices have been divested of all but the most essential functions. This means that when a company runs into problems, or seeks to exploit new opportunities, it is likely to have to look outside for specialist advice and skills.

- The growth in self-employed consultants has been partly facilitated by the 'downsizing' of companies and also by additional forces encouraging self-employment such as the enterprise culture, government subsidies or incentives for small business start-ups, companies sub-contracting non-core activities, and new technologies (e.g. computers, faxes) enabling individuals to carry out work independently of support staff.

- The growth of the professions. A growth in the number of professions and in people working in professional and managerial occupational groups has been a direct consequence of the expansion of knowledge and the increasing complexity of society. The 1991 Labour Force Survey shows there were 27.9 million economically active people in Great Britain; of these, 25.6 million were in employment. If we look at occupations and employment during the 1980s, we see that the managerial and professional occupational grouping underwent a dramatic rise of 24 per cent or 1.7 million between 1984 and 1991. Numbers increased to 8.6 million. This growth is projected to continue. If we assume that many of these people provide some sort of professional advice, either as professional consultants or in consulting activities as part of their role, we can see the importance of promoting consultancy skills. Examination of changes in industry structure over the 20 years reveals that much of the growth in the employment of professionals was provided by the business and miscellaneous services sector which increased its share from 9 to just over 21.5 per cent. It is predicted that by the end of this century around 40 per cent of science and engineering professionals, 34 per cent of health professionals, 5 per cent of teaching professionals and 43 per cent of 'other' professionals, will be employed within the business and miscellaneous services sector (Bosworth *et al.*, 1992).

HOW DO PROFESSIONALS ACQUIRE COMPETENCE TO PRACTISE?

Admission to the rights and privileges of full membership of a qualifying organisation indicates to the public that the candidate has reached, by examination and experience, the degree of competence required of practitioners. Indications of competence are the use of designatory letters after one's name. As a member of a professional association, the individual accepts certain responsibilities towards clients, colleagues and the general public. It is not surprising therefore to find that the growth in the professions has been accompanied by a similar growth in qualifying associations. Prior to 1800 these numbered seven. Between 1800 and 1900 an additional 42 associations were formed. From 1901 to 1962 a further 109 came into existence. There are now more than 400 professional bodies in the U.K.

Hazel Bines (1992) provides details on three models of professional education: apprenticeship, technocratic and post-technocratic. In the 'apprenticeship or pre-technocratic' form, professional education occurs mainly 'on the job' with some additional instruction being received through block and/or day release in a training school or institute of further or higher education. Delivery of the curriculum is by experienced practitioners, although some input may be made by subject specialists. Mastery of facts, practical routines and gaining understanding of one's place in a hierarchy of authority are key elements in learning.

'Technocratic' education is the form that has been adopted by a large number of professions in the last 20 years or so. It is characterised by the separation of professional education into three main elements. First, the development and transmission of a systematic knowledge base; second the interpretation and application of the knowledge base to practice (including analysis and problem-solving activities, and socialisation into expected values and behaviours). A third element is supervised practice in selected placements.

This model has been criticised on a number of counts. For example, people might hold differing concepts about a profession and different institutions may adopt differing policies and practices with regard to education. These can lead to wide variations in what is deemed to be evidence of 'competence', what sort of knowledge needs to be imparted, what types of methods should be used and what level of student choice should be provided. Most importantly, it can lead to the disjunction between theory and practice. Academic knowledge and its teachers are given higher status and priority over 'practice knowledge and practitioners.'

However, the key criticism has come from Donald Schön (1983, 1987) who suggests that this model is based on a 'technical rationality' which fails to acknowledge the nature of professional knowledge and action and the ways in which professionals really develop their practice. Indeterminate situations, unique cases and messy problems usually involve a conflict of values in the shaping and setting of problems; this means that practitioners cannot merely apply technical theories and knowledge in the resolution of these conflicts.

A third form of professional education, termed the 'post-technocratic' model, is therefore in the process of evolving. This emphasises the acquisition of professional competences in a practice. Bines argues

> competences are primarily developed through experience of practice and reflection on practice in a practicum within which students have access to skilled practitioners who act as coaches... the practicum is thus the key and integrating element of the course and the professional education tutor and the practice tutor become major educational figures... there is also a greater emphasis on individual student learning and progress and on a partnership of higher education institutions, services and employers.   (1992, p.16)

There are a number of key features of this developing model. First, the identification and description of a range of discrete competences, usually described in behavioural terms, which may be acquired and assessed in a practice setting. Second, an emphasis on the development of a capacity for critical reflection in – and on – action. Third, constructing training *partnerships* between all interested parties and negotiating to resolve conflicts due to competing definitions of the professional role and of what constitutes 'good practice'. Fourth, the linkages between pure and applied knowledge – professional practice – are made overt and connections between practice and theory are deliberately structured as an integral part of course design.

A number of problems need to be overcome for this model to be successfully adopted. These are fully examined in Bines's book.

Professions can be characterised by their knowledge systems and degree of abstraction (Abbott, 1988). At present it would seem that some types of consultancy use the first model of professional education, i.e. the apprenticeship or pre-technocratic form, others are using the second model and a few are moving to the third (cf Male, 1990; RICS, 1984, and PRS, 1987). It will only be possible for consultancy to develop as a profession when the current knowledge system expands and the degree of abstraction increases. This latter characteristic is not, however, static – as Abbott points out 'As social work and nursing have become collegiate professions, medicine has become postgraduate. How abstract is abstract enough to become professional?' This issue is critical to professionalisation, since Abbott argues abstraction is the 'ultimate currency' in competition between professions. Abstraction allows problems to be defined or redefined in that particular profession's terms, e.g. it has enabled medicine to adopt a wide range of problem areas including alcoholism, mental illness, obesity, and hyperactivity in children.

There is a lack of empirical studies of how professional work really proceeds within its everyday context. Lennart Svensson (1990) used case studies of architects and psychologists at work to survey 'the means and resources which professionals use and try to control in their work, against the background of their positions at work and their acquired knowledge'.

For Svensson, competence 'is equivalent to being able to mobilise resources of different sorts for particular working tasks'. He distinguishes between two sources of resources – organisational and professional. Tasks which utilise the former source (termed organisational assets) include interpreting rules and regulations, applying administrative routines, or deciding where a given case belongs. These tasks determine the extent to which a professional's work is regulated, standardised and formalised.

Tasks which utilise the second source (termed 'skill or credential' and professional assets) include giving explanations on scientific grounds, and with using certain skills and techniques. These tasks impinge on the professional's education and affiliation and their own system of rules – including ethical rules, which are specific to the profession and individuals within that profession.

It is important to emphasise that

> Problems are posed and solved in a conceptual framework. These concepts and their relation to one another tend to be used by convention in one way and not in another, and those who have the appropriate education or training know how to use it... within the knowledge base, the ability to handle the conceptual instruments forms part of a 'discourse'. This discourse provides a basis of mutual understanding among professionals, which is not shared by others (Torstendahl, 1990).

THE NEED FOR A SOUND KNOWLEDGE BASE FOR USE IN THE TRAINING OF CONSULTANTS

Management consultancy as such is not yet a legally recognised or chartered profession. Those who are involved in consultancy independently of any professional body are striving to become recognised as a profession. In the UK an embryonic body is the Institute of Management Consultants (IMC). The IMC, founded in 1962, is the recognised professional institute of individual management consultants in the UK. Its membership is comprised of more than 3500 individual consultants and 300 registered practices. Some individuals are sole practitioners, others come from partnerships, or small, medium and large consultancy firms. Most functional and industry skills are covered by their membership. It is estimated by the IMC that they probably have between a quarter and a third, as members, of people practising management consulting in the manner which the Institute would recognise.

This embryonic profession will have a set of skills which differentiates itself from other professional bodies, and a set of skills which it shares with others who are in the consultancy business as defined by us in Chapter 1. The latter are the core skills which are critical in the process of meeting client needs, in making clients feel that they have been helped. Agreement does not exist as yet as to the delineation of this generic set of skills, partly because of the difficulty of the task, but more importantly because of the lack of research relating to the scope and nature of these skills and to their acquisition.

The importance of stimulating relevant research is becoming urgent in the light of the growth and economic significance of consultancy activities, and in the seemingly inadequate training in consultancy skills. In a pilot survey of some 20 UK professional associations (e.g. engineers, accountants, architects) we found that consultancy skills training was not systematically promoted. In none was it recommended, and only in one was it under discussion. Opportunities for receiving training in for instance presentational, counselling, project management, negotiation and influencing skills were sparse.

The IMC is interested in raising the quality of professional service to the client through the encouragement of effective individual experience, development and accreditation. The MCA is actively encouraging member firms to gain the UK quality standard BS5750 or its European and International equivalents (EN2900 and ISO9000).

As a nation the UK is noted for its relatively poor record on training, and no doubt consultancy as a whole is no exception! Yet, because effective consultancy depends upon the acquisition and development of particular skills, planned rather than *ad hoc* learning is crucial. Large firms are more likely to meet this requirement – a third of those working for firms employing at least 60 consultants received an average of four to eight days of training a year, over the last three years (IMC, 1990). Smaller firms and sole practitioners are not so fortunate.

As we describe later, experts can acquire and develop consultancy knowledge and skills either through 'trial-and-error' learning (often at clients' expense), or through experiences via craft apprenticeship and formal training. It is important to emphasise that merely possessing expertise, as for example in management, engineering, tax or other profession, is not sufficient to practise as a consultant. Extra knowledge and skills are needed if consultants are going to develop those superior client-oriented skills which make clients feel that they are being helped. This book highlights the roles that consultants will need to master in order to achieve this goal.

3 Consultancy Roles

No two consultancy assignments are the same, even if they fall within the same technical area. The major factors contributing to this uniqueness are situational differences, including client needs. In order to master such diversity, consultants have to be trained to recognise client needs and expectations and the forces impinging upon their client's behaviour, and be able to respond appropriately. Models of consultancy roles can serve as useful aids when training individuals to display the competences (i.e. the knowledge and skills) we associate with the effective consultant.

In this chapter we shall outline the essentials of the consultancy process, including the element of choice as to target and style of intervention, discuss representative models which have been put forward to help understand the nature of this process and identify some of the limitations of these models for training purposes.

THE CONSULTANCY PROCESS

Figure 3.1 portrays the essentials of the consultancy process. This simplified model highlights the importance of the consultant understanding the client's needs, and in turn being able to help the client understand how he or she can be of help to the client. Three important features of this process are not conveyed by the model. First, identifying client needs can be difficult because the client may be uncertain or even unaware of their 'true' nature. Second, client needs are dynamic and may change over the course of an assignment. Third, identifying the consultant's need-satisfying resources and expectations is not straightforward, and few clients are likely to possess the level of skill required. This puts even more responsibility on the shoulders of the consultant to ensure that effective communication takes place.

The effective consultant is more likely to be able to fathom out client needs, and to respond in a manner which is appropriate to the context in which these needs arise. Conceptual aids are required for the less skilled so that the process of developing superior skills will be as smooth and efficient as possible. One such aid would be a model of consultancy roles geared to discover and meet client needs.

In order to service a client's needs, a consultant has to intervene in the way the individual client thinks or does things, or in the activities and systems over which the client has responsibility. There are a

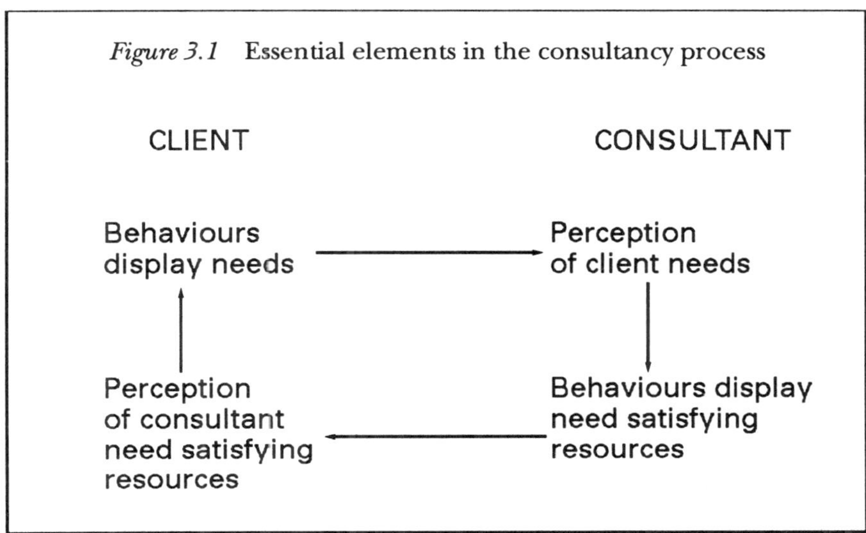

Figure 3.1 Essential elements in the consultancy process

variety of ways in which this can be done. For example, the consultant can act as an expert and give appropriate advice to the client; or as a friendly tutor by listening and asking questions; or as an extra arm by carrying out tasks on behalf of the client. In each case the consultant is displaying a set of behaviours which we readily associate with a stereotype or role.

The important thing to recognise is that consultants are in a continuous choice situation with respect to roles. It is this rich choice facing consultants, and the significant consequences of their selected behaviour, which has led practitioners and academics to identify typical roles and to develop taxonomies or models.

CONCEPT OF ROLES

The term 'role' has at least three meanings, in addition to its theatrical sense (e.g. the role of Hamlet in Shakespeare's play). First, in the occupational context it is used to refer to a generally recognised occupational category, e.g. a managerial role, a doctor's role, a consultant's role. We often develop strong stereotypes of individuals filling these roles: that is, we expect them to behave in certain characteristic ways. Stereotype labels are often used to describe particular roles, or types, or styles of intervention used by consultants.

Second, in the social psychology theory context it is used to analyse individual and group behaviour (Katz and Kahn, 1978). Thus consultants take roles according to the expectations that they think the client has of them, their superior has of them, their subordinates have of them and so on. 'Role' in this context is being used in a technical and theoretical sense to gain understanding of the behaviours of two or more people interacting with each other.

Third, the term may be used interchangeably with function. Thus, in training we may use a case study to show how situational factors make certain demands on the consultant which have to be met if the assignment is to be successfully accomplished. These demands may be expressed in terms of functions to be met or roles to be taken – these are two sides of the same coin. It is in this sense that we are trying to identify the roles (or functions) that consultants may be required to fulfil in the course of an assignment.

All three interpretations of roles (let us call them stereotype, theoretical and functional) are applicable to the study of consultancy. But we need to be clear as to which meaning is being used when exploring models of consultancy roles for training purposes.

MODELS OF CONSULTANCY ROLES

The most frequently quoted models fall into two main categories: contingency models, and ideal style models. The former are essentially saying that if 'x' situational factors are present then 'y' rather than 'z' role is the most appropriate response; the ideal style models are saying that there is a single role response that is appropriate for most situations.

Contingency Models

A good example of this is that of Schmidt and Johnson (1969). They identify three typical consultancy roles: facilitator, consultant and executive. Underlying these roles is a continuum of behaviours ranging from the non-directive (e.g. listens, interprets) to the directive (e.g. proposes criteria, recommends). In the former, the maximum use is made of the client's experience and knowledge; in the latter, it is the consultant's specialised experience and knowledge which dominates. The model provides guidelines as to what situational factors to look for when deciding which role and associated behaviours are most appropriate.

This model is essentially focusing on the 'style' of intervention, and the situational factors identified as relevant in determining which style to adopt include: what the client wants (e.g. to understand and learn about the problem), and what the client has (e.g. little experience);

what the consultant wants (e.g. client to grow and develop), and the consultant has (e.g. high understanding of client); the nature of the client–consultant relationship (e.g. little empathy); and other situational factors such as the urgency of the problem.

Another example is Lippitt and Lippitt's (1978) role continuum. They identify eight roles spread across a similar non-directive/directive continuum indicating the level of consultant problem-solving activity: reflector (asks questions to help clarify or change a given situation); process specialist (observes and gives feedback on problem-solving processes); fact finder (gathers data and stimulates thinking); alternative identifier (establishes criteria for assessing alternatives); collaborator in problem solving (participates as a peer in decision-making); trainer/educator (designs learning experiences and trains the client); technical expert (provides information and suggestions); advocate (through suggestions and persuasion influences the problem-solving process).

Champion *et al.* (1990) put forward a model consisting of two dimensions: consultant responsibility for client growth, and consultant responsibility for project results. These form a grid within which are located nine separate roles, reflecting different combinations of low, moderate or high interventions by the consultant. Thus, the hands-on expert role reflects high intervention by the consultant and low intervention by the client, since the task is undertaken by the consultant on behalf of the client. The counsellor role is the reverse, since here the client performs the task with the consultant providing indirect help in the form of clarifying goals, maintaining positive motivations and so on. The other seven roles are: modeller (consultant carries out the task but the approach is sufficiently visible to encourage learning through modelling); partner (consultant has high responsibility for results and growth); coach (moderate responsibility for results but high for client growth); teacher or trainer (moderate responsibility for both); facilitator (low task but high growth responsibility); and reflective observer (low task and growth responsibilities, in that consultant confined to feeding back observations).

As with the previous model, Champion *et al.* provide guidelines as to the circumstances in which particular roles are likely to be most effective. These are based on a reading of four situational variables: the organisational situation (i.e. the extent to which there is an immediate need for results); characteristics of the client; characteristics of the consultant; the client/consultant relationship (e.g. whether it is one of trust and openness).

A fourth model by Wooten and White (1989) tries to bring together the roles played by consultants, by clients and by both parties. The roles in the last category are identified as: problem solver, diagnostician learner, monitor. The consultant roles are defined as: educator/trainer, model, researcher/theoretician, technical expert, resource linker. These particular consultant roles were arrived at by a thorough review of the more influencial theorists and practitioners in the organisation development field (e.g. Lippitt *et al.*, 1958; Lawrence and Lorsch, 1969; Argyris, 1970; Bennis, 1973; Steele, 1975; Blake and Mouton, 1976; Lippitt and Lippitt, 1978). The main contingency aspects of this model are introduced via a table which indicates the particular combination of roles (of the consultant and the client) which are likely to be most appropriate at different stages of the consultancy process. Thus at the early 'clarification stage' the critical consultant roles are researcher/theoretician, the client roles of supporter/advocate and information supplier, and the roles shared by both, namely learner and problem solver.

On the basis of an examination of the literature (particularly the work of such people as Schein, 1969; Margulies, 1978; Steele, 1975; and Lippitt, 1969), Steven Stryker (1982) identifies seven dominant roles found in the consultancy process:

- *Doctor* who diagnoses situation and prescribes a cure.
- *Marketer* who attempts to sell client packaged services.
- *Scientist* who observes and reflects on a problem in an objective manner, and acts as a catalyst for change.
- *Detective* who focuses on gathering evidence to resolve problem.
- *Expert* who has the latest knowledge on problem and advocates the course of action.
- *Broker* who shares with the client equal responsibility for resolving problem, and helps client to develop skills for defining and resolving future problems.
- *Sanitary engineer* who assists in maintaining the status quo.

As with the Wooten and White model, Stryker relates his taxonomy to the various stages of the consultancy process, by showing that certain roles exert a larger influence in one or more stages of the process. Thus the doctor or scientist roles are likely to be more prominent at the beginning of an assignment. At the pathway or solution implementation stage the scientist and broker roles are likely to have greater impact (Stryker, 1982, p.32).

Another set of models which fall within the contingency category are those which can be labelled the career progression models. An example was recently put forward by the Institute of Management Consultants as part of a scheme prescribing the training and experience which consultants should receive at different stages in their career (IMC, 1993). The four roles identified and their underlying knowledge and skills, were arrived at by a process of distilling 'the wisdom and experience of a number of practices, and of specialist training-consultants, to arrive at what must become the definitive statement of the training a consultant needs at every stage of his or her career' (IMC,1993, p.1). The roles are:

- *Analyst*: a mainly research-based role that is likely to involve minimal client contact and reporting to a senior consultant.
- *Consultant*: a role which carries with it responsibility for the design and implementation of assignments.
- *Engagement manager*: as for the consultant role, plus responsibility for selling and supervising consultants on projects.
- *Practice manager*: this role carries with it responsibility for a business area within the consultancy, plus the tasks of the engagement manager and responsibility for market development, career development of staff and the meeting of profit targets.

Such a model seeks to cover roles which go beyond our area of interest, i.e. client–consultant interactions once an assignment has commenced. It is the second career role of the 'consultant' that we are primarily studying in this book.

Ideal Style Models

Several other authors have produced taxonomies of consultancy types or roles, and express a personal preference for one type on the grounds that they (and others) have found it most effective in achieving their objectives. Roles are used here in their occupational sense, since the labels used are selected for their stereotyped associations.

Edgar Schein (1969, 1987) puts forward a typology of role models based on the literature, and on his own experience:

- *The expert* (or the purchase model): this model assumes the client knows what he wants, and requires to purchase information and/or a service.
- *The doctor–patient*: here the client invites the consultant either to give them a check-up to see in what condition of health they are in, or to help them overcome a weakness or illness by finding out what is wrong and recommending a programme of therapy.

- *The process:* the emphasis in this model is on helping clients to help themselves, not on solving their problems or giving expert advice.

For Schein it is the process model which is normally the most effective when trying to develop and change social systems, because it results in the client becoming more self-sufficient and able to cope with future problems. Although he uses the term 'process' to emphasise the essential difference between this approach and the others, Schein could very well have labelled it the 'counsellor' since it is the approach which most typifies the stereotyped image of the professional counsellor.

Charles Margerison (1988) identifies four basic role models which consultants adopt:

- *The doctor:* a common model based on the medical analogy, where one assumes the client or client system has some illness or malfunctioning. The consultant carries out an expert diagnosis, and then prescribes some operation or treatment as the solution to remove the cause of the illness or malfunctioning.
- *The detective:* the underlying principle here is that something is wrong and there is a need to find out who are the offending individuals so that they can be changed or removed. This model may be seen at work in consultancy assignments relating to safety at work, particularly after an accident. This model concentrates on searching for clues which will account for a series of undesirable events, so that appropriate preventive measures can be taken.
- *The salesperson:* the underlying assumption here is that the consultant has the right product or service that will help solve the client's problem. One often finds these products or services have been developed by consultants because they see a ready market for them, and this tends to generate fashionable solutions to a wide range of client problems. Such solutions include: management by objectives, job enrichment, payment by results, total quality management, and so on.
- *The travel agent:* this approach assumes the client is on a journey, but may not be clear where he wants to go or how to get to a particular destination. The consultant's job is to clarify the client's objectives and to work out the best means of reaching the desired destination.

For Margerison it is the travel agent model which characterises the approach with which he is most comfortable, and which he feels is most appropriate for the assignments which he is usually asked to tackle.

Peter Block (1981, p.18) identifies three roles which consultants adopt with line managers: the expert, a pair-of-hands, or a collaborative role. He discusses the characteristics of each one, together with their consequences. The expert is similar to other uses of the term already given. In the second role the manager sees the consultant as an extra pair of hands, the manager making the decisions and retaining control during implementation. As in previous schemes the collaborative role is one of shared responsibility between the client and the consultant. Block recognises that the choice of role will depend upon individual differences in management style, the nature of the task, and the consultant's own personal preference, Block concludes that 'the more the consultative process can be collaborative, the better the odds for implementation after the consultant has left' (p.23).

LIMITATIONS OF EXISTING MODELS

What are the advantages and disadvantages of using these various models of consultancy roles as training aids? The contingency models are attractive because they stress the importance of situational needs, and the need for consultants to respond differentially to them. They also provide guidance as to the critical cues to respond to in the client situation, and the most appropriate roles to undertake in a given situation. These conceptual frameworks enable trainees to learn many of the skills required to manage the consultancy process.

However, the more popular contingency models have three potential disadvantages. First, the dimension(s) on which the contingencies are based are highly selective. Thus, the Schmidt and Johnson (1969) model is based on a single directive/non-directive dimension of roles. The Champion *et al.* (1985) model builds on the two dimensions of responsibility – for project results and for client growth. The Wooten and White (1989) model differs from the other two in being mainly based on the stages of the consultancy process (i.e. initiation, clarification, specification, diagnosis, action planning, systems intervention, evaluation, alteration, maintenance, termination).

Given that these authors have been influenced in their thinking by models developed for other purposes (e.g. leadership style), it is legitimate to ask whether other dimensions may be more critical for learning about consultancy competences.

Second, and related to the last point, the consultancy context in which these authors are operating is that of organisation development (OD). OD has a particular theoretical orientation, value system and technical base. It may be that certain consultancy roles have not been identified as worthy of mention because of this bias.

Third, the consultancy roles identified result from a review of the literature plus the personal experience of the authors, rather than any programme of scientific research.

An exception to the above criticisms is the IMC career progression model – analyst, consultant, engagement manager and practice manager. This model has been specifically put forward as a basis for a modular programme for training consultants at different stages in their career. As such, it is not strictly comparable to the other models. It is also a model that rests on a wealth of experience in the consultancy industry.

The ideal style models have a lot to recommend them, but only where the prescribed roles match situational needs. Here again the influence of OD-type consultancy, with its heavy emphasis on process rather than content, is discernible. The ideological basis (and implied inflexibility) of these models limits their value for training individuals in generic consultancy competences.

In the light of these observations there is clearly a need for further research which is more open-ended, scientific, and spans a greater mix of consultancy assignments. The last is particularly important because the models of consultancy roles in the literature derive mainly from an examination of OD-type assignments. This is not surprising given that most of the literature on change agents falls within this area of knowledge, and that some people use the terms consultants and change agents interchangeably.

The need for further research was reinforced by the conclusions that we drew as a result of our own personal observations:

- Consultancy roles change over the years as a result of the changing needs that clients experience (e.g. requiring help to implement recommendations, operating in new markets abroad);
- There is an unanticipated tendency for the nature of assignments to change once they get under way.

Both these phenomena create additional difficulties for those responsible for training consultants. The changing nature of the consultancy market may mean that models that were once valid training tools are no longer so. The unexpected twists of assignments indicates the need for comprehensive and flexible models of consultancy roles.

These were some of the considerations which led us to initiating research into consultancy roles.

Part II
The 1+7 Model of Consultancy Roles

4 An Empirical Investigation

PILOT STUDY

A pilot study was carried out in 1988 to see the extent to which our ideas were shared by others in the consultancy industry in the UK. We interviewed senior people in seven consultancy firms and in four professional associations, including the British Consultants Bureau and the Institute of Management Consultants.

The principal points that we covered with the people we talked to were:

- Their main current business concerns;
- Whether in their experience consultants during recent years have to take on roles that involve a much higher degree of interaction with clients;
- What these roles are and what abilities they called for;
- How the new requirements are reflected in what firms do about selection and training;
- What they consider are the main factors likely to inhibit profitable growth in the future.

Despite consultancy firms being swamped with applications, one of the main problems was getting staff of the right calibre – those who could deliver all the competences required. The gaps were perceived to be mainly in the areas of interpersonal skills, broad business knowledge and personal effectiveness. As one respondent put it:

> Getting people with the technical skills is not a problem, but there is a great shortage of those with the other basic skills we need. The things that are missing are the ability to relate their technology to general business management, and interpersonal skills especially persuasion. The more technical the area, the more difficult to find the latter.

Most of them considered that there had been changes in recent years in the demands made on consultants in terms of the roles that they had to undertake. The two or three who did not agree with this said that they thought some of the demands might have changed a bit but that the core skills were the same as ever. Those who believed that there had been changes were asked to describe the new functions that consultants had to carry out. Descriptions such as facilitator, politician, sub-contractor, negotiator and persuader were used frequently.

The answers to the questions about selection and training indicated that the main priorities lay in finding people who already had the full range of abilities needed. Training methods varied. Some ran extensive in-house courses, others relied largely on training on the job; some had precise systems for programming training and monitoring performance and others adopted a more informal approach.

To our questions about the factors that were likely to inhibit future profitable growth, four of the eleven indicated staffing problems as their main concern and four others that these were one of their secondary concerns. Three said that profitability was their main concern, two mentioned some aspect of organisation effectiveness and the other two some aspect of marketing.

A key point as far as we were concerned is that we had no reports of a detailed analysis having been made of the roles that constituted the changes in the demands more recently being made of consultants, with follow-up training programmes designed to create the relevant abilities. It is important to emphasise, however, that this does not mean that appropriate action was not being taken; in some firms at least it was highly probable that relevant on-the-job coaching was given. What was apparently missing was a comprehensive and dedicated analysis of the roles that would lead to full identification of training needs.

We had set out to check assumptions that had been based on our own working experience: that consultancy has been changing and continues to change; that important new abilities were being demanded of consultants and that these abilities were scarce and not fully understood; and that a principal symptom would be a shortage of staff of the right calibre, able to take up the range of roles that consultancy situations now frequently demand. The pilot study provided the positive reinforcement needed for us to initiate the main study described below.

MAIN STUDY

Orientation

Our approach was influenced by three objectives:
- To focus on what consultants actually did during the course of an assignment (i.e. the functions that they tried to fulfil and the behaviours displayed);

- To base our observations on a heterogenous group of assignments (diversity rather than representation was a guiding principle);
- To study assignments 'with a twist', that is, those which contained a significant development which had been difficult to spot when the assignment commenced.

Case Histories

Given these objectives, it seemed appropriate to collect the research data on the basis of case histories. A semi-structured interview approach was used, and the main consultants involved in the assignments studied were always interviewed. The interview schedule was designed to ensure that the following topics were explored: general background of client and project; project history from initial contact to closure; the activities and roles undertaken by the consultants (particularly the difficult and unexpected ones) and the skills, knowledge and understanding required for their successful execution; with hindsight what would have been done differently and why.

Each case history was written up, and checked with the respondent(s) for accuracy and confidentiality. Most of the case histories are reproduced in Chapter 9, and abstracts of several of them appear in Chapter 5. The identities of the consultancy firms have been disguised by the use of pseudonyms of a flowering shrub or tree. The identity of clients have been suitably camouflaged.

Sample

The size of the consultancy firms from which these case histories were obtained, and the nature of the assignments, are shown in Table 4.1.

Obtaining case histories from consulting firms is not an easy task, given the problem of confidentiality and encroachment on the fee-earning time of individual consultants. The British Consultants Bureau and the Institute of Management Consultants kindly gave our research some publicity in their newsletters; a number of firms approached us as a result of this. In addition, we wrote to all consulting organisations that had had recent contact with the Business School, including its Career Service. Altogether we were in contact with 37 organisations. Of these, 22 offered us help; two of these subsequently dropped out owing to business reasons. Of the remaining 20, two offered us two case histories each. The study is thus based on 22 case histories.

Table 4.1   Some characteristics of the sample

Size of firms (number of employees)		
Up to 50	3	
51–100	3	
101–500	6	
501–1000	6	
Over 1000	4	
Total	22	
Type of assignment		
Management, strategic consultancy		8
Engineering, construction		5
Information technology		5
Design consultancy		4
Total		22

It will be seen that the coverage was reasonably widespread, but it cannot be claimed to be representative. Small firms are under-represented, and the type of assignments undertaken are not representative (e.g. legal or chemical engineering assignments are not included).

ANALYSIS AND FINDINGS

Given that we have carried out a qualitative study, it is important to understand the approach we adopted in arriving at our model of consultancy roles. Figure 4.1 summarises the approach in terms of six steps.

Step 1   We have already described the collection of research data through the case histories. The next four steps were interactive and culminated in the 1+7 conceptual model.

Step 2   We analysed each case history, listing those behaviours which the consultant had perceived as critical and/or which we perceived as such. The long list of extracted elements had then to be condensed into a logical framework. We found we could categorise

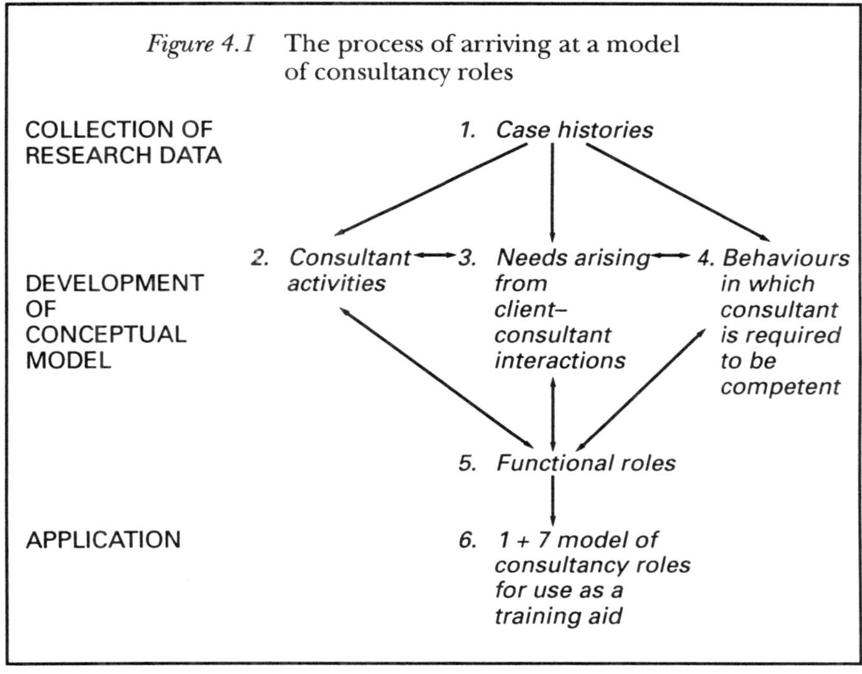

Figure 4.1 The process of arriving at a model of consultancy roles

the behaviours under three main activity headings, and nine sub-headings. A summary appears in Table 4.2.

This initial analysis brought home to us the extraordinary scope of consultants' activities. The problem-solving activities are ones which we readily associate with consultants, but perhaps we tend to under-estimate the extent to which their activities are concerned with managing and influencing.

All the identified activities can in fact be related to the problem-solving paradigm, which is no surprise given the frequency with which the consultancy process is conceptualised in terms of the para-digm (i.e. the cycle of problem definition, problem diagnosis, gen-eration of alternative solutions, selection of solution, implementation of solution, and evaluation). The attraction in applying it to the consultancy process stems from its logical appeal, its empirical and theoretical justification, and its widespread use in describing assign-ments retrospectively and in structuring ongoing interventions (see for instance: Kolb, 1983; Wooten and White, 1989).

One of the authors has suggested elsewhere (Williams, 1987) that in order to counter the criticisms levelled at the excessively

Table 4.2   Critical activities and behaviours

---

1. **Primarily Managing Activities**
- *Contracting* (e.g. checks that all parties agree to contents of contract)
- *Planning, Organising, Monitoring, Controlling and Adapting* (e.g. regularly reviews progress through meetings with interested parties)
- *Leading* (e.g. acts as mentor to others in team)

2. **Primarily Problem-Solving Activities**
- *Information Generation and Problem Definition* (e.g. carries out a diagnostic study which identifies the sources of problems)
- *Solution Generation* (e.g. shows how a technique used elsewhere can be adapted to client's organisation)

3. **Primarily Influencing Activities**
- *Negotiation* (e.g. deals with other interest groups on behalf of client)
- *Consulting and Persuading* (e.g. initiates meetings for briefing and consultation)
- *Teaching and Facilitating* (e.g. helps clients to think through and build a model of the business)
- *Politicising* (e.g. uses steering committee to influence the activities of others)

---

tidy and rational image of the problem-solving paradigm, it is more fruitful to conceptualise the consultancy process as iterative, i.e. it consists of several intertwined mini problem solving cycles within a macro problem-solving cycle. Each mini cycle progresses the overall consultancy assignment a little further in the macro cycle. Each stage of a mini or the macro problem-solving cycle will require certain needs to be met. The skilled consultant will perceive what these needs are, and the extent to which they can be met by the client, by the consultant, or by both. It is the consultant's diagnosis of these needs that will trigger off the particular roles he/she will display.

Steps 3 and 4   On the basis of the actual activities of consultants, and within the context of the problem-solving paradigm, we inferred the needs that arose from the consultancy process, and the behavioural implications that these have for the competences required of consultants.

Step 5 A list of functional roles resulted from the earlier analyses. The identified roles did not logically emerge at the end of a tidy sequence of activities. Given the nature of our data there was no statistical way in which we could arrive at them. The process was a judgmental one, and in the process of identifying roles we were influenced by the following explicit criteria:

- They should account for a significant functional need within the consultancy or problem-solving process (i.e. we were not concerned with the roles which consultants performed within their own firms).
- Overlap between the roles should be minimal.
- The naming of a role should be informative in itself, in that it reflected the pattern of behaviours (or stereotype) associated with the name.
- The set of roles identified should cater for all the critical behaviours discovered in one or more of the case histories.

Figure 4.2 lists the eight groups of needs arising from client-consultant interactions, and their corresponding functional roles.

Step 6 The final step was the creation of a model that summarised our findings, and at the same time was simple, memorable, and an informative training aid for achieving superior performance in consultancy. In order to achieve the latter aim it was necessary for the model to incorporate not only our findings, but also conclusions to be drawn from the general literature on consultancy. They include:

Figure 4.2 Client–consultant interactions viewed as problem-solving activities

Needs arising from client–consultant interactions	Functional roles
• To provide specialist information or advice ⟶	EXPERT
• To manage or control assignment ⟶	EXECUTIVE
• To gather, analyse and interpret information ⟶	RESEARCHER
• To help clients arrive at own informed decisions ⟶	TUTOR
• To impart knowledge through formal methods ⟶	EDUCATOR
• To get individuals/groups in conflict to work together ⟶	CONCILIATOR
• To change the balance of power within client system ⟶	POWERBROKER
• To enhance the effectiveness of existing work units ⟶	SYNERGIST

1.   Giving prominence to the role of expert.   It is, after all, a consultant's expertise which makes him or her attractive to a client in need. The minimum requirement for selecting consultants is that they are expected to have the expert knowledge and skills of, for example, an organisational psychologist, an engineer or a management consultant.

2.   Recognising the multi-role nature of consultancy.   You can be a good organisational psychologist in academia, but a poor organisational psychologist in consultancy. In order for one's expertise to be instrumental in solving a client problem one needs to mobilise additional competences or skills. The actual competences required at a particular point in time will depend upon situational factors. Our findings show that key competences needed may be categorised under seven additional roles.

3.   The nature of consultancy assignments are such that it is necessary for a consultant to be competent in all eight roles.   The characteristics of assignments which justify this statement include:

- The unpredictable nature of the course that assignments may take as a result of changing client needs and circumstances. Initially the client and consultant may have misunderstood each other's needs and expectations. Clients may hide their true motives until a climate of trust has been established. Only when the consultant's own diagnosis of the problem is complete is its true nature revealed. Less controllable factors may also be at work. These may include changes in key client personnel, or in economic, social or political forces.
- The social and political consequences of many assignments. Consultants often take on a temporary position in a social system in order to procure change. Change in social systems brings about winners and losers. Consultants must learn to deal with these client emotions in the process of applying their expertise.
- Some assignments may span several stages of a major change within the client system. Models of organisational change generally recognise Lewin's (1951) three stages of unfreezing (antecedent), moving (implementation), and refreezing (reinforcement). Consultants will find different patterns of role responses being triggered according to the stage of an intervention.
- Consultants are often on their own in having to deal with unexpected client needs, and cannot depend upon their professional colleagues to make up for their deficiencies.

The model in Figure 4.3 is a visual attempt to incorporate the three features we regard as important. Thus it gives prominence to the role of expert by the title 1+7 and the central position allocated to the role; it gives equal weighting to the seven additional roles; and it conveys the idea that the role of expert can only find expression in conjuction with the other roles in the model (in other words, that a consultant's effectiveness in the role of expert is dependent upon his or her performance in the seven other roles).

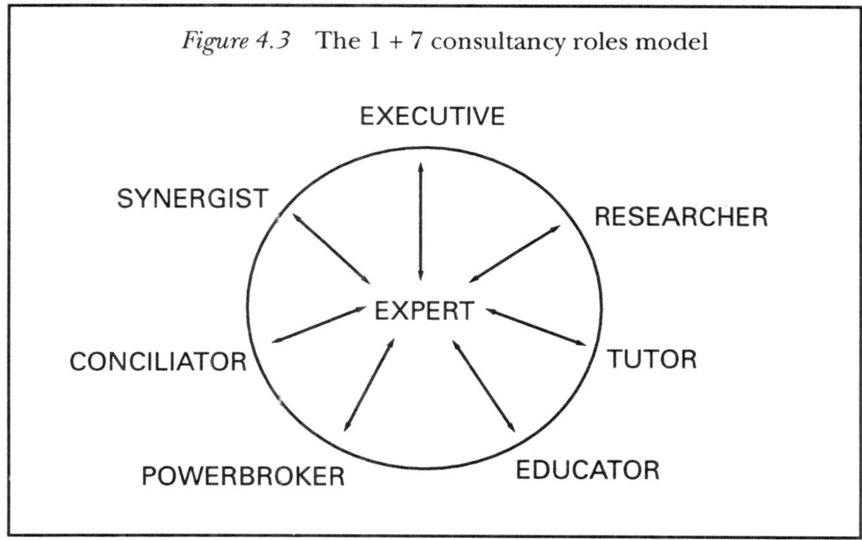

Figure 4.3   The 1 + 7 consultancy roles model

The abstract of the Neanthis case history in Box 4.1 will illustrate the multiple and dynamic nature of consultancy roles. The consultant started off as a 'tutor' to a managing director, helping him to understand more about total quality management (TQM); to this was soon added the role of 'expert' on strategy, and the role of team-builder or 'synergist'. The same adaptive behaviour of the consultant can be seen in the other case histories in Chapter 9. Thus in Deutzia the consultant started off in the straightforward role of an 'expert' in salary administration systems, but soon found himself having to take on a 'tutor' role *vis-à-vis* the area directors in an effort to change their attitudes. In Forsythe the consultant's initial roles were those of 'expert' and 'researcher', but he subsequently found himself undertaking roles akin to an 'executive' (managing a project) and a 'tutor'.

Box 4.1   Abstract of Neanthis case history

The managing director of a large organisation in the services industry asked Neanthis for advice on whether and how total quality management (TQM) could be used in his business.

They arranged an appreciation programme for him. In the course of it, they showed him that TQM is most effective when it is used to implement business strategy and that to have a valid strategy it is essential first to have a clear and agreed understanding of the organisation's mission and vision. The Managing Director and his Board asked Neanthis to help them work this through.

The task proved to be very difficult, mostly because the Board had not previously been used to getting together to tackle such issues. It took a series of meetings extending over some months to produce a statement to which all were fully committed. But they succeeded in re-defining the goals of the business and developed a strategy to achieve them. The strategy utilised TQM and necessitated a change in the corporate culture. Throughout, Neanthis structured the agenda and managed the process. They also helped in the follow-up implementation.

It is worth remembering here that a label is attached to a particular role because the set of behaviours being referred to is a subset of behaviours we would normally associate with experts in that role. The use of the label of 'researcher' is not intended to imply that all the skills and behaviours of professional researchers are needed by all consultants.

The value of the 1+7 model of consultancy roles will become clearer in exploring the competences underlying the roles. This will be done in the next chapter, when we shall be in a better position to evaluate the model in the light of current knowledge.

5 Competences Underlying Effective Role Performance

We have described consultancy as a process in which a consultant provides a service to a client for the purpose of meeting the client's need. We have also conceptualised this process in terms of the problem-solving paradigm, i.e. viewing the client's need as a problem to be solved. In the course of this problem-solving process the consultant may undertake a variety of roles according to his or her interpretation of the needs of the situation. The value of the 1+7 model is that it identifies (in a readily assimilated form) the *key* roles which consultants should be able to undertake in the process.

The model must now be given more substance if it is going to be useful in training. We need to answer questions such as:

- What competences are associated with the eight roles identified?
- How are these competences acquired?
- How can individuals learn to apply these competences so as to achieve superior performance on assignments?

The first question will be tackled in this chapter. The second and third questions will be tackled here and in later chapters. In relation to the third question it is worth reminding the reader of our central argument: the 1+7 model is intended as a training aid for achieving superior performance by seeing what is needed and responding appropriately.

COMPETENCES, SKILLS AND EFFECTIVENESS

A clarification of terms. So far we have been talking about 'knowledge and skills', 'skills', and 'competences' without demanding tight definitions of the different meanings which they may convey. We are saying that in order to be able to meet the needs of a client, a consultant should be skilled or competent in an identifiable range of roles. Each of these roles requires the consultant to display behaviours that 'relevant others' will judge to be evidence of particular competences. (By relevant others we mean clients, supervisors, trainers and educators). Our use of competence is therefore compatible with, although not synonymous with, the technical definition given to the term by the Employment Department's Training Commission:

> Competence is a wide concept which embodies the ability to transfer skills and knowledge to new situations within the occupational area... An element of competence describes what can be done; an action, behaviour or outcome which a person should be able to demonstrate. Or an element of competence may describe such things as the knowledge or understanding which is essential if performance is to be sustained, or extended to new situations within the occupation. Each element of competence has associated performance criteria which define the expected level of performance. (Training Commission, 1988, pp.14, 15)

The main criticism levelled at the Department of Employment's work on competences is that it is too mechanistic and analytical, and insufficiently organic and holistic. In other words, the fact that Smith has acquired a particular *mix of competences* does not necessarily make him or her an *effective* consultant. When we are judging a consultant's performance as effective, we are implying that his or her performance is instrumental in achieving a planned end result or goal. This requires the consultant to have the appropriate mix of competences, and the professional judgement and expertise to bring them to bear on the needs of the situation so as to achieve the 'right' planned goal. Figure 5.1 will clarify this difference even further. It shows that the effectiveness with which a consultant adopts the roles required by typical assignments is a function of situational needs, superordinate goals and the relevant competences acquired by the consultant.

Within the context of this framework the following questions will indicate the criteria for judging the effectiveness of a consultant:

- Does the consultant's client actually feel helped?
- Are the consultant's goals achieved without compromising recognised ethical codes?
- In helping clients to bring about change are the processes managed in ways which avoid *unnecessary* conflict, resistance to change, human and financial costs?
- Does the consultant cope successfully with new (and perhaps unexpected) demands from clients?

While we are spelling out these criteria within the context of giving meaning to the concept of effectiveness, we should also point out that these are the criteria we would select to define a truly *client-oriented consultant*. The first criterion is critical: if the client does not feel helped then it is difficult to see how the consultant's contribution was worth the fee to the client. The second criterion reminds

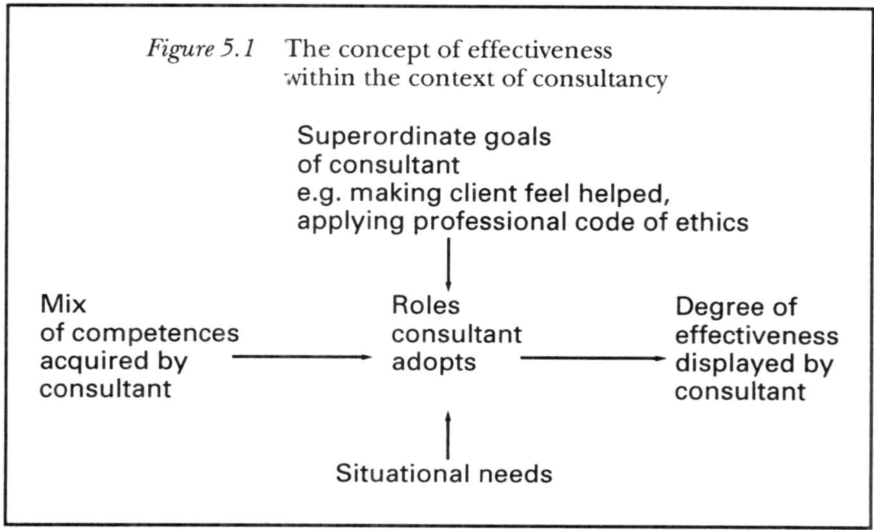

Figure 5.1 The concept of effectiveness within the context of consultancy

us of the main purpose of a code of ethics to a profession, i.e. the protection of the client's interests and the importance of consultants ethical behaviour (Allen and Davis, 1993). The third criterion accepts that in most assignments the consultant is involved in helping the client to procure change, but through appropriate competences the client-oriented consultant will be concerned to bring about planned change with minimal damage to the client system. The fourth criterion refers to an observation we have already highlighted elsewhere, that there is a tendency for clients to make new demands during the course of an assignment. This behaviour is usually justified in terms of changes in the felt needs of clients. Consultants must be able to respond positively and constructively to changed circumstances.

What is the relevance of the off-the-job learning situation to becoming effective? Our use of the term 'effectiveness' is such that it is inseparable from performance on the job – it is a judgement made by relevant others about consultants on assignments. Effectiveness comes as a result of accumulated practical experience across a range of clients and situations. On the basis of their experiences consultants will arrive at personal generalisations which guide their subsequent behaviour (the work of David Kolb, 1984, and Donald Schon, 1983, have been particularly helpful in increasing our understanding of the processes involved and will be discussed in Chapter 7). An example of such a generalisation could be the belief that a preparatory educational process must precede any major change, and that this must include a participative review of the current situation so that staff can see for themselves the need for change.

The emphasis given to practical experience in becoming effective must not be allowed to overshadow off-the-job learning experiences. As every trainer knows, integrating on-the-job and off-the-job experiences reduces the period of trial-and-error learning involved, to the benefit of clients! The essence of high quality training is somehow to bring together first-hand experiences and second-hand experiences (i.e. the relevant body of knowledge which has accumulated from the experiences of others, including scientific studies) so as to enrich the practical knowledge of individual consultants.

The quality of this practical knowledge is likely to be variable where training and development are undervalued, or where the content covered and the methods used are uninformed. It is to the content issues that we now turn (methods will be discussed in Chapter 7). The objective here is not to outline details of courses, with appropriate syllabuses – that is the task of the trainer. Our aim is to give more meaning to the consultancy roles we have identified by indicating typical behaviours associated with these roles, and highlighting some of the knowledge and competences underpinning these behaviours. This should give greater insight into the nature of the 1+7 model.

THE 1+7 ROLES

Expert

A client approaches a consultant because he or she is perceived as an expert in a particular field (e.g. human resource management, marketing, civil engineering, software engineering) and/or as an expert in a particular context (e.g. financial services sector, the motor industry, the Middle East, Eastern Europe, project management).

In the professions there are well-defined routes for gaining recognition as an expert capable of delivering a service. Full membership of a professional body usually indicates that the competences and effectiveness criteria have been satisfied, as assessed by a combination of examinations and relevant experience. Every profession is therefore involved in the consultancy process, and every consultant adopts the role of expert. Professionals who choose to work in particular contexts further develop an applied expertise.

The consultant in the expert role is illustrated in Box 5.1. This is an abstract of the Forsythe case history, where an in-depth knowledge of IT and its integration within the business was clearly essential for the consultant to meet the particular needs of the client.

Box 5.1   Forsythe and the expert role

Forsythe, an IT consultancy, were asked to do a failure study of a £1 million software project that would not run. They were called in by the people who had prepared the software, the IT division of a major organisation then owned by the UK government. The software had been commissioned by the organisation's Sales Director.

Forsythe located the problem quickly enough. However, because its origins lay in the function specification (i.e. in the basis on which the software had been built), all the work already done had to be aborted and a new specification written. The Sales Director asked Forsythe to stay on and manage the project.

To produce the new specification, Forsythe had to help the Sales Director and his colleagues do two things. First, develop a much better understanding not only of what IT could do for their business but also of what its limitations were. Second, build a model of their business so that they could establish what information they needed in order to run it with maximum effectiveness. Working with a client who was eager and quick to learn, Forsythe moved the project rapidly to success.

The sort of behaviours we would expect consultants to display when they are in the expert role are encapsulated in the following statements:

Is persuasive when providing advice in his/her area of expertise

Is able to speak knowledgeably about the client's business

To merit a high rating by self and/or others on items such as these requires significant learning experiences. We would expect those who have achieved full membership status in their professional body to be able to speak with appropriate expertise in their specialist area. Knowledge of the industry in which the client operates is another matter, and this is most likely to be accumulated by a combination of planned formal learning and actual involvement in assignments within that industry.

There are clearly different levels of expertise with respect to both scope and depth. While professional bodies lay down certain minimum criteria, the level achieved by different consultants will largely reflect the mix of practical experience accumulated.

Executive

An executive or managerial role involves responsibility for achieving defined goals, given certain constraints relating to authority, resources and time. Within the 1+7 model the term is applied to occasions when a consultant carries out an activity or project on behalf of a client, and/or is required to meet the needs of the situation by displaying behaviours and skills we normally associate with an executive.

The abstract of the Laurus case history in Box 5.2 is a good example of this role in operation.

Box 5.2   Laurus and the executive role

> Laurus were engaged as project managers by a food manufacturer for the construction of a new highly automated warehouse. On behalf of the clients, they engaged other specialists (architects, engineers, etc.) to work on the project and appointed the contractor – who was to operate on a part-design-and-build basis.
>
> The project appeared to go well for the first nine months of its scheduled 12 month duration. It then became clear that there would be cost and time overruns – and the quality of the contractor's work deteriorated. Laurus put the contractor under pressure, intensified the level of scrutiny and took a greater role in the supervision of activities. They also had to handle the knock-on effects on client relationships. By adopting this increasingly executive role, they brought the project round and restricted the time overrun to three months.

Statements relating to typical behaviours associated with the role are given below. It will be noticed that the first group of items are more task related, and the second group more people related:

Prepares accurate cost and time estimates for assignments

Checks that all parties agree to the terms of a contract

Reviews progress through meetings with interested parties

Creates structures for coordinating and controlling an assignment or project

Is sensitive to the difficult and prolonged negotiations which may occur in foreign cultures

Selects suitable individuals for the job in hand

Provides encouragement and support for his or her team

These behaviours are only a sample of those we expect to be mastered by executives or managers. They are highlighted here because they emerged as critical behaviours in the case histories. They underline the importance of:

1. Agreeing a formal contractual relationship which is appropriately resourced, well planned, and clearly understood by all parties.
2. Setting targets, and monitoring and controlling progress against these targets.
3. Regularly informing and consulting appropriate parties so that they are aware of developments, and the effectiveness of their contribution to these developments.
4. Making good use of human resources by allocating tasks/jobs to appropriate individuals.
5. Building up teamwork by developing norms that are conducive to supportiveness and high-performance goals.
6. Adjusting own expectations and behaviour to local culture (i.e. the normal ways of doing business in that locality or country).

Displaying appropriate behaviours in each of these areas will be facilitated by a mix of experience and formal learning. The latter approach is particularly important. The knowledge, skills and attitudes underlying effective performance in each of these areas are well understood, as are the methods facilitating their acquisition. There are good management textbooks covering these areas (e.g. Bartol and Martin, 1991; Hellriegel and Slocum, 1992).

Many individuals entering consultancy have had management experience. Where this is the case they may already have acquired the competences associated with the executive role. But there are other professionals, such as financial or engineering specialists, who may require formal training in these competences.

Researcher

The stereotype of the researcher is someone who generates hypotheses, tests out their validity by collecting data and analysing data, and draws appropriate conclusions from the results. Implicitly or explicitly this process is involved in all consultancy assignments which are viewed as problem solving. However, within the context of the 1+7 model we need to distinguish between the consultant in the role of an expert researcher, and the consultant in the role of a researcher. In the former case we may expect the competences associated with someone trained to research in their area of speciality, possibly to PhD level; in the latter case we only expect the more universal researcher competences to be present.

The consultant is most obviously in the researcher role when he or she is trying to gain insight into the nature of the client problem, since this usually involves forming tentative hypotheses, collecting, analysing and interpreting data, and accepting, modifying or rejecting hypotheses. The abstract of the Jeharna case in Box 5.3 illustrates the researcher role.

Box 5.3   Jeharna and the researcher role

A £500 million construction project in a Third World country ('Jeharna') was going wrong. It had fallen badly behind schedule and no one could identify the reason why. Juniper were asked to help put it right. They realised straight away that any attempt to impose an executive solution would fail; success lay only in working with the Jeharnians and helping them to put it right themselves. This approach became paramount throughout the assignment.

First, they located the main cause of the hold-up. It lay in the project's organisation structure. Second, they identified that, though the project staff were all highly competent, there was a need for the people in charge of key areas to be able to call on a resource of highly expert practical help. With delicacy and empathy, they solved the first problem by helping the Jeharnians to select and install an alternative structure that would be more effective. They met the second need by bringing out experts from Juniper whose task was to act as mentors – a role that was new to them.

In the unusual circumstances – and with their contract up for renewal every six months – the Juniper team had to work hard, diligently and diplomatically to keep the momentum going and the climate of opinion favourable. After four years, the project was successfully completed.

There are three relevant comments in relation to this case. First, from their initial observations the consultants formed hypotheses about the culture of their client, one of which related to the ownership of the solution. Second, the consultants were involved in certain activities which enabled them to diagnose the cause of the hold-up. Third, they identified a resource gap. All three outcomes would have involved research-type activities.

The sort of behaviours one would expect consultants to display in the researcher role include:

Proposals and reports are well written

Absorbs information quickly and accurately

Distinguishes between valid and doubtful data

Puts interviewees at their ease

Uses a planned approach in the collection of data

Many more behaviours could have been identified. The problem is to locate the dividing line between those competences which people in consulting roles in general should possess, and those which we would only expect the expert or professional researcher to possess. Those included are competences which our case histories suggest are important in determining the outcomes of client–consultant interactions. For these reasons it would, for instance, be inappropriate to include competence in the statistical technique of factor analysis. Many introductory texts have been written on research methods (e.g. Bryman, 1989) and although not written with consultants in mind much of the contents are relevant.

For consultants to be effective in the researcher role they will need to be able to:

1. Communicate clearly through the two types of documents-cum-presentations which we associate with researchers, i.e. proposals and reports. The skills of writing reports and giving presentations can readily be taught.
2. Gather information, i.e. data which is as reliable and valid as possible given the purpose of the assignment and the constraints of the situation. The skills of formulating questions, interviewing and recording responses are relatively easy to acquire through formal learning. Knowing what questions to ask may be part of the researcher role or part of the expert role, depending on whether specialist knowledge is a pre-requisite.
3. Interpret quantitative data. This requires a certain facility with figures, and a knowledge of basic statistics. These are teachable.

More sophisticated interpretation of data which requires a technical knowledge of sampling and research design belongs more to the expert role.

4. Interpret qualitative data. This is an activity which the consultant is constantly carrying out. Consultants need to be aware of the nature of qualitative data, the role of various cognitive elements (e.g. expectations, concepts, attitudes) in the interpretation of such data, and the need for confirmatory evidence (i.e. basing one's interpretations on evidence from multiple sources, so as to minimise the effects of perceptual selectivity and distortion). Other requirements for the interpretation of qualitative data are likely to depend upon the possession of specialist knowledge, and therefore belong more to the expert role.

Tutor

Our stereotyped image of the tutor is a sympathetic and supportive person who helps individuals solve their problems through a face-to-face discussion. In the tutoring process there are two different styles of help which can be discerned. First, there is the *directive approach* in which the tutor listens and tries to understand what the tutee's problem is, and then makes suggestions as to what could be done. Second, there is the *non-directive approach* whereby the tutor skilfully gets the tutee to explore the problem so that insight into the problem and its solution is achieved by the tutee. In the former situation the tutor is coming close to the expert and executive roles, and in the latter he or she is coming close to the stereotyped image of the professional counsellor.

In the 1+7 model we are using the term 'tutor' to cover those occasions when the consultant is trying to help the client to resolve a problem through discussion and support, using either or both approaches as the situation demands. The abstract of the Berberis case history in Box 5.4 will illustrate this role in action.

The success of this assignment partly depended upon the effectiveness with which the consultants were able to fulfil the requirements of the tutor role when interacting face-to-face in a private discussion with the Executive Vice President.

The competences we would expect a consultant to display in this role would include:

Makes a determined attempt to understand an individual client's point of view

Helps an individual client to clarify the problem by asking probing questions

Box 5.4   Berberis and the tutor role

The Executive Vice President(EVP) of the client, an American mineral extraction company, had doubts about a proposal, prepared by his head of computer services, to install a large new computer system. He contacted Berberis, an IT consultancy in UK, and asked them if they would vet it.

A Berberis Director and a colleague went to the USA to discuss the matter with the EVP. They had a private and crucial meeting with him, in which a high level of mutual trust was quickly established. Exchange of views about the proposal led on to a confidential discussion of the future of the company's business (on which the proposal might impose constraints) and of the ability of senior management to make effective use of IT. The conversation revealed that the EVP had previously had no one with whom he could discuss his private thoughts freely and constructively. He extended the scope of Berberis' remit.

Berberis' investigation showed that the proposal was inappropriate and confirmed the EVP's views about the structure of the business. They recommended a full strategic IT study, the strengthening of the IT function and the introduction of an IT training programme for senior management. Their recommendations were subsequently accepted and they played a large part in implementing them.

Creates opportunities for clients to discuss their needs

Is comfortable in using a counselling or non-directive approach in helping an individual client understand a problem

Helps clients gain new insight into problems by skilful questioning and answering

For consultants to be effective in the tutor role they will need to:

1.   Be good at active listening.
2.   Be able to use appropriate strategies to discover client's ways of thinking.
3.   Recognise the importance of developing and maintaining a relationship of openness and trust with the principal clients.

4. Have other basic counselling skills. These skills can be developed through formal training.

Some useful texts exploring this area include Gerard Egan's *Exercises in Helping Skills* (1990) and Anne Munro *'Counselling – The Skills of Problem-Solving'* (1989).

Educator

The stereotyped role of the educator is someone who tries to develop or change individuals or groups by creating formal learning situations which will facilitate the acquisition of new knowledge, skills or attitudes. The term educator is normally used in preference to trainer when the goals of learning are more open-ended, general and long-term. In the 1+7 model this meaning is expanded to include the activities we would normally associate with a trainer, i.e. where the goals are more work related or focused on an immediate work problem. One of the main aspects in which the educator role differs from the tutor role is that in the former case clear learning objectives are agreed between consultant and client, whereas in the latter there is a cooperative exploration with uncertain outcomes. An example of the educator role is given in Box 5.5.

Box 5.5   Corylus and the educator role

Corylus were asked to review the structure of the Education Department of a major English county, against a background of changes imposed by the Education Reform Act. Corylus's investigation revealed that the Department would be able to function even more effectively if major changes were introduced in its employees' attitudes about the way they worked together; and in particular in its structure, the availability and use of its resources and the way its policies were developed and communicated.

Using skills and techniques he had acquired as a teacher, Corylus's lead consultant organised a workshop at which these issues could be examined and discussed. He believed that, given a positive and fact-oriented ambience, those involved had the ability and courage to take on ownership of the problems and solve them. Many doubted this, but he insisted. The success of the workshop far exceeded everyone's expectations. Combined with further input from Corylus, the Department was able itself to introduce changes that enabled it to become more effective and adaptive.

In this example the lead consultant had actually had the benefit of professional experience in the educator role, but he was here acting out the role as an educator not an educational expert. He was using formal classroom methods to bring about the change that was needed. What competences do we expect consultants to have if they are going to be effective in this role? They include:

Gives interesting and easily understood presentations

Translates technical jargon into business or non-technical terms

Designing workshops (or similar events) to help others learn concepts and frameworks crucial to the achievement of an assignment's objectives

Helps client to see a problem in a totally new light

Enables the client to make a significant value or attitudinal shift

Introduces new factors or ideas so as to challenge a client's existing perceptions

For consultants to be effective in the educational role they will need to:

1. Set learning objectives.
2. Be good at face-to-face communication.
3. Design courses and arrange conditions so as to achieve learning objectives.

Powerbroker

This label does not refer to a recognised work role, and therefore has no established stereotype. The consultant undertakes this role when he or she identifies a need to influence the balance of power in the client system in order to facilitate the achievement of the assignment's objectives. Most consultancy assignments are interventions which involve change, and change in any social system has implications for relationships and for the balance of power. In more complex assignments (as opposed to run-of-the-mill standard procedural and rule driven ones) consultants cannot avoid becoming embroiled in this process if they are to be of help to a client. The Deutzia case history in Box 5.6 illustrates this role in operation.

Box 5.6   Deutzia and the powerbroker role

For a client in the equipment-hire industry, Deutzia were asked to produce a new salary administration system. The client's Managing Director (MD) and Head of Personnel commissioned the work. The existing system, they said, had two main faults: it created anomalies; and salaries were not geared to the market rate.

Deutzia's investigations confirmed both points. However, they also found two other main problems. First, the client's culture: it was not performance oriented. Second, the client's structure: it was dominated by the powerful, profit-accountable, autonomous Regional Directors who ran the operations. So when it became clear that paying the market rate meant putting more money on the table, the Regional Directors wanted something in exchange for better performance. But the culture was against change in this.

Deutzia's assignment was extended to review performance. But who was the client? The MD was not willing to push things through and the Head of Personnel was now out of favour with the Regional Directors. Deutzia solved the problem by working individually with Regional Directors, starting with those who could be persuaded to see the need for change and were ready to do something.

In this assignment the consultants realised that those who had the power to resist or to facilitate change were the Area Directors; they therefore dealt directly with them rather than through the Managing Director or the Personnel Director. This tactic had the effect of strengthening the Area Directors' power in relation to the assignment, and diminishing the power of the Managing and Personnel Directors.

The sort of behaviour and competences which appear to be required for effective performance in this role include:

Identifies individuals and groups who wield power within the client system

Gains the support of those who have the power and influence to facilitate or to inhibit change

Empowers individuals or groups in the client organisation to change their situation

Uses structures such as steering groups to influence those in power

For consultants to be effective in the powerbroker role they will need to:

1. Understand the sources of power in social systems.
2. Be skilled at diagnosing the power of those with whom they deal.
3. Be skilled at mobilising or harnessing those sources of power which can determine the success or otherwise of an assignment.

Larry Greiner and Virginia Schein (1988) have written a useful text in this area.

Conciliator

This is a recognised work role, although it may not be a widely recognised profession. We tend to associate conciliators with arbitrators; many of their skills are identical but their function is quite different. Both try and resolve a problem or dispute between two or more parties. While the goal of the arbitrator is to try and arrive at a decision which involves apportioning blame and/or reward (thus having a winner and a loser), the goal of the conciliator is to bring the parties together, and through a process of facilitation, to try and get them to arrive at a mutually acceptable solution.

The role of the conciliator in the 1+7 model is similar to the stereotype for the role with respect to the competences required, but the exercise of the role will be in a more subdued and informal setting than would be the case when a consultant was being used as an expert conciliator. The key element is getting people to work together effectively when previously they had not done so. In this role the consultant will try to eliminate (or at least markedly diminish) feelings of hostility, fear or mistrust between individuals or groups in the client organisation or within a wider social system of which the client is a part. Box 5.7 illustrates this role.

In this case we find that by successfully combining his executive and conciliator roles the consultant was able to meet the needs of the situation and achieve the desired outcomes.

The competences we would expect a consultant in the conciliator role to display would include:

Wins the trust of individuals or groups in conflict

Gets those in dispute to come together to resolve their differences

Initiates activities that result in individuals and groups seeing the point of view of others

Box 5.7 Olearian and the conciliator role

Olearian were asked by a quasi-government body to review a major IT project, for which the Prime Contractor (PC) was a large software house. The project was running badly behind schedule.

They found a history of muddle, personality clashes between PC and client and a lack of adequate project control procedures. They recommended that proper procedures should be installed and changes made in key staff of both client and PC. They were subsequently asked to stay on and manage the project. They put in one of their senior consultants as project manager. The role was an executive one but, in a highly charged political situation, the limits of his authority were left to be defined by what he could win through his own technical, managerial and personal skills.

He built bridges with and between the key people, put in good control procedures and used committees and friendly persuasion to equip himself with the clout he needed to get things done. Inevitably, challenges to his authority came, but by then he had won the confidence of the top people in the client and they backed him – eventually without question. The PC was helped to do a good job and the project brought to a successful conclusion.

Can negotiate positively in a setting of unpleasantness and animosity

Shows tolerance and understanding toward those resisting change

For consultants to be effective in the conciliator role they will need to:

1. Win the trust of others.
2. Show empathy for the positions of all parties in conflict.
3. Show patience and tolerance in difficult and frustrating situations.
4. Be skilled at increasing understanding and commonality between conflicting parties.

Walton (1969) has written one of the few texts which are helpful in understanding more about the knowledge and skills required in the conciliator role.

Synergist

This is another unrecognised occupational role, although the function it serves is met by every good manager. The key element of the role (within the context of the model) is creating situations that enable individuals or groups to work together in new ways so that new uses are made of their talents, and the overall effects are greater than the sum of their previous talents. The abstract of the Kerrian case history in Box 5.8 will serve as an illustration.

Box 5.8   Kerrian and the synergist role

Kerrian were asked by a steel manufacturer to review a large investment plan. The decision that the clients had to make was not only vital to their business; it was also emotionally loaded for many of those who had to make it.

Lack of reliable information about future markets made it very difficult for Kerrian to find an analytical approach that would lead to a solution to the question that they had been asked. However, they were able to identify another, previously unconsidered, strategy that would open up an alternative and possibly very profitable market. This they proposed to the clients. While accepting the logic of the alternative, the clients found it very hard to decide whether to adopt it - and asked Kerrian to make the decision for them.

Kerrian felt strongly the clients should make the decision. It was critical for the future of the business and the clients would have to live with the consequences, so it was essential that they were fully committed to whatever decision was made. The clients pressed, but the consultants stood firm on the issue. In the end, Kerrian were able to find a method that enabled the clients to reach the decision for themselves. It involved an alternative decision-making solution which made new use of talent at a level just below the Board.

In this example the consultants were in effect combining their roles of powerbroker and synergist. In the powerbroker role they were instrumental in getting a lower level of management to have a greater influence on decision-making than formerly. In the synergist role they brought together a number of individuals to merge their separate talents to resolve a problem.

The competences we would expect to be displayed in the synergist role include:

Helps Board and other key structures to work together as a team

Generates new impetus in client system by bringing together individuals or groups with common interests

Strengthens the feeling of togetherness in the client system by facilitating the emergence of superordinate goals

Strives to achieve consensus in decision-making

For consultants to be effective in the synergist role they will need to:

1.   Have an understanding of organisational behaviour, including group dynamics.
2.   Be skilled at team building.

Synergist skills are likely to be acquired through practical experience. Useful texts on teambuilding include Katzenbach and Smith (1993) with their emphasis on accountability and Dyer (1987) who looks at group dynamics. Organisational behaviour texts include Huczynski and Buchanan (1991) and Szilagyi and Wallace (1990).

6 An Appraisal of the 1+7 Model

SUMMARY SO FAR

We argued that the consultancy industry is vitally important to the economies of advanced industrialised countries, using the British economy as an example. Therefore any means of enhancing its competitiveness deserves examination. We initiated the research which is reported in this book because we believed *(a)* that the roles that consultants were required to undertake in the consultancy process itself were changing, and *(b)* that if consultancies and interested others became more aware of the nature of these changes, and reflected this knowledge in their training and development programmes, they would enhance their competitiveness.

Many academics and practitioners have attempted to conceptualise the consultancy process for the purpose of increasing our understanding of its dynamics, to identify the skills involved and to facilitate their acquisition. However, the difficulties of conducting scientific research into this process are such that most of these models are either too subjective in origin and/or too specific in their application.

Our task therefore was to establish what it was that consultants actually did during an assignment which was perceived as important, to infer the roles which this required them to play, to identify the associated competences and to indicate how these can be acquired.

A pilot study confirmed our beliefs that changing demands were being made upon consultants, that there was a shortage of consultants with the necessary range of competences or skills, and that staffing problems were recognised as one of the main obstacles to future profitable growth.

Three principles governed our main study. First, we focused on what consultants actually did during the consultancy process: that is, how they went about meeting the needs of a client or delivering their service. Second, assignments from a variety of situations and consultancies were studied. Third, assignments with unexpected twists were selected for analysis because they were perceived as triggering roles critical to competitive success.

Given our aims, resources and current knowledge, the most suitable method of research was the case history. We completed and content-analysed 22 case histories. These analyses were then used to help us infer the functional roles and associated competences which we hypothesised underpinned effective performance in the consultancy process. This sequence of activities was summarised diagrammatically in Figure 4.2.

THE ESSENTIALS OF THE 1+7 MODEL

On the basis of our research, and a review of the consultancy literature, we are putting forward a model which is predicted to enhance the performance of consultants in managing the consultancy process. We propose appraising the model by (a) examining the main assertions and assumptions it is making, and (b) reviewing its merits in the light of other models available.

The main assertions and assumptions are:

1. In a consultancy assignment it is the needs of the client which should always take priority, and using the problem-solving paradigm as the overall framework for managing the consultancy process will help achieve this objective.
2. Client needs will only partially be satisfied through the consultant's exercise of his or her expertise (i.e. that body of knowledge and skill which sets off one group of consultants from another group, such as consultant civil engineers from consultant corporate strategists). This expertise has to be delivered in a way which aids rather than inhibits the problem-solving process or, alternatively, which progresses rather than retards the satisfaction of client needs.
3. The consultancy process requires that the consultant readily slips into seven additional roles, i.e. those labelled executive, researcher, tutor, educator, powerbroker, conciliator and synergist. The model stresses that each individual consultant should master the competences required for effective performance in all eight roles, hence the 1+7 model of consultancy roles!
4. The competences underpinning performance in the consultancy process can be acquired through appropriately planned learning experiences. However, acquiring individual competences is necessary but not in itself sufficient. The superior consultant is one who is consistently effective in satisfying client needs, and this requires the development of judgement and professional expertise so that an appropriate amalgam of roles are played according to situational needs.

Client-Oriented Problem-Solving

The value of using the problem-solving paradigm is considerable: it focuses consultant activities on client needs; it provides a systematic framework which reminds us of the steps for successful problem resolution; and it is already well used by practising consultants. The disadvantages come when the paradigm is applied inflexibly or incorrectly, such as when the problem-solving process is thought of as encompassing problems and not opportunities, or when the problem-solving process is conceived as a tidy smooth progression rather than a messy discontinuous development, or when care is taken to meet the requirements of one stage in the process (e.g. clarifying the nature of the problem) but not another equally critical stage (e.g. implementing the solution).

We are not solely concerned with problem solving as an individual activity. Within the consultancy setting it is predominantly a social process. In the simple two-person situation the consultant is trying to influence the cognitive structure and behaviour of individuals in order to achieve certain goals, and this may require intervening in the relationships between the individual client and others. In the wider group and organisational situation the consultant is also trying to influence behaviour; this may require intervening in their strategy, structure, culture and staffing (Williams *et al.*, 1993). This makes the task of the consultant formidable, and raises a number of ethical issues.

Argyris (1970) has rightly argued that the task of the consultant is not only to help solve a problem but to ensure that the problem remains solved. This may mean persuading the client of the need to intervene in additional parts of the client system or to use particular methods of change so that:

- those in favour of change have enhanced power (consultants can facilitate this through the powerbroker role);
- those responsible for the implementation and maintenance of a solution own the solution and understand the reasons for it (through the non-directive aspects of the tutor role the consultant should preserve two of Argyris's three basic requirements for intervention, i.e. free informed choice by the client, and the choices made by the client are done in such a way that internal commitment to these choices is high; through the researcher and educator roles the consultant should be able to ensure Argyris's third requirement is met, i.e. the generation and sharing of valid data);

- those working in the client system who are responsible for the consultancy contract recognise there may be a need to employ consultancy resources during the implementation of a solution (with implications for the consultant's executive role competences).

There are a number of ethical issues here, e.g.: How deeply should a consultant intervene in the client system? How far should consultants see it as their responsibility to train clients to learn how to solve their own problems in the future, with minimum reliance on external help? The ethical aspect of these issues is important and needs more attention than we can give it here.

If we accept Argyris's proposition that a consultant should not only help solve a problem but ensure that it remains solved, then it becomes even more obvious that a consultant cannot just be an expert giving out advice or carrying out a task on behalf of the client. The consultant needs to understand the context in which the problem or opportunity arises and the situational variables which are likely to affect the implementation and durability of solutions. Moreover, while learning about these contextual features, the consultant must share this learning so that clients become more capable in meeting their own needs in the future. In order to achieve these goals the roles we have identified from our case histories take on a new importance.

The All-Rounder

It is not sufficient to assume that a consultant only has to be competent in a given field of expertise and in *some* of the seven additional roles, with colleagues brought in to make up for deficiencies. As we have seen, many assignments have unexpected twists as they progress and clients have changing needs. Individuals who feel uncomfortable or incompetent in some of the roles will either not recognise the cues triggering them or will rationalise their relevance away. Consultants striving for superior performance need to learn the key competences which underpin effective performance in all eight roles. This is the only way that a consultant can be truly client-oriented in practice as well as in aspiration.

The 1+7 model is therefore quite distinct from the managerial role models found in the literature. For both Mintzberg (1973) and Belbin (1981), their managerial role models are also functional models (i.e. they are all necessary in order to meet the requirements of the situation) but they are best played by several people rather than a single individual. The reasons include: the managerial situation requires teamwork rather than individual brilliance; and differences between the personalities, abilities and experiences of managers means that some will be more competent at certain roles (Schroder, 1989) and some will prefer certain roles (Belbin, 1981; Stewart, 1982). The 1+7 model asserts that consultants should be competent in all eight roles. In Chapter 5 we indicated the competences which a consultant will need before he or she is an effective consultant. As a set of competences they are challenging. But so are clients, with their overt and covert motives, their differing capabilities and resources and the widely diverging situations in which they are found. Helping to satisfy a client's needs is a major challenge and demands complex skills. It is reassuring to note that in a competences-based study of 32 consultants carried out by Gordon Lippitt (Lippitt and Lippitt, 1978, pp.96–7) the findings are similar to the present study with respect to areas of knowledge (e.g. management and organisational behaviour, educational and training methodologies), and of skills (e.g. listening and reporting, teaching and persuading, counselling, forming relationships based on trust and working with a great variety of persons and groups, data collection methods, locating sources of power and influence). The most noticeable differences are in the attitudinal areas. Lippitt lists a number of personal characteristics such as integrity, self-confidence, open-mindedness and a humanistic value system. We have avoided specifying these qualities, preferring instead to focus on measurable activities and outcomes.

Planned Learning

Any individual who has met the requirements of a professional body, and is therefore a recognised expert in a given field, should be able to acquire the competences underpinning effective performance in the seven additional roles. Knowledge relating to the methods for acquiring these competences is available although not necessarily used. What is less well understood is when to play these different roles, and how to weld their underlying competences together so as to achieve planned results. It is this display of professional judgement and expertise which we implied is the distinguishing feature of the effective consultant in Chapter 5. It is the consultant who consistently earns this label who will be recognised as a superior performer as opposed to an adequate performer.

Experience on a range of assignments is a necessary way of acquiring the practical knowledge of the effective consultant, but on its own it is sub-optimal because of its dependence on trial-and-error learning. This latter method of learning is emphatically not a *client-oriented* approach to superior performance. Breaking down and analysing holistic performance in terms of activities, and then building the picture up again with the use of such concepts as competences and roles helps us to understand the ingredients involved, and the recipes which lead to effective performance. These ingredients and recipes can most efficiently be learned through a combination of practical experience and theoretical and simulated learning. Off-the-job experiences involving case histories, role playing and the like may fall down on realism, but conditions are better controlled and the learning outcomes more predictable. Why and how simulated learning through case histories and role playing can help to develop the effective consultant is the topic in the next chapter.

RELATIVE MERITS OF THE 1+7 MODEL

As a training aid will the 1+7 model be more or less useful than others in the literature? To what extent is the model compatible with our general knowledge of the management of change? A strategy for answering these questions is to remind ourselves of the 'logical' reasons for favouring the use of the 1+7 model in training, to identify the main differences between this and other models in terms of the roles identified, and to account for these differences within the context of managing change.

The two main reasons which led to the development of the 1+7 model of consultancy roles were:

1. the restricted ideological base of existing models (i.e. their OD derivations), and
2. their weak scientific foundations (i.e. based largely on personal experience rather than objective studies).

The present study is a modest move in the direction of rectifying these weaknesses: it analyses a mixed range of assignments carried out by others, and it shuns the prior adoption of an established theoretical framework. For these reasons the 1+7 model offers something different to existing models, with respect both to comprehensiveness and to generalisability.

We are sceptical of the general value of encouraging trainees to apply a mechanical set of guidelines indicating when particular roles should be played. This is likely to happen when using contingency models such as those of Schmidt and Johnson (1969) with their continuum of facilitator, consultant and executive; or Wooten and White (1989) with their contention that particular roles are more relevant to certain stages of an assignment. These models, together with those promoting an ideal style of intervention such as that of Margerison (1988), may have their place in a training programme when a particular approach to an assignment is being discussed. But they carry the danger of being dysfunctional to the *inexperienced* trainee when used as general models of consultancy roles.

We would argue that it is a safer and more efficient strategy to get trainees to learn to become sensitive to the range of client needs they will encounter within their chosen area of expertise, and to practise the repertoire of roles which are instrumental in satisfying these needs. This is the approach we are encouraging because it is designed to be more client-oriented. The approach recognises the complex nature of the client and the complex process whereby effective change is initiated and implemented. For these reasons the 1+7 model should be a useful training aid.

SIMILARITIES AND DIFFERENCES IN IDENTIFIED ROLES

How does the 1+7 model compare to others referred to in Chapter 4? Not surprisingly, a common characteristic of all models is that consultants should expect to undertake multiple roles including that of 'expert'. Models based on OD-type assignments will invariably include the roles of educator/trainer, researcher/fact finder, expert/adviser, process counsellor/helper, or their equivalents. They may also include resource linker, and role model (Wooten and White, 1989). The 1+7 model uses labels which can readily be equated to these roles. The inclusion of 'role model' by Wooten and White is a reminder of the OD roots of these taxonomies, where the client learns new behaviours by modelling himself or herself on the consultant. The informal learning goals of this role indicate that it would be covered in the 1+7 model by the tutor role.

The 1+7 model differs most obviously from others with respect to the prominent position given to the role of expert, and to the presence of the roles of executive and powerbroker. Given the qualitative nature of the research upon which the model is based we need to explore these differences, and to see the extent to which they can be justified in the light of general knowledge relating to consultancy and the management of change. The reason for exploring the validity of the 1+7 model within the context of managing change is not hard to understand. Consultants will agree that virtually every assignment they have tackled has been concerned with change – advising about the need for change, helping to formulate plans for change, helping to implement change, and/or evaluating change!

Expert Role

The single most influential textbook on management consulting in Europe has been that of Milan Kubr which was first published in 1976, and revised in 1986. We shall compare and contrast our conception of the expert role with that of others through his presentation of the more authoritative views of the role. He identifies two basic consultancy roles: the resource role (also called the expert or content role) and the process role. In the former the consultant helps the client by providing technical expertise and doing something for and on behalf of the client (e.g. supplies information, diagnoses organisation, designs a new system, trains staff in a new technique etc.). In the latter the consultant, as the agent of change, helps the organisation to solve its own problems by making it aware of organisational processes, their likely consequences, and of intervention methods for stimulating change. Kubr acknowledges the contribution of Edgar Schein (1969) in developing and promoting the process role in consultancy. He goes on to say that nowadays pure resource consulting is relatively rare, and that the two roles should more and more be seen as complementary. The resource consultant needs to have some of the behavioural skills when involved in implementation. The process consultant's contribution to helping client change is likely to be modest if he or she does not understand certain technical, financial and others factors in the client organisation. While recognising the need for a consultant to switch from a resource to a process role and vice versa according to situational needs, Kubr adds 'no one should try to play a role which is alien to his nature and in which he will be less effective' (1986, p.45).

This dual role model is then further refined by Lippitt and Lippitt's (1978) model of eight roles distributed along a directive/non-directive continuum (as we described in Chapter 3). The directive role involves those behaviours where the consultant leads or initiates activity; the non-directive role where he or she provides data for the client to use or not to use. This supplementary model enables Kubr to illustrate how consultants can adjust their behaviour to take into account situational variables.

As we saw in Chapter 3, this portrayal of our state of knowledge is widely reflected in the literature. The rise in importance of the process role owes much to the OD movement, which provided the theoretical and practical impetus to its development and application (Schein, 1969). The OD movement in its turn owed much to the non-directive counselling approach pioneered by Carl Rogers (1951). An influence of the OD literature has been to encourage the development of a paradigm of 'content or process', and in which process consultancy is seen as superior to content consultancy where change is the goal.

The 1+7 model can readily accommodate this knowledge, but does so in a significantly different way. It views all consultants as 'experts'. It is those competences which differentiate one type of consultant from another (e.g. a consultant engineer from a marketing consultant, or an IT consultant from an OD consultant) and defines the particular expertise they are offering a client. An OD practitioner may in fact be hired for his or her expertise in process consultancy. But in playing the role of expert, or in delivering this expertise, the consultant interacts with the client in an amalgam of roles. The most effective amalgam or mix of roles will depend upon the immediate and longer term needs of the client. In terms of the 1+7 model a consultant cannot just interact with the client through the role of expert; he or she must at the same time display elements or behaviours which more typically belong to other roles in the model.

If we were pressed to present the 1+7 model in terms of a dual role theory, we would express it as 'content + process' rather than the more common 'content or process' paradigm implied by much of the literature. The paradigm suggests to the inexperienced consultant that each is independent of the other. For superior performance in consultancy you cannot have one without the other.

In case proponents of OD may feel that the 1+7 model risks putting the clock back by playing down the importance of process, it is worth pointing out that the 1+7 model has a strong developmental flavour. Satisfying developmental needs is intuitively part of a consultant's repertoire, but few agree as to what this encompasses. In the 1+7 model the developmental needs are catered for by five of the eight roles – tutor, educator, powerbroker, conciliator and synergist. These are the roles which we tend to associate with process consultancy.

Why this apparent preponderance of process-type roles? We can think of three good reasons:

- For the last 50 years the most significant contribution to the consultancy process has been made by behavioural scientists straddling the worlds of academia and consultancy. Their major discovery was that in helping a client to change, a process-oriented role was more effective than a content-oriented role. All our case histories have in some way been concerned with creating and/or adapting to change.
- Competition within the consultancy industry is very strong. The developmental roles are the ones that are more likely to

enhance a client's problem-solving capability for the future as well as helping in immediate problem-solving. The effective consultant is aware of the competitive edge to be gained in catering for both time horizons.

- The case histories upon which the 1+7 model is based are derived from rich and complex assignments. These are the assignments in which we would expect the developing roles to be at a premium, and experienced consultants are aware of this.

Powerbroker Role

At first sight Kubr's framework does not appear to cover our power-broker role. But in fact he does complete his chapter on roles with a section headed 'Methods of influencing the client system' (1986, p.49). He points out that it may be impossible to help change practices or performance without influencing certain people, and discusses a range of methods through which this can be achieved. He acknowledges that some of these ideas originate from Fritz Steele (1982). They include: demonstrating technical expertise; exhibiting professional integrity at work; using assertive persuasion; developing a common vision; using participation and trust; using rewards and punishments; using tensions and anxieties (e.g. predicting the negative things that would happen if change is resented or delayed). These are some of the ways in which we expect the power-broker role to be played out. The two frameworks that Kubr has used to account for the roles that management consultants adopt have not enabled this category of influencing behaviours to be explicitly named.

The powerbroker role resided uncomfortably with the early OD pioneers. Trust and openness was valued and anything associated with manipulation condemned. Throughout its early history OD appeared to neglect the power variable, except for aspirations to increase the power of the individual employee and to promote an egalitarian philosophy. The subsequent analyses of change processes, particularly by sociologists, are placing the power variable near the top of a consultant's agenda.

Executive Role

No consultant will deny that part of their activities on any sizeable assignment involves them in planning, monitoring and control. Kubr (1986) discusses these aspects of consultancy in a chapter devoted to 'Controlling the assignment'. He, along with many others, place those behaviours under the label of the expert role or at the directive end of the directive/non-directive continuum. We would argue that the executive role requires an independent identity, since the behaviours associated with this role will be required in most situations regardless of whether a consultant is adopting a content or process-oriented approach.

Change Agent's Expertise

A valuable contribution to understanding the roles of the consultant has recently been made in a book by David Buchanan and David Boddy (1992). Their arguments lend support to recognising the importance of the powerbroker and executive roles, and indeed of the general thinking underlying the 1+7 model. They have analysed the expertise of the change agent, building on relevant knowledge and a study they carried out which sought to establish the competences of the effective change agent. The study focused on project managers. They use 'project manager' and 'change agent' interchangeably, pointing out that it is difficult to argue that a project manager is not a change agent, given the nature of their task. Also, most consultants advocate some version of a project management approach to the implementation of their recommendations for organisational change.

The main theme of their book is that change agents have to support their 'public performance' based on the rational problem-solving approach and the democratic participative approach, with the 'backstage activity' of intervening in the political and cultural systems. The latter is concerned with the exercise of 'power skills' (1992, p.27), and the authors acknowledge the contributions made to this area by Andrew Pettigrew (1985, 1987), and Rosabeth Moss Kanter (1983). In any setting the change agent has to cope with three parallel agendas:

- The content agenda: requiring technical competence with respect to the substance of the changes being implemented (corresponds closely to our expert role);
- The control agenda: requiring competence with respect to such things as planning, resourcing, monitoring, and target setting (corresponds closely to our executive role);
- The process agenda: requiring competence in such things as consultation and influencing skills, team building and dealing with resistance (corresponds particularly with our roles of powerbroker, conciliator and synergist, but also to the roles of educator and tutor).

This conceptual framework is compatible with the 1+7 model, although Buchanan and Boddy's three parallel agendas are replaced by a central agenda (the expert role) and seven radiating agendas (the other seven roles)!

There is one further relevant observation to make in relation to their model of the change agent's expertise: the change agent's agenda priorities depend upon the *context* in which they are operating. The particular situational factors shaping the context and therefore the role of the change agent are: the frequency with which management goals change, the complexity of organisational dependencies, the ambiguity of ownership or responsibility for change and the degree of support or hostility provided by senior management for the changes in hand. The less favourable those factors are, the more vulnerable is the context, and the more important is it for the *process* and control agendas to be given priority. The more favourable those factors are, the less vulnerable the context, and the more appropriate becomes the *content* and control agendas. The clear recognition of the power variable (our powerbroker role), and the presence of the control agenda (our executive role) in the two extreme contexts, are supportive of the distinctive features in the 1+7 model.

Conclusions

The 1+7 model does not replicate already existing models, but it is not in conflict with current knowledge about the consultancy process and the management of change. As a training aid we believe it has advantages over alternative models. The potential value of incorporating conceptual aids of this nature into training programmes for consultants, and some suggestions as to how this can be done, are themes of Chapters 7 and 8.

The reasons for the differences found between the 1+7 and other models of consultancy roles can be explained as follows:

- Unlike some model creators we eschewed an ideal style approach, selected a mix of assignments as the research database, analysed the data so as to identify what consultants actually did in assignments, and expressed their behaviours in terms of readily understood roles.
- Some of the assignments involved OD-type approaches, some more conventional approaches, and some project management type approaches. This mix enabled certain roles to emerge which otherwise might have remained indistinguishable.

- We deliberately set out to develop a model which would be useful for training purposes. This meant that the behaviours observed, and the competences inferred, had to be grouped under role headings so as to facilitate their learning.
- During any given stage of an assignment, we assumed that a consultant would be playing an amalgam of roles rather than an all-embracing single role. There is no generally desirable profile for this amalgam, since an effective consultant's behaviour (or 'role profile') will adapt to client and situational needs.

Part III
Developing Superior
Client-Oriented Skills

7 Learning Theories and the Development of Expertise

In previous chapters we have shown how consultancy has developed into being more than simply providing specialist information or advice. We have presented a model of roles that consultants are adept at playing, and indicated some of the key competences underlying these roles. We have also shown that, for training purposes, the 1+7 model has advantages over other models. In this chapter we are concerned in giving readers greater insight into the process of learning, so as to increase their understanding of the value of such models as training aids and ways of incorporating them into a training programme.

THEORIES OF LEARNING

A generally accepted definition of learning is that it is a relatively permanent change of behaviour that results from practice. Consultants will become more effective in the various roles they adopt as a result of the learning that takes place on assignments. But as we have pointed out it is inefficient to rely on this method of learning, because of the minimal control over conditions of practice. Greater control is possible in the classroom situation, where learning principles can be applied that stem from established learning theories. The two main groups of theories are the stimulus-response and cognitive theories.

Stimulus–Response Theories

Much of the early work on learning was undertaken by the behaviourists who postulated that actions should be explained in terms of observable variables, using terms such as stimulus, response and reinforcement, without recourse to any hypothetical mechanisms such as thought and ideas or images (cf. Pavlov, 1927; Skinner, 1953). Hence a 'black box' exists between input (sensory stimulation or 'stimuli') and output (behaviour or response). Behaviourists believe that the law of association is the mechanism by which knowledge can be acquired and, therefore, learning takes place. This involves the notion that simple ideas originate by the copying of sense impressions into the memory store. One type of learning is habituation where repeated exposure to the same stimulus makes for sluggish responses or lack of response, for example, learning to ignore the ticking of a new clock or the sound of trains passing nearby. In habituation, the behavioural change is that the person ceases to respond to or notice a stimulus.

It is thought that many of our emotional responses have been conditioned in an involuntary way. People can produce a variety of emotional responses to visual symbols, words, and situations without, in many cases, knowing why or being consciously aware of their existence.

In exploring learning we need to consider factors which retard as well as facilitate learning. It is a well-recorded fact that 'the majority of people suffer from bad learning experiences and these can set up blockages which seriously inhibit any learning taking place' (Downs, 1992). Key blockages are worries and fears about learning induced by past experience. Many people shy away from computers or mathematics because of such emotional blockages.

Whereas the development of emotional responses may be conditioned in an involuntary way (through classical conditioning) an alternative form of conditioning is where people choose to learn responses because these operate upon or affect their environment (termed operant conditioning). For example, when a person performs a specific behaviour, the likelihood that it will be repeated depends upon its consequences. A new recruit to a consultancy firm will be quick to learn what behaviours are acceptable (through positive reinforcement such as praise) or unacceptable (through negative reinforcement such as a frown or negative comment like 'that's not how we do things here!'). Shaping of people's behaviour is achieved through the technique of reinforcing only those variations in the responses of the learner that move in the direction desired by the trainer or employer.

Cognitive and Constructive Theories

In contrast to S–R theorists, cognitive theorists do away with the 'black box' and propose that the crux of learning lies in a person's ability mentally to represent aspects of the world and to operate on these mental representations. In some cases, associations between stimuli and events are simple representations, while in other cases more complex representations such as cognitive maps (e.g. an image of how to get from A to B) and abstract concepts (e.g. consultancy roles) occur. Cognitive theorists emphasise perception, insight, the development of understanding, and the generally constructive nature of the mind (Kohler, 1929; Neisser, 1967; Tolman, 1932).

It was Sir Frederic Bartlett, in 1932, who first argued that memory is not simply a copy of the perception of what the person has seen. Rather, it is a symbolic representation or 'schema' or mental model, of the external world. Mental models can represent a class of people (e.g. our stereotype of clients), objects (e.g. tables) and events or even situations. Perceiving and thinking in terms of mental models enables us to process large amounts of information quickly and economically. They also affect how we perceive our world. We may take longer to respond to novel settings because we need to absorb a lot of information from the situation (i.e. perception is a data-driven, bottom-up process). However, in familiar settings our beliefs, prior knowledge and expectations enable us to take short-cuts in making sense of the situation (a top-down schema driven process). This is why we often don't notice changes in familiar situations, until they are pointed out to us.

Social Learning Theories

A lot of work has been conducted over the last 25 years into aspects of complex learning, and while previous schools of thought focused on learning through personal experience of the environment, much learning is of a more vicarious sort, as in learning by observation (Weiss, 1990). This has led to social learning theories which look at the importance of social interaction and imitation in the learning process. Learning is thought to come about through the continuous reciprocal interaction of our behaviours, various personal factors and environmental forces.

A proponent of social learning is Albert Bandura who recognises two modes of learning: enactive learning, which is learning through experience and observational learning, which is also termed modelling. For him, 'learning is largely an information processing activity in which information about the structure of behaviours and about environmental events is transformed into symbolic representations that serve as guides for behaviour'. (Bandura, 1986, p.51)

Thus we use verbal and imagined symbols to process and store experiences in representational forms. These can serve as guides for future behaviour. Additionally, people make inferences about rules of behaviour by observing what people do and what happens to them in particular situations. Modelling is a complex process and a key characteristic is that people do not simply produce behaviours that imitate those of others. Often, novel behaviours are produced as a result of observing and synthesising behaviours of multiple models. Thus observation differs from imitation because behaviours can be deferred for a long time and they can be the product of an amalgam of a number of observations of different models.

Social learning theory has been applied in the field of training in the form of behaviour modification training programmes. There is some evidence that providing a positive and competent model (e.g. an effective consultant) can help to accelerate the learning of appropriate behaviours, particularly if there are opportunities to try the new behaviours in supportive settings with appropriate feedback. Some studies suggest that behavioural modelling is the most effective method for acquiring interpersonal skills (cf. Decker, 1980) but there is conflicting evidence as to whether these skills are retained beyond the training session (Baldwin and Ford, 1988). The notion of vicarious learning also suggests that consultants are likely to draw conclusions about prospects for rewards/punishments and successes/failures not only from their own experience but also from observing other consultants.

Some Implications of Theories of Learning

The stimulus–response and cognitive theories we have examined enable us to increase our insight into the processes of learning. The principle of reinforcement helps us to understand why it is we come to acquire certain habits and attitudes, and how we can utilise this knowledge to shape our own behaviour and that of others whom we are trying to train. Both classical and operant conditioning theories have helped us to understand and to deal with some of the emotional problems that become entangled with learning.

Cognitive theories give us insight into more complex learning. They show the importance of mental models, which we develop in the process of learning to cope with familiar and unfamiliar experiences. Some of these mental models are acquired in childhood and are very deep rooted. Others are learned through a combination of training and experience. One of the goals in the training of managers, consultants and other professionals is to give trainees a 'standing start' by introducing them to valid models at an early stage in their career. Valid models in this context are those which have been shown to be helpful in achieving effective performance, according to accepted criteria. Thus, the inclusion of the 1+7 model in a training programme is intended to bring about superior performance in consultants at an earlier stage than would otherwise be the case. It does this by helping consultants to perceive their interactions with clients in terms of a set of roles, and related behaviours and competences.

One of the difficulties with most work-oriented models is that they are more likely to be valid in some situations than in others, and under present rather than future conditions (given the rapidly changing world we live in). It is important for trainees to appreciate the strengths and limitations of different models, and to learn to use them as a means of enhancing learning rather than as a sacrosanct blueprint. The methods used in learning about these models should facilitate this process. More on this in a moment.

The word 'model' is used in a different sense in the context of social learning theory. A trainee may model himself or herself on an individual whom s/he perceives as being a successful consultant. There is no doubt that learning through modelling is an important vehicle for learning, particularly where roles are involved. This vehicle for learning has clear potential in the consultancy situation.

One of the points about learning which has not come across in this brief discussion of theories is the importance of active learning in a social context. Traditional approaches to education view the learner as a passive recipient, with the teacher having control over what is to be learnt and how it is to be learnt. The primary aim is to transfer information/knowledge from the 'expert' (i.e. teacher) to the students who are deemed to absorb facts and ideas like sponges filling up with water. Interchange between students and teacher involves question and answer sessions, with little or no interaction among students and most communication taking place through the teacher.

This education system has for a number of years produced students who did not master a variety of learning strategies, and hold incorrect beliefs about their learning abilities. Criticisms such as these have led to attempts to introduce major changes at all levels of education. These changes are based on an alternative model of education which goes by various names including active learning, self-directed learning, self-managed learning, learner-centred education. All propose that people need to be actively involved in the learning process. In addition it has been shown that learning activities conducted using realistic contexts and opportunities for social interaction are often superior to traditional decontextualised abstract learning. The relevance of active learning for developing the superior consultant, and the methods of facilitating this, will become clearer below.

FROM NOVICE TO EXPERT

Development from novice to expert consultant can involve three learning contexts: project assignments, relationships and formal situations.

Project Assignments

Assignments are an important context for the development of consultants (Maister, 1984), particularly when they involve challenging tasks. The experience of being challenged results from a gap between the skills or competences of the consultant and those required by the client or situation; this leads to the feeling of being 'stretched' by the assignment. Experiencing this gap motivates the consultant to learn what is necessary to carry out the roles required.

The case histories included in Chapter 9 highlight some of the key elements of challenge. Obviously our requirement that consultants provide us with a case which involved an unexpected twist is one type of challenge, but the perceptive reader will be able to identify others.

Experiencing challenging assignments can lead to a variety of behaviours, such as seeking new sources of information, trying out new behaviours or building new relationships. Practice at these can lead over time to competence in a new role, but this is conditional on a number of factors. These include: reflection takes place; feedback on success or otherwise of new activities occurs; and new behaviours are reinforced. Differences between people on characteristics such as self-esteem, past experience and learning orientation are likely to influence how a consultant will react to challenge and how much is learned from it. We will discuss this further when we introduce the notion of experiential learning.

Different assignments provide consultants with a diversity of experiences which can lead to them developing a broader perspective on how they progress, how organisations are run and other cause–effect considerations. They help consultants develop an appreciation for inter-relationships between various parts of an assignment, and also assist them in forming a network of contacts in client and other organisations.

For learning to occur it may be important that consultants remain long enough in an assignment to fully understand the situation, and to be able to act upon their new understanding rather than upon their past experience. In cases where consultants are moved in and out too rapidly, it is unlikely that changes based on learning will be well enough consolidated to make the experience developmental.

There are risks involved in placing consultants on challenging assignments for developmental purposes. There is the possibility of client dissatisfaction when it is apparent the consultant does not have the required competences; the learning and adjustment period may prolong the length of the assignment or unforeseen problems may arise because of the inability of the consultant to cope with the needs of the situation. A more senior, experienced and costly consultant may need to spend time advising a junior on what needs to be done. Finally, the worst scenario is that the assignment will fail.

Yet it is through experiencing difficulties that consultants are provided with opportunities to learn about themselves and their effectiveness, about others and about assignment requirements. From this reflection they can develop an improved understanding about their practice and how it might be improved (Schön, 1987). Being able to learn from mistakes, being willing to examine one's behaviour and its effects, recognising the conflict between the theory of behaviour which one espouses and the actual theory in use, are all needed in the processes of learning and development (Argyris and Schön, 1974).

Robin Snell has proposed that in order for people to learn from 'hard knocks', including failure to overcome challenges, three general stages seem to be necessary. The first stage is enduring the psychological blow or shock and not being completely demoralised by it. The second coping stage entails resisting immediate aggressive or self-destructive urges, retreating instead to a private place to release the shock out of one's system. Often this stage can be helped by the non-directive support of a colleague or partner. The final stage comes only after the psychological trauma has subsided: this is concerned with reflecting and thereby drawing lessons from the experience (Snell, 1991).

He also draws out from his research examples of non-painful ways of learning on the job. These suggest attitudes like 'taking nothing for granted' and behaviours of being alert, active, questioning, scanning for early signs of problems and contemplating unfavourable scenarios. Other activities include using a network of informants; allowing oneself to be mentored; adopting reciprocal counselling; watching the fate of colleagues and significant others and keeping a regular diary of important learning points. A key finding of this research is that although these non-painful learning channels exist they are not widely used in his sample of managers and administrators. Are consultants any different?

Relationships With Others

Relationships play an important part in development. Four different relationships in the work situation may contribute to consultant development: mentor, supervisory, peer and client. A more experienced consultant may form a mentoring relationship with a junior consultant; this is usually an informal and voluntary arrangement whereby the mentor keeps an eye on the learner – helping to ensure that developmental opportunities, support, resources, feedback and counselling are all present when required. This developmental role may also be played by a person's supervisor or peers. Indeed individuals may regard some supervisors as mentors. But generally speaking the supervisory and mentoring relationships sit uneasily side by side. The former cannot consider the development of the individual as a priority, divorced from the needs to evaluate and improve the performance of all staff. This is not to say that the supervisory relationship plays a minor role in the development of a subordinate. On the contrary, through his or her power to place a consultant on particular assignments, to appraise and provide feedback through a performance appraisal system, to approve participation on courses, and to provide rewards and reinforcement through praise, merit awards and promotion, a supervisor has a very important developmental role to play!

The phenomenon of modelling of course enables learners to benefit from their encounters with any or all of these four relationships.

Typically, the consultant–client relationship is presented from the perspective of an uneven relationship, with the client learning from the consultant. But the expertise of clients and consultants often overlap, and this is a trend which is likely to increase within management consultancy at least as a high standard of management training becomes the norm for all managers. In these more even relationships, we might expect development to be taking place concurrently as each party parries and spars ideas and observations with the other during the various stages of problem solving.

Relationships with others can thus provide a useful learning context for increasing one's understanding of how the world operates (e.g. by modifying mental models); of the behaviours and roles which lead to success (e.g. through modelling); for gaining knowledge of one's strengths and weaknesses (through feedback and counselling); and for practising new skills (through challenging assignments).

Formal Situations and Methods

How should one influence the learning process in formal training situations in order to facilitate the acquisition of the competences underlying effective consultancy performance? Above we have been exploring learning 'on the job' by observation, by undertaking challenging tasks and assignments and through relationships. This approach has been labelled *craft apprenticeship*, as opposed to *cognitive apprenticeship* (i.e. learning through formal learning situations and activities) to which we now turn.

> cognitive apprenticeship methods try to enculturate students into authentic practices through activity and social interaction in a way similar to that evident – and evidently successful – in craft apprenticeship ie. constructive learning processes should be embedded in contexts that are rich in content, resources and learning materials; that offer opportunities for social interaction; and that are representative of the kinds of tasks and problems to which learners will have to apply their knowledge and skills in the future' (Brown *et al.*, 1989, p.123)

In Chapter 9 we present a number of case histories which can be used in this approach to learning. In order to help ensure that these cases are used effectively, there are four additional concepts relating to learning theory which are worth exploring. They are: meta-cognitive learning skills, discovery learning, experiential learning and scaffolding. These concepts are defined and discussed under appropriate headings below.

Meta-Cognitive Learning

Cognitive apprenticeship recognises that in today's rapidly changing world, professionals need not only to 'know about' but be able to 'do', and be able to learn 'how to learn'. The latter notion of learning how to learn relates to meta-cognitive or self-regulatory skills. It is a higher level of learning which results in us applying models or strategies which prove to be particularly effective in the process of learning. Influential psychologists such as Jerome Bruner and Albert Bandura have enriched our understanding of meta-cognitive or self-regulatory skills, and thereby enabled us to account for the changes in performance and effectiveness that take place as the novice develops and becomes an experienced consultant.

In a seminal study in the 1950s, Jerome Bruner and colleagues (1956) reported in their book *A Study of Thinking* that people adopted different focusing and scanning strategies in order to discover concepts or ideas. Since then numerous strategies have been identified (Weinstein *et al.*, 1988). Common orienting tasks designed to improve a person's constructive approach include questions (reviewing), note-taking (categorising), mnemonics (for remembering key ideas), paraphrasing (elaborating), analogies (integrating and differentiating).

One distinction between these strategies concerns whether they lead to *deep* or *surface* processing during learning. Depth of processing may be a core construct to which other strategies connect (Snow and Swanson, 1992). The notion of surface and deep strategies arose from work by Ference Marton and colleagues (1984). In the surface approach, people concentrate on remembering facts rather than attempting to understand the author or speaker's argument. In the deep approach, people look for the principal ideas or themes and try to develop a good understanding. Surface processors seem to attend to the sign, i.e. the text itself and the words and phrases which constitute it. Deep-level processors look for the message; they make active attempts to incorporate the reading or listening activity with existing knowledge and personal experience. For Marton 'meaningful learning is a qualitative change in one's way of understanding reality'. An example is that in reading, active readers back-track in the text to pick up missed information. They recognise comprehension problems so they read more slowly at points of difficulty while they check out their understanding, and they put a lot of effort into encapsulating the gist of what is being said.

Another way of looking at this is through considering the notion of schema introduced earlier. Since it is our mental models that are used to interpret what we see and know, it is plausible that surface processors fail to organise new material in the light of prior knowledge and experience and that lack of elaboration fails to improve upon existing schema. These learners would operate at a lower level of learning, i.e. they may be able to identify, list, name and recite but they would not understand or apply or operate at any of the higher levels of learning (cf. Bloom and Krathwohl, 1956).

A text (or talk) is like a painting – it has many possible meanings. The particular meanings that a reader gains from the text will depend upon the goals he or she has been following when reading, or listening (Strang, 1987). This relative view of meaningfulness reflects a phenomenological perspective and puts the reader's intentions as central in identifying meaningful learning.

Since we are arguing that our mental models of reality are constructed from existing knowledge and abstractions interacting with new facts and ideas, it is important to acknowledge that learners bring 'naive' theories into the learning situation. It is also important to note that research shows that people's 'naive' theories are rather resistant to change – why is this?

There are two kinds of learning that affect our mental models. The first is learning that *enriches* prior knowledge by increasing the sophistication of existing mental models. A second form of learning is one which requires the *restructuring* of an existing schema. In most cases the process of knowledge and skill acquisition relates to the first kind of learning. However, when we are faced with major anomalies that our existing schemata cannot accommodate then a new structure is required (Vosniadou, 1992). There are different levels of change in structure, going from a perceived improvement in skills or a change in standards down to a fundamental change, which can mean the complete replacement of one's world-view of an area with another (Porras and Silvers, 1991).

Knowledge and skill acquisition takes effort and elicits emotions. Each level of change will exert a greater cost in terms of effort and emotion. We start the knowledge acquisition process by constructing certain beliefs based on observations consistent with everyday experience. If these are reinforced they become entrenched with time, and are robust and difficult to change. Some beliefs constrain the mental models which people can form and restrict inferences which they can draw.

Articulation and the restructuring of mental models or schemata can be aided by discussion with others. When we have articulated our existing beliefs, and heard others introduce and explore alternative frameworks, we can then determine which ones might better describe, explain or predict 'reality'. However, research shows that when people are exposed to information and ideas that contradict their experiential beliefs they find it difficult to change their views and may compromise through constructing a series of 'synthetic models' – or misconceptions. These synthetic models permit them to retain as many as possible of their experiential beliefs.

Deeper levels of change in existing mental models can be attempted through a number of methods, including discovery and experiential learning.

Discovery Learning

This is learning that occurs through free activity in rich environments, with a minimal amount of structuring to facilitate learning, and has a long history. The general orientation is that learners find something out for themselves without initially having it explained by others. There are many variations of discovery learning, including: autonomous and enquiry (self-directed and self-managed).

Autonomous discovery learning (Ausubel *et al.*, 1978) has a number of situational characteristics:

- a considerable level of uncertainty;
- ill-defined procedures;

- encouragement for learning from errors;
- the need for the learner to decide on goals, devise procedures that work, discern relevant from irrelevant information.

In autonomous discovery learning, active processes are proposed as the major mechanism for learning and these include both the construction of knowledge and understanding and the application of competent learning strategies.

A number of approaches feature 'enquiry' as a central theme. There is an assumption of a need for concrete experiences, the teaching of strategies for making inferences from experiences or data and, in some cases, a need for the acquisition and development of concepts through less active means such as lectures and teacher-prepared materials. Two examples of enquiry approaches are self-directed and self-managed learning.

One of the main proponents of *self-directed* learning is Malcolm Knowles, who argues that there must be a change of focus away from 'teaching' towards how we learn (1975, 1984). This approach seeks to provide a structure whereby learners can achieve their own goals through focusing on relevant problems. The structure may have many forms but typically it involves the need for a climate of support for learning, and for learners to: identify and clarify their own goals; plan programmes based on available resources and produce evidence of achievements and make judgements about the degree of success of their self-managed programme. The 'learning contract' is a widely used device for those who are supporting and assisting learners to manage their way through the learning path. These contracts are not rigid, but are continuously re-negotiable (Knowles *et al.*, 1984).

Ian Cunningham and colleagues provide a variation in their self-managed learning. They argue that learning to learn involves fundamental changes in the whole person and in one's attitude to learning. Skill-based training approaches can fail because they are based on the notion of an expert telling learners how to learn. In self-managed learning people are given the freedom to control their own learning. In this approach to learning, we need to think about how we have learned in the past, and propose learning strategies to try out in the present. We need to consider how well we are meeting our goals and therefore the effectiveness or otherwise of our learning. We need to manage the way we change.

In this process of meta-learning the individual gains insight into *how* they personally learn and what alternatives there might be to their current learning habits (Cunningham, 1988). Variants of self-managed learning have been applied in the management development field through action learning (cf. Mumford, 1991; Pedler, 1991; Revans, 1982).

Experiential Methods

David Kolb (1984) has devised a model of how we learn through action, based on the 'experiential learning cycle' of Kurt Lewin. It consists of the four stages of:

1. Concrete experience;
2. Observations and reflections;
3. Formation of abstract concepts and generalisations (i.e. hypotheses);
4. Testing implications of concepts in new situations (practice in the new situation provides fresh experience and so the cycle starts again).

This model incorporates notions of both the importance of learning from experience and that of people being 'intuitive scientists'. In the model, action, reflection, theory and practice are all accorded importance, but the starting point for learning begins with action rather than theory. In other words, through enquiry.

For David Kolb, and others who have provided variations of this model, identifying the preferences which people have in one or more of these activities is important because it has implications for people's success in learning a task. Weakness in any of these areas may prevent learning from occurring (Honey and Mumford, 1986; Revans, 1980).

Reflection is, however, a key element in learning. As described above, much of the learning that we engage in requires active processing whereby new ideas interact with existing mental models. Learners process experiences they have and reflect on them. This process of reflection needs to be made explicit.

Experiential learning can take place within the context of actual assignments or through classroom simulations. These latter include activities such as group exercises, role playing and case studies. Some simulations provide learners with knowledge of an area such as the financial industry, others develop self-knowledge or interpersonal skills, and yet others are useful for learning diagnostic skills or analytical skills. The key point is that the emphasis is on active learning in a salient context to acquire both conceptual and procedural skills and knowledge.

Scaffolding

Learning by scaffolding involves the control of learner responses by an external agent, together with attempts to reduce opportunities for error. It is in many ways a compromise approach, which incorporates elements of several methods we have discussed. Although somewhat like shaping (i.e. reinforcing responses which progress behaviour toward the desired goal), it differs in that in this learning situation the activity is presented as a whole rather than in parts. The external agent (i.e. parent, teacher, trainer, expert professional) provides support in one of three ways: first, when learners are unable to perform a particular activity, the agent takes over and does it for them. In this case only spurious performance occurs. In the second approach, the agent can stimulate the necessary activity by providing hints (i.e. directing attention). In this situation the learner uses the hints and can practise the role of active learner and self-regulation. The third situation is where the agent can provide a model or simulation. Here the learners gain skills in regulating their actions, and also learn about situations where it is appropriate to apply the skills.

Scaffolding as a learning approach is underpinned by theoretical work conducted in the developmental area by Ivan Vygotsky and Jerome Bruner. Vygotsky's work in the 1930s provided the view that learning first occurs in social interaction and is then internalised. The metaphor of the scaffold describes the idea of an adjustable temporary support that can be removed when no longer necessary (Glaser and Bassok, 1989). Research suggests that a contingent approach is needed so that tutoring is contingent on learner performance; more scaffolding is needed for less able learners and less scaffolding for more able learners. In the extreme, the external agent can range between 'mastery' style direct instruction and guided discovery depending upon the variability of individual performances in the group (Brown *et al.*, 1989).

The principles underlying such work, namely, 'a structure of joint activity in a context where there are participants who exercise differential responsibility by virtue of differential expertise' (Cole, 1985) is a framework whereby we can explain how people are encultured into a profession.

Professionals have specific ways of doing things and they espouse values both particular to their specialism and to the craft of being a professional. Novices acquire, through craft apprenticeship, and often in an unconscious manner, the cultural aspects of their profession. Novice consultants usually work on a project alongside people with more experience than themselves.

Accordingly, many consultants experience successive steps towards the mastery of consulting within an overall activity and hence they are 'immersed' in the whole process. Before taking responsibility for any of the stages, 'experienced novices' have observed most of the consulting process over a number of occasions. When given responsibility for an activity, e.g. data collection and analysis or writing a proposal, they start to practise what they already know (Bruner, 1966). Thus consultancy experience gained in project groups or other informal learning situations of a 'craft apprenticeship' variety enables novices to work hard in those productive activities of which they are capable, while getting exposure to and practice in subsequent activities related to the next stage of developing capability.

Similarly, in discussions between novice and more experienced consultants, talk is focused at the beginning on the level of the novice's personal skills and the specific task being undertaken. Much of the conversation relates to the experienced consultant identifying what needs to be done and telling the novice to do it. As the novice gains experience and actions become more skilful, talk shifts to discussion of salient aspects of the work in progress. With yet additional experience, talk is directed to judgemental issues.

Learning programmes and activities incorporating scaffolding are deemed to work because

> they are designed to externalise mental events in a collaborative context...an audience monitors individual thinking, opinions and beliefs and can elicit explanations that clarify points of difficulty...overall, by sharing it, a complex task (the process of consultancy as a whole or particular aspects of it) is made more manageable without simplifying the task itself. The *group* achieves understanding until such time as its members have acquired the skills themselves (Glaser and Bassok, 1989, p.644).

SUMMARY VIA AN EXERCISE

The theoretical content of this chapter makes it more difficult to understand than the others. Given the nature of the principles of learning discussed, it is appropriate for readers interested in the process of becoming a more effective consultant to summarise the main points covered for themselves. This 'active learning' element will aid learning, as will any opportunity that is engineered for discussing one's summary with those of other readers. Table 7.1 presents the minimum of scaffolding in tackling this task!

Table 7.1 Summary of principles for learning role-effectiveness in a formal environment

1.

2.

3.

4.

5.

6.

7.

8.

9.

10.

8 The Case Method of Learning

This chapter introduces the essentials of the case method of learning and includes examples of exercises for using the case histories in Chapter 9. Seventeen out of the twenty-two case histories from which our model was developed are included in that chapter. Five have been omitted because of space considerations.

We use the term 'case history' to describe an assignment which actually happened, as seen through the eyes of the principal consultant. For the purposes of our research we specifically asked consultants to provide us with a case history describing an assignment that was a good example of a 'project with a twist', in which the consultants concerned had found themselves having to take up roles that they had not expected at the start of the assignment. This material was then used to build the 1+7 role model and to help identify key competences required. Each case illustrates a unique amalgam of roles and exposes the complexities of client-consultant interactions.

The case-study method of learning covers a variety of actual approaches, but they share common characteristics, including:

- Using actual events as learning material. This gives the case study face validity. Novices feel that they are getting as near to the real thing as possible, without actually carrying out a live project. Also the writers of the cases can take into account the purposes to which the cases will be put, and present them in such a way that the trainer's task of getting the learner to draw out the appropriate lessons or skills is made easier.

- Encouraging active learning. As we have seen from our discussion of various theories, effective performance as a consultant is best achieved by using active learning methods. The case-study approach does this by requiring the learner to view a problem through the eyes of one or more characters in the case, and to arrive at certain decisions or recommendations. A variation often used is to ask the learners to take on different characters and to act out the roles as they would in real life. This type of role-playing simulation exercise is an excellent way of gaining insight into, and practising, certain competences such as listening skills.

- Developing problem-solving skills. Some case studies consist of a problem in a particular setting that requires a solution. Others are more or less complete stories (such as our case histories); they require analysing in order to identify critical elements which lead to specific outcomes such as success, failure, time delays, further assignments, and so on. In both types simulated practice is provided for in several elements of the problem-solving process, e.g. clarifying a problem, identifying appropriate roles to be played, generating suitable solutions.

- Legitimising pluralistic solutions. One of the main lessons trainers will want individuals to learn from cases is that there is no single right solution. There are solutions which are likely to work or unlikely to work; and there are solutions which looked as though they worked or looked as though they did not work. Like management, consultancy is an art impregnated by science. This state of affairs puts a premium on the validity of the ingredients used by learners: in particular, the mental models or schemata which they draw upon in the problem-solving process. It also provides scope for experienced consultants to disagree with each other, thus enabling them to recognise the legitimacy of viewing the same data in different ways, of developing their professional and ethical sensitivity, and to practise their interpersonal skills such as persuasion and negotiation. Perhaps most important of all for experienced consultants, disagreements within a group create opportunities for individuals to question certain assumptions they habitually make on assignments. As we have seen, the first step in acquiring more valid beliefs and mental models is to become more aware of their vulnerability when set against plausible alternatives.

If these characteristics are to facilitate planned learning it is obviously necessary that the cases be well researched (i.e. are valid and reliable accounts of events) and presented in a way which will enable the learning objectives to be achieved. Also the cases need to be incorporated into exercises designed to encourage active learning, i.e. learning in situations which demand an exchange and sharing of opinions relating to the case histories, plus any relevant experiences on assignments, and prior theoretical knowledge.

Each case in Chapter 9 is included because it is regarded as being a valid and reliable account of events as seen by the principal consultant. Examples of the sort of exercises which meet the criteria of active learning are given below. These are intended to provide the minimal guidance to whet the trainer's appetite to design their own exercises around the cases. Relevant theoretical knowledge is provided in this book through the 1+7 model, and the many references at the end of the book.

Why include as many as seventeen of the cases in Chapter 9? One of the potential weaknesses of the case-study method is that learners may attach too much importance to the learning gained from a single case. Each case is unique, as each consultancy assignment is unique. By tackling a variety of cases, particularly through exercises which require the study of two or more cases, learners will discover lessons to be learnt from disparity as well as similarity and uniqueness. The scope for designing exercises from the cases is considerable. The exercises below are just a few examples.

Table 8.1 is designed to make the task of the trainer or self-managed learner a little easier in selecting cases for particular purposes. It is a matrix showing which assignments are a good example of which roles in the 1+7 model. An omission of a role against an assignment does not mean that it was not present, just that it was not so visible as others.

Table 8.1 Case histories which are good examples of particular roles and some of their underlying competences

	Expert	Executive	Researcher	Tutor	Educator	Power-broker	Conciliator	Synergist	Page no. in the book
1. Acacia	*	*							106
2. Berberis				*					112
3. Corylus			*		*			*	118
4. Deutzia	*				*	*			126
5. Escallon	*	*							131
6. Forsythe				*	*				138
7. Garryan			*		*			*	143
8. Hammamel		*							147
9. Ilex			*			*	*		152
10. Juniper		*		*		*			159
11. Kerrian			*		*	*		*	167
12. Laurus		*							174
13. Neanthis				*	*			*	180
14. Olearian		*					*		186
15. Romney	*					*			192
16. Spatius	*				*				196
17. Tamarisk			*	*					203

EXAMPLE OF EXERCISES BASED ON THE CASE HISTORIES

Objective: To increase insight into the nature of the 1+7 model, and in particular to the interdependence of the role of expert and the other roles, and how the importance of this interdependence may be affected by contextual factors.

Pre-reading: Relevant chapters in *The Competitive Consultant,* and the relevant case histories in Chapter 9.

Procedure: Participants to divide into convenient syndicate groups of, say, five or six per group. Each group to nominate a chairperson whose task is to ensure the completion of the 'activity' within the time allowed by the trainer, to draw together the agreements and disagreements of his or her group in relation to the questions posed, and to present these findings in a plenary session. Each 'activity' below should be led by a different person, participants should tackle the related questions on an individual basis initially, then come together to exchange and discuss their findings.

Activity 1:   The consultant from Acacia was a technical expert engaged to provide civil and structural design services. The consultant from Romney was also a technical expert engaged to provide space-planning and design services. Both were in the situation of being a member of a project team.

How did they differ in their provision of expertise in a multi-disciplinary team situation? How were they similar? What were their apparent strengths and weaknesses?

In both cases the consultants worked without having full control over what was happening in the engagement. What effect did this factor have for the roles they found themselves playing? What key competences can you identify as being needed for superior performance under these conditions?

Activity 2:   In Deutzia, consultants were engaged to develop and implement a reward structure for senior and middle management. In Escallon consultants were engaged to provide advice on automating procedures and controls and help develop and implement automated systems. In Spatius consultants were engaged to review existing human resource management policies and procedures and develop ones which would help the hospital succeed in their application for Trust status.

These three cases illustrate very well the interdependence between the consultancy roles when assignments are concerned with procuring change.

Compare and contrast these three cases. What, in your opinion, are the strengths of Deutzia compared to the other two cases? What additional roles and competences might have been useful in Escallon? What roles did the consultants in Spatius adopt with a view to improving their performance?

Activity 3: Corylus were asked to review the structure and resources of the Education Department of a major English county, against the background of changes imposed by the Education Reform Act. They proposed their approach to the assignment would be an analogy of the 'medical check-up' that healthy people sensibly ask for. To do this they divided the task into five stages.

Garryan were asked by the R & D (research and development) Division of a large plc to review expenditure on IT equipment and related services and advise if they were getting good value for money. In response they undertook a fact-finding programme.

What research-type activities did consultants undertake in these two assignments? What are the competences underlying the research role that you can identify from these cases?

Activity 4: Ilex were asked by the client, an insurance company, to review the adequacy of the architecture of a proposed new local area network that was part of a large and critically important IT project. Garryan were asked to review expenditure on IT by the R & D Division of a large plc.

Ilex and Garryan are situations where the information needed to determine the adequacy or effectiveness of a process was not available.

Compare the responses of the consultants in both situations. What are the implications in terms of both expert and researcher roles and competences?

In Ilex, a project director was in overall charge. Comment on her performance in light of the 1+7 role model.

Activity 5: Olearian were asked by a quasi-government body to review a major IT project, for which the Prime Contractor (PC) was a large software house. The project was running badly behind schedule. They undertook researcher activities, made recommendations and were subsequently asked to stay on and manage the project.

The lead consultant's role was an executive one but, in a highly charged political situation, the limits of his authority were left to be defined by what he could win through on his own capability.

In order to effect his executive role, what other roles did the consultant undertake? What competences were called for? How does this case compare with that of Hammamel? What do they have in common?

Activity 6:   Forsythe, an IT consultancy, were asked to do a failure study of a costly software project that would not run. They quickly located the problem and were asked to stay on to manage a new project. Part of this involved producing a new specification. In alternating roles of expert, tutor and educator, the consultants helped their client develop a much better understanding, not only of what IT could do for their business, but also of what its limitations were.

The Managing Director of a large organisation in the services industry asked Neanthis for advice on whether and how Total Quality Management (TQM) could be used in his business. They arranged an appreciation programme for him. Again, this case included expert, tutoring and educator roles.

Compare and contrast how clients' needs were met by the consultants undertaking these two assignments. What competences were demonstrated?

Activity 7:   The educator role involves the consultant undertaking formal classroom-type methods to bring about a change in client knowledge, skills or attitudes. Clear learning objectives are agreed between consultant and client.

Corylus is a case where the consultant organised a workshop where issues identified through the researcher role could be examined and discussed.

For a client in the equipment-hire industry, Deutzia were asked to produce a new salary administration system. This they did, but it was clear that the client's culture was not performance oriented. The consultants began to run a series of workshops to try to educate the Regional Directors about the need to change culture.

Under the guidance of Garryan a task force was set up to organise a series of workshops for (mostly) Divisional managers. The primary aim was to stimulate user management into taking ownership of IT and this resulted from the consultant undertaking powerbroker and synergist roles. In its educator role, the workshops aimed to help managers decide the priorities for expenditure and provide the information that would enable the Board to set more effective IT budgets annually.

In Neanthis the consultants arranged to introduce the Chief Executive of their client company to companies who were implementing TQM so that he could see it in operation.

Read these cases and identify some of the key competences required for the educator role.

Activity 8:   The key element in the conciliator role is getting people to work together effectively when previously they had not done so. Ilex were asked to conduct two studies relating to the same system. For their second assignment, as a result of what they had learned from the first, they wrote the terms of reference with care. Their remit allowed them wider range over the whole project and gave access to a higher level of management than would otherwise have been needed. It also ensured that different parts of the client organisation would have to work together and that Ilex would be there to smooth the way.

Compare and contrast Ilex and Olearian. What structures did consultants in the conciliator role introduce? What competences did they exhibit?

Activity 9:   In the synergist role, the consultant seeks to create situations that enable individuals or groups to work together in new ways.

Corylus organised a workshop using competences related to the educator role. Additionally, one of the objectives resulting from the synergist role was for the workshop to bring individuals together to develop common ownership on which an action programme could be built.

The Managing Director and his Board asked Neanthis to help them develop a clear and agreed understanding of the organisation's mission and vision. Neanthis adopted a synergist role and helped the individuals on the Board to come together and work effectively as a team.

Compare and contrast Corylus and Neanthis case histories with Spatius. What are your conclusions?

9 Case Histories

1. ACACIA ENGINEERING CONSULTANTS

This case history is about the construction of a leisure complex in a major town in south-west England, which is developing rapidly as a result of industrial expansion. The main parties in the case history are as follows.

Acacia Engineering Consultants is a medium-sized, privately owned professional firm. Established for over 50 years, it has a high reputation, especially in civil and structural engineering.

On Acacia's side, the two people principally involved were: Malcolm Drew, the Project Director, and Harry Conrad, the Project Engineer, a structural engineer in his mid-30s. Both are professionally qualified chartered engineers and had been working for Acacia for many years. Malcolm led the Acacia team that won the assignment. Once the contract had been signed, he handed over to Harry the responsibility for leading Acacia's activities. Harry had previously been the Project Engineer for other assignments, but none of these had involved the engineering complexity or the responsibility for handling client relationships of the present case. Acacia's fee for the project was fixed as a percentage of the eventual capital cost of the project. So, whatever the cost, fees were accordingly determined – and there was to be no abortive fee. The contract required them to produce all the civil and structural design services that were necessary for the project.

Adnock Leisure Developments is a major division of Adnock Property Corporation plc, a UK-based company operating in all aspects of property development. The division specialises in leisure centres. Often working closely with local authorities, it identifies business opportunities for leisure centres, most of which comprise restaurant and entertainment facilities. It arranges planning permission, buys or leases appropriate sites, arranges demolition and construction, and then either operates the sites via another division of the parent group or sells or leases units in the completed centres to the eventual operators. It has operated in this field for some 20 years and is well respected in its market. It is a major contributor to the profits of the parent group.

Those involved in the case on Adnock's side were: Hugh Peters, Head of Project Development and a Director of Adnock Leisure; and Len Ventnor, the Project Manager. Both are qualified quantity surveyors. Len had had similar responsibilities on several previous Adnock sites.

The site, which is in the centre of the town, includes a cinema, restaurants and a night-club. Demolition had already been completed. A site survey had shown that, though the sub-soil was clay, no major geotechnical problems would be encountered, given adequate piling. Construction costs (using information provided by Acacia) had been estimated at £10 million. This became the budget for the project. Len had only limited authority to increase costs without reference to Hugh. Construction was to go ahead to a tight schedule. Design work was to begin in October 1986 and the centre was scheduled to open in December 1987. Adnock regarded the site as an important one, partly because the area was fast-growing with a lot of commercial potential but also because early completion was required in order to assist cash-flow.

Acacia scheduled a team of design engineers and engineering technicians to work on the project. The team would reach 12 at peak. All were under the management of Harry.

Adnock's organisation was more complex. They had their own team of architects and a separate team of interior designers. Also, in addition to Acacia, they appointed a firm of quantity surveyors and a firm of mechanical/electrical consultants to work on the project. These all came under the management of Len. Also involved were Adnock's own specialist cinema division, which included architects and interior designers, specifically for cinema lay-out and decor. Further, after work on the project had begun, Adnock appointed a firm of managing contractors whose services included not only the actual construction itself but also design input, the nature of which was not fully specified.

In October 1986, Acacia began work on the project.

The first problem emerged almost immediately. The architects had not completed their design work and in particular they did not at that stage know precisely the weight of the total building or how it would be distributed over the site via the main columns. Knowledge of this kind is essential if the piles, which are driven into the ground and support the columns, are to be designed and located in a way that attains the necessary engineering strength at minimum cost.

However, if the required completion date of December 1987 was to be achieved, it would be necessary to start the work of driving the piles in November 1986. That in turn meant that the design of the piling programme (specifying what piles, and where) had to begin at once. There was only one other option available, and that was to over-design, or in other words to put in more and stronger piles than was absolutely necessary. This would give the architects some flexibility in their eventual choice of design but it would add about £500 000 to the cost.

Harry summarised the situation as it stood then:

Adnock were faced with a choice. They could either put back the completion date by the amount of time it took for the architects to come up with the information we needed, or they could pick up the bill for the cost of the over-design. We discussed the whole thing fully at one of the early project meetings. These meetings, which were to be held regularly, were chaired by Len; I attended them to represent Acacia. When we discussed the piling problem, I explained the options and put our point of view. Then we talked it through. Adnock definitely did not want to put back the completion date and therefore it was decided that the over-design solution was the better one available in the circumstances. That was their choice – so I was a bit concerned to hear afterwards someone on Adnock's side saying that 'the engineers were responsible for upping the cost of the project by half a million'.

The second problem emerged very shortly afterward. The architects found that, because of some information that came to them late, it would be necessary to lower the floor level of the basement of the building in order to provide more height there. This was a change to the original design that had been given to Acacia and again it would cost money because it meant additional excavation and additional construction.

Harry explained how problems of this kind are tackled.

It is quite normal in any construction project, whether large or small, for work on site to begin before every single detail of design has been completed. Design work and site work continue in parallel. One of the benefits of working like this is that some changes in the design requirements can be made at a relatively late stage.

Consulting engineers expect this and indeed it is part of our expertise to accommodate such changes at minimal cost. As long as the changes required are not major ones that affect, for example, the strength of the building as a whole, we will find an engineering solution – but inevitably there are usually cost implications. Whenever we are told of changes of this kind, we discuss the position thoroughly at meetings back in our own offices. We look at the engineering implications and we develop and explore a range of solutions. The approach is essentially logical with the emphasis on both sound engineering design and the minimisation of the cost to the client. What comes out of our discussions is a carefully thought-out professional solution.

In the case of the basement problem, the best solution we could devise would still add about a hundred thousand to the overall cost. It was the architects who had required the change, but I had to be the bringer of bad news to the project meeting – and it did not go down well.

It was not long after this that I began to find the atmosphere in the project meetings very different from what I had expected or could wish for. The emphasis there was on pushing ahead hard to achieve the completion date, on reducing costs to a minimum – and on laying blame on anyone whose work negated either. And the people at the meeting did not seem to be always willing to give time to examining carefully who it actually was who had been responsible for causing increases in costs or delays to the programme. What seemed to matter more was who could fight his own corner better and who had the 'committee-man' dexterity to convince the others that he was blameless. There's no doubt that our firm was being made to take an unfair share of the blame for some of what was happening.

The managing contractors had by now got the site work well under way. Some of their methods proved to be unusual. They had, as is normal on a large project, divided the total site work up into a series of 'packages'. Their manner of doing so did not however always suit the method of construction that Acacia had assumed would be the case and it was in general carried out in a somewhat uncoordinated way.

It is important to emphasise that, in the production of their designs, consulting engineers take careful account of how the actual work on site will be carried out, both in detail and in general. It is no good producing designs that require the contractor to operate in a sub-optimal way. The skills of designing for effective and efficient construction form an important part of the training of professional engineers and are part of the expertise of a good firm. Of course, assumptions have to be made as to how the contractor will go about construction; the consulting engineer expects to have very close links with the contractor so as to be able to explain the assumptions that have been made.

In the early design stage on this project, Acacia did not have as close a link with the contractors as is often the case. Partly as a result of this, a major problem arose in the construction of the basement. Harry described what happened.

We had assumed that the whole of the basement construction would be treated and built as a package. We had therefore designed it as an entity – a box-like structure in which base, walls and roof all contributed to the strength of the whole. The managing contractors decided to treat the base and the walls as a package and then place the roof on after as a part of a different package. Without the roof on, the walls would not be able to take the sideways thrust imposed on them by the adjoining earth, particularly if heavy plant was working nearby.

By the time this was discovered, the base and the walls had already been built, so the only way to deal with the problem was to shore up the walls and to restrict the access of heavy equipment in the vicinity. Doing this took time, added to the costs and meant that over a large part of the site the contractors would have to work in a way that was different to and less efficient than the way they had planned.

The effects of this problem were two-fold. First, the expected completion date had to be put back to early 1988. And second, the entire contingency for the project was by now exhausted.

Inevitably, the blame for this had to be laid somewhere. Harry found himself being forced to defend Acacia's position and reputation, both in project meetings and outside them. Relationships with the client became increasingly difficult and began to take on the nature of conflict rather than co-operation. It appeared to Harry that none of those at the project meetings lost any opportunity of attributing the cause of a delay or cost escalation to Acacia if there were the slightest ground for doing so. He was continually put on the defensive and he found this situation very hard to handle, especially as he noticed that others seemed to be able to manipulate a potentially awkward spot to their eventual advantage.

Meanwhile, other problems occurred. Harry explained:

There were quite a number of them. For one, the local planning authorities, late in the day, found fault with certain safety aspects of the design, and demanded changes – and in addition Adnock revised part of their brief in a way that affected planning consent. Then the interior designers called for changes to the detailed construction of the inside of the building, which necessitated some re-design by us and the use of higher quality steel – and that of course was more expensive. On top of this, the cinema specialists decided to place additional air-conditioning plant on the roof, so that meant it also had to be re-designed. And other changes were called for that involved new designs for some of the brickwork and columns inside the building.

But there were also problems of a different kind – problems with communications. Len was under increasing pressure from his senior management to get results and his way of dealing with this was to deal more and more on an individual basis with all the many different parties involved in the project. It didn't help matters when the managing contractors – and you'll remember that the nature of their design input to the project had never been clearly spelt out – started to take on some of the roles that are traditionally handled by architects, because these particular architects had not previously worked in this way and they found it very difficult to deal with.

Sometimes it was really quite hard to find out who was representing whom, and who had authority to decide what. So when it was necessary to get a decision made in order to be able to progress our work, I tended to go to Len in the first place.

As the project moved toward completion, costs continued to rise and flags began to be raised. At times it seemed to Harry that as far as Len was concerned the over-riding consideration was the earliest possible completion date, if necessary regardless of cost. Nonetheless, there were a number of project meetings at which reviews were made of ways of reducing the ultimate costs of the different packages, when it could be expected that comments would be made like: 'As we had to spend so much on the ground' (i.e. on sorting out the basement problems) 'others will have to reduce their costs'. And there would be sidelong looks at the engineers.

Despite the difficulties, the project went forward to eventual completion. The leisure centre opened in May 1988, five months after the intended date. The full cost of the project is known only to Adnock, but it is certain that the original budget was exceeded by more than 15 per cent.

In reviewing the project, Harry drew out three aspects for particular comment.

The main point to be made is that many of the time and cost problems that arose in the construction of the leisure centre occurred because the overall design of the centre was not sufficiently developed before work began. So it follows from this that it is essential to emphasise to clients that difficulties with time and cost overrun are inevitable if changes are made after important decisions have been reached and acted on.

The second point relates to the fact that, during this project, I spent much more time and energy than I had expected in haggling, negotiating and defending myself and my firm. I have really come to appreciate how useful these kinds of skills are. And

I have learned to be wary of silver-tongued people who have a knack of putting others in the wrong.

And the last point is that I have learned the importance of not only doing your best for your client but also *showing* your client that you are doing your best.

2.   BERBERIS CONSULTANCY PLC

This case history is about an information technology assignment in the USA. It shows how an apparently small engagement can become a major source of business if the consultants concerned are able to handle all the roles that are required of them at the early stages. The companies and people involved are as follows.

Berberis Consultancy plc is one of the largest UK-based computer consultancy companies. Founded in the early 1960s, it has over 2000 professional staff and its services cover the whole range of information systems and technology (IS & T) including: the development, installation and operation of computer-based information systems; auditing existing and proposed systems; and the provision of training. Specially relevant to this case history is its emphasis on the need to match IS & T planning to corporate plans and goals.

Berberis's consultants involved in this assignment were: Richard Wilkes, a Divisional Director in his early 40s who has many years experience in industry and commerce covering line management, data-processing management and as a consultant in IS & T; and John Legge, a Principal Consultant in his late 30s. Both had previously worked on assignments in which the objective had been to determine clients' business information requirements and turn them into IS & T systems that fulfilled the needs identified.

Buckingham Products Inc is a publicly owned company based in Harrisburg, Pennsylvania. It operates about 30 mineral extraction sites located along or near the eastern seaboard of the USA from Massachusetts to Virginia. It also has about 20 manufacturing sites, which convert the extracted material into products that are sold to industrial customers and through retail trade outlets. The manufacturing units are mostly located close to the extraction sites and serve the markets in their regions. Each region was managed by a Regional Vice President who had a high degree of autonomy. The company was founded in the 1930s by the father of the current President and Chief Executive Officer, Harold C. Buckingham. Its annual turnover was around $400 million and it was generating a moderate level of profit.

At the time when the assignment began, Harold Buckingham was in his mid-60s and had been running the business for 20 years. His style of management was essentially paternalistic. He delegated extensively to his Regional Vice Presidents (VPs) and kept a firm but kindly eye on them. War service had interrupted his education and he did not graduate. He went into the family business in 1945 and took it over on his father's death. He was not unsympathetic to modern business systems but was somewhat naive about them – and this included his approach to information systems technology.

There were less than a hundred staff at the corporate headquarters in Harrisburg. Most came under the control of the Vice President Finance, including the Head of Computer Services, Steve Wrokla. Steve had been working there since 1968 and had been in charge of the computer system for most of that time. Harold Buckingham had himself been responsible for selecting the original computer system and, for largely patriotic reasons, he had chosen a US company to put it in for him. The association with that company had continued thereafter, because it was a comfortable relationship. Harold had not required, nor the computer company suggested, that the system be constantly up-dated to best modern practice; indeed, Steve's brief was to keep costs to a minimum because the system was effectively regarded as an overhead. All computer facilities were located at Harrisburg; the input to the system came from documents that were forwarded daily by the regions.

On Buckingham's side, the key person in this assignment was Brian F. Weltmann. He had joined them in 1985 when they had acquired the company of which he had been Chief Executive Officer. He had recently been given the title of Executive Vice President of Buckingham's, which effectively made him deputy to Harold Buckingham. He had an accounting qualification and was in his mid-50s at the time.

The assignment began in March 1987 when Brian put through a phone call from Harrisburg to Berberis's head office in London. The call was referred to Richard Wilkes, as the senior Director available.

Brian told Richard who he was and outlined his company's business. He mentioned that in 1980 he had hired Berberis to do a software job for him and had been very pleased with the result. He now had, he said, a problem on his hands in which Berberis might be able to help. He had a report on his desk that had been prepared by Steve Wrokla. It proposed that Buckingham's should spend about $4 million installing a completely new computer system, with distributed hardware at all the regional sites and offices linked to a main computer at Harrisburg. A feature of the new system was that it would use common systems for both the extraction and manufacturing parts of the company's activities. He knew, he said, that the company needed to up-date its IS & T but, despite the fact that the proposals had been endorsed by all the Regional VPs, he was not at all sure about them. He wanted a second opinion and wondered whether Berberis could provide this.

Richard asked whether, as a first step, he could look at the report. Brian agreed, and a copy arrived on Richard's desk the following day. Having read it through, he could certainly see the cause of Brian's concern: the report did not adequately spell out the benefits that the proposed new system would bring to the business. He phoned back and they talked about the problem.

Richard said that, going by what he had read, he shared Brian's unease about the proposals and whether they were really tied in to the business needs of the company. 'Just what I felt myself', replied Brian, 'It makes no business case and maybe we ought to throw it out.' Nonetheless, Richard suggested, there might be more behind the document; it could have been a good study but a lousy report. 'That's a very professional response,' said Brian. They discussed further the report's recommendations about the use of distributed hardware and the use of common systems, and noted that the shape of the systems was not clearly defined. But, while they agreed that the report was inadequate, the question was what to do next. 'Can you come here and look the whole thing over?' asked Brian.

It looked to Richard as though this would be a 10–12-day assignment and he would need the help of John Legge. So he negotiated a fee of $12 000 and by the end of the month he and John were sitting in Brian's office in Harrisburg.

To begin with, the conversation focused on the existing business, the existing system and the report. It was when Richard commented that he found it hard to believe that a common system could really fit both the extraction and manufacturing parts of the business that the talk got a lot deeper. Brian said he was not at all sure that the two aspects of the business should be so closely linked organisationally and that maybe they were in fact better treated as two separate businesses. In any case, he went on, what would happen if the business were to expand out of its present geographical confines? Richard said it looked as if the report assumed that the business would stay more or less as it was, operating in the same kinds of markets in the same broad area; the proposed system would constrain, not encourage, expansion. Yet the report had had the endorsement of the Regional VPs, who formed the company's senior management; he wondered whether that was the way they really saw the company's future. Brian revealed that he did in fact have plans for expansion and that in turn meant that he was looking for people capable of taking new slots. He had been concerned about the Regional VPs' endorsement of the report and wondered how much they really understood of what they were apparently supporting. It was something else on which he needed to take a view.

At the end of an hour-and-a-half's discussion, the brief that had originally been discussed over the phone had been amended somewhat. Within the same time-scale, Brian asked Richard to report on: whether there was any body (or depth) to the report and if not what action he should take; and whether the senior managers knew and appreciated the full implications of what they had signed. He said he wanted a verbal report with minimal written back-up.

It was clear to Richard and John that a high level of trust had been established.

Richard had reason to be unsure how the forthcoming interviews would go. The Vice President Finance, Adam Voysell, for example, had sanctioned the original report by Steve Wrokla – who himself was not likely to welcome the review by Berberis. And the Regional VPs might well see the review as interference. In fact, most of the interviews went very well. Adam took both the Berberis people out to a meal and set out his stall immediately. He had been with Buckingham's only eighteen months and fully appreciated the need for changes. He saw Brian, he said, as his 'white knight' who had procured the review that the whole situation demanded. He gave every help that he could. Of the other interviews none proved to be difficult except that with Steve Wrokla, who was obstructive.

At the end of two weeks, Richard and John made their report to Brian. They made three key points.

First, that the mineral extraction business was essentially different from the manufacturing business and that as the Regional VPs ran both in their areas they needed two different information support systems. Second, that the original report 'made no case'.

Third, that while there was a high degree of commitment and concern within the company, there was a general lack of appreciation and knowledge about the whole area of IS & T – of what it offered, of how to match it to business needs and how to manage and control it. This led to three recommendations: that the company needed an IS & T executive reporting directly to the Board and that it would be necessary to recruit that person from outside; that a programme of education in IS & T was needed, which should start with senior management; and that there was a need for a full strategic study to be made, using the services of outside people.

Brian received this report thoughtfully and warmly. He thanked them for what they had done and said he was very pleased with the assignment. They packed their bags and left for London.

Two months later, Richard received a phone call from Brian. He said that Harold Buckingham had stepped down as Chief Executive Officer and that he, Brian, had taken over. He wanted to implement immediately the recommendations that Richard had made. He asked if Richard could go over to Harrisburg as soon as possible to stand in for six months as the head of IS & T while a new executive was recruited. He also asked that Berberis should undertake the strategic study recommended and organise the training programme. Lastly, he said that there were to be major changes in Buckingham's: the extraction businesses were to be separated from the manufacturing businesses, reporting separately to the Board; the company would expand by acquisition as far as the West Coast; and the head office would move to central USA.

Berberis went ahead with this work. The total fee involved was about $800 000.

Richard took up temporary residence in Harrisburg. He supervised the recruitment of the new executive and managed the strategic study and the development of the training programme. When the study had been completed, Buckingham's commissioned Berberis to assist them in providing the new system and managing the (always difficult) process of change. Meanwhile the old system, based on the computer at Harrisburg, continued to do its job. A transition period was obviously needed between the old and the new – especially as the latter was to be based at the new corporate head office in Kansas City. Berberis were asked to take over the running of the old system during this period (a facilities management contract), thus allowing Buckingham's to concentrate all their resources on the new system. Berberis's fee was about $18 million, spread over four years.

In reviewing the assignment, Richard made a number of points.

First of all, he emphasised the great importance of the success of the first meeting in Brian's office in March 1987. He and John Legge had gone there essentially to discuss the technological aspects of Steve Wrokla's report. But, encouraged by Brian, and themselves encouraging him, their conversation had then developed into an unexpected and wide-ranging review of the nature and future of Buckingham's business, its strengths and weaknesses, and of the corresponding capabilities of its senior management. Brian, who up till then had been largely isolated from anyone with whom he could discuss his plans and hopes, had found an opportunity to open up, and thus to develop his ideas and strengthen his determination for change.

It was, said Richard, a very sensitive discussion.

We were not certain that we got on well with him at first. On the surface we were talking the same language and using the same words. But had we really understood him and had he really understood us? It was only when we found that things we said encouraged him, and vice versa, that I knew we had a real meeting of minds.

What was it that enabled Brian to trust these two people from a foreign country whom he had not met before? Richard said:

First we had to convince him that we were pragmatic professionals, able to talk about complex technological matters in straightforward business terms. We had to test each other out; after all, despite the use of buzz-words, neither side initially accepted that the other was necessarily as well informed as he talked. The skill you have to have is the ability to grasp very quickly the essence of the business, and the role and nature of the person you're talking to. In this, knowledge of a particular industry can be a very good door-opener but it can also be a hindrance if applied too rigidly because you can both get tied up in the same old traditional beliefs. Also it's difficult to tell a Chief Executive something he hasn't thought of when you both have the same background. So sometimes knowledge of related industries is better.

And then there's the ability that we call 'tapdancing', which is essentially thinking on your feet. When a client comes up with a problem, a good consultant is able to help him conceptualise, and can put forward possible options that help progress things towards a solution.

Of course you have to have the ability to listen and of course you must be oriented towards the business aspects; being well rounded in business is one of the secrets of success. The wrong kind of person to have sent to Harrisburg would have been someone who was very technically oriented and who was not able to talk in terms that were easily understandable. But on top of this there's no denying the old saying that age does speak to age, and in the case of Brian the fact that I had some American experience undoubtedly helped, as did the sales training that I got in this company.

What it comes down to is that a kind of chemistry develops between you and the client. And it doesn't always work. I can think of a case, an important job that Berberis in fact won, when the clients accepted our offer but said they didn't want the Director who led the sales effort to be involved in the job.

To win an important IS & T assignment, you have to be able to understand the underlying business elements. Where is the client going to? Where has he come from? What are the essential organisational aspects? And so what information does he really need in order to succeed?

3.   CORYLUS MANAGEMENT CONSULTANTS

This case history is about a management consultancy assignment in which the client was a major English county council, and it focuses on that county's Education Department. It shows how the consultants, by extending the roles originally required of them, were able to help the client secure important and unexpected improvements in the organisational climate of the Department. The organisations and people involved in the assignment were as follows.

Corylus Management Consultants forms the consultancy division of a well-known company in the financial services sector. It has been established for over 10 years and employs upward of 500 professional staff. It provides a full range of management consultancy services.

Corylus consultants involved in this assignment were: John Western, a Managing Consultant in his late 40s who has over 20 years' experience in education both as a qualified teacher and as a line manager in education and educational publishing, and had been with Corylus for about a year at the start of the assignment; Jonathan Pierce, his Director; and Philip Collins, one of Corylus's most experienced lead consultants. Philip, who was around 50, had worked as a professional consultant for 15 years and had specialised in assignments that involved education and health services. He had special expertise in cost/benefit analysis and in evaluating the difficult area of non-tangible benefits. Three specialist consultants (in financial management, property, and information technology) also took part in the assignment.

Claine County conceals the name of a major English county. In terms of its annual budget, which is over £400 million, Claine County Council is one of the 10 largest counties in the country. Two-thirds of its budget is spent on education.

Its Chief Executive was Donald Greaves. In his early 50s, Donald is a man of very considerable energy, intelligence and forthrightness whose strong personality has made him a very influential figure in the affairs of the Council. Its Chief Education Officer, Ken Turner, had had a long period of service in Claine and was coming up to retirement. An intelligent, educated and cultivated man, he was well respected and liked. The county's Chief Finance Officer was Jack

Thorsby, a man of high professional reputation whose dedication and willingness to work long hours enabled him to keep a tight control over all aspects of Council expenditure.

Four other people from Claine were to play important parts in the case history. Michael Anson and Jim Harwood were the two Deputy Chief Education Officers – and formed something of a contrast in styles. Michael, the younger of the two, put a lot of emphasis on delegation and innovation in management; Jim, enormously liked by his colleagues and very amiable, gave himself wholeheartedly to his task and worked himself so hard as to risk his health, liking to be directly concerned with detailed application. Also directly involved were two elected Councillors, Tony Ellis and Terry Collins. Both had been on the Council for over 20 years; both had an industrial relations background; and both had a strong commitment to the young people of the county.

The origins of the assignment are to be found in a meeting of the Policy Committee of the Council in late 1986. This committee, of which both Tony and Terry were members, had wide powers of overview on all the Council's activities. So it was natural that the Education Department, which was the Council's biggest spender, should come under its scrutiny, particularly as the Education Reform Act was on the horizon. Many county education departments, because their work is largely governed by legislation, run with a high level of autonomy. They tend to develop a mystique and a habit of keeping outsiders out. (Sometimes they are known as 'The Secret Garden'.) Thus often only the most inquisitive councillors gain a full understanding of what their education departments do and how they operate.

Claine's Department was certainly more open than most and, what is more, it was regarded by most of the Councillors as being well run. Nonetheless, without in any way indicating criticism or unease, or with a view to cost-cutting, the Policy Committee felt it was an appropriate time to reconsider the structure and resources of the Department to see whether there were ways in which it could become more effective in a period of major change.

They decided to call in outside consultants and prepared standard terms of reference for competitive tender, the essence of which was 'To advise the Council on a structure for the Education Department that would be robust and flexible enough to deal with the expected changes arising from the Education Reform Act.' Several consultancy firms, including Corylus, made a bid for the job. Each was invited to visit Claine before submitting their offer in writing. Selected firms were then asked to make a verbal presentation to a sub-committee that was drawn largely from the Policy Committee.

In their presentation, Corylus emphasised that their approach to the assignment would be an analogy of the 'medical check-out' that healthy people sensibly ask for, and that they would focus on four areas in particular: policy formulation; resource planning; organisation structure and functions; and communications.

The sub-committee chose Corylus to do the job. John Western was later to be told by Tony Ellis that it was the understanding, enthusiasm and commitment that they demonstrated at the presentation that won the day for them. It was anticipated that the project would be completed in six months and the contract was made at a fixed fee of around £50 000.

John explained how Corylus set about the task.

To start with, our views of the main contributions that we could make were, first, to help the Authority get a better understanding of its Education Department and, second, to re-shape the Department so that it was more effective in implementing policy rather than being a vehicle for administration.

It's important to remember that local authorities have a number of far-reaching policy decisions to make about the schools and colleges in their areas. They must decide whether schools should go or remain comprehensive, what the age of entry to schools should be, whether schools should be re-organised so as to reduce surplus places, and what the total size of the educational budget should be.

We divided the task into six stages. The first stage, which in terms of the use of our time was the greatest, would be to make a thorough investigation of the situation. This would involve us in a study of all the relevant documents and in conducting a series of interviews with those people who could contribute to our understanding – the key Officers (including departments other than Education, such as Finance and Personnel), the key members of the Council, a sample of school and college heads, and another sample of the area administration officers. With the information we needed then at hand, we could go on to the next stage, which was to make our analysis and prepare a series of papers setting out the main issues as we saw them.

The third stage would be a workshop. At this we would get together all the Claine people, or their representatives, for whom our report would have an important bearing. We would put before them the issue papers we had prepared and invite them to discuss each one in whatever depth seemed appropriate. It would be a way of checking our first perceptions with them, of helping them to explore each issue and look at the implications, and of giving us some feedback on what we could and should highlight in our eventual report. Most important of all, it would give them a chance to contribute to what the final shape of that report would be. After all, people tend to support what they have helped to build.

The next stage would be the preparation of our draft report, and after that its review with some of the key people involved. The final stage would be the presentation of our report to the Policy Committee.

If there were to be any difficulties in all this, they would centre on our credibility within the Education Department. We had to show them, right from the start, that we had a real understanding of their side of things and a real contribution to make. If they started to see us as partly informed generalists or worse still as accountants, we were lost.

Work began on the assignment in mid-1987. Philip Collins, Corylus's lead consultant, undertook most of the interviews, with John handling some of the sensitive ones himself. All the interviews followed a similar pattern. First, the people being interviewed were asked to explain their roles and functions and to say what they thought the main issues were in developing the education structure within the county. Three questions then followed: What are your problems? What are your criteria for success in your own job? And if you could wave a magic wand, what would you wish for?

In addition to these interviews, the three specialist consultants made their own investigations in the areas of financial management, property and information technology.

John asked each of the consultants to write a first-draft paper on each issue that had emerged in each of the areas they had been looking at. From these, he found that three items came up repeatedly: organisation structure, the availability and use of resources, and policy and communications. He knew that it would be important to ensure that the papers that went to the workshop participants put their points across in a way that was both objective and sensitive. He therefore prepared further drafts himself and took them to Claine for discussion with the key Officers there. They asked for a number of amendments to be made so that the 'implied criticisms' in them were reduced. He found that he had a very strong reaction from the Finance Department who thought that they were wrongly criticised. After these discussions he wrote the final versions.

He prepared for the workshop with great care. First, he re-checked its objectives. He had in mind the following quotation from Berkhard:

For change to be possible and for commitment to occur, there has to be enough dissatisfaction with the current state of affairs to mobilise energy towards change. There also has to be some fairly clear conception of what the state of affairs would be if and when change is successful.

The objectives, he decided, could now be clearly stated as follows:

1. To test and verify the observations;
2. To stimulate participants to agree where change was needed and the direction and main features of change;
3. To consider the key resources needed for change and identify any constraints on change;
4. To develop a consensus about and a sense of commitment to change, through common ownership, on which an action programme could be built (but the workshop would not be asked to produce the action programmes themselves).

Deciding the format of the workshop now became easier. He grouped the identified issues by subject area (policy formulation, organisation structure, resources and communications) and allocated time for each group in the two days the workshop was to take.

About 30 people were expected to come to the workshop. This included the Chief Executive, the key Officers and some of their subordinates, members of the Policy Committee and representatives of the teaching professions and trade unions. With this many people and with the amount of material to be covered in the two days, John knew that expert chairmanship of the workshop would be vital if things were to go well and the full agenda covered. His Director, Jonathan Pierce, had agreed to chair it and John briefed him extremely carefully. Using the skills he had learned as a teacher himself, he set objectives for each of the different parts of the workshop. Firm and fair chairmanship, which on the day would be an essential ingredient of success, involved not only controlling the discussion with sensitivity. People needed to know why they were there and to acknowledge each other's presence. They had to have a clear understanding of what they were expected to do and to realise they had enough information to do it. And they needed to know what they had done so that they had a sense of achievement in a task completed.

Every participant in the workshop was to receive a briefing document about 40 pages long. In it, each issue to be discussed was set out. The format used followed the pattern suggested by the aims that John had identified. First, there was a statement of the consultants' observations, phrased so as to be comprehensive but free of any 'blaming' content. This was followed by a series of questions for discussion that would help participants decide the relative importance of the issue, whether change was needed and if so what direction it might take, what resources would be required to effect it and what constraints there were. These questions also were very carefully and sensitively phrased so as to be broad, open and non-leading. It was left to the workshop to distinguish the real issues from the non-issues and to do the work of sorting out the options and selecting those that they wanted to follow up. (But, John decided, the Corylus people would go to the workshop with prepared options to put before participants in case things got sticky.)

Naturally, the list of issues ranged widely. Three examples will suffice to indicate the kind of subjects that participants would be asked to address: the way that information flowed or did not flow in the lead-up to policy formulation; the operation of the management accounting information system; and the area administration structure.

Meanwhile at Claine some of the key Officers were beginning to have doubts about the way things were going. There was a distinct danger, they thought, that the workshop would open up too many issues, that it might well create more problems than it solved and that it would become a scene for political in-fighting with little accomplished but damaged feelings and greater departmental entrenchment. It might be better, they said, if the consultants simply followed the normal course of events and put their recommendations in a report for the Policy Committee to consider.

John had to work hard and persuasively to keep things on track, and he succeeded. Eventually, after some delay, the dates for the workshop were firmly fixed.

John and the full Corylus team went down to Claine on the evening before the workshop started. He and Jonathan Pierce had dinner with Donald Greaves and they found he was still not optimistic about the coming two days. 'There'll be blood on the walls tomorrow', he predicted as they parted.

But it turned out very differently.

Because of the way that things had been structured, and because of the way that Jonathan chaired the meeting, the unexpected began to happen. The whole tone of the discussion was constructive. People came out from behind the barricades they had erected over years and started to communicate openly and without 'side'. They found it possible, as attitudes began to shift perceptibly and publicly, to reach a consensus on most of the issues. They talked as if they themselves, not somebody else, owned the problems. They began to commit themselves to change.

When the workshop closed on the second afternoon with the agenda completed, the consultants were able to go home with a sense of considerable achievement. They had not, it was true, been able to get as much agreement as they might have hoped on the action implications of many of the issues, so they would have to develop these themselves. And they had found that the level of importance attached to many of the issues was very different from what they had expected. But they knew that they now had a client who not only accepted the need for changes but also had greater confidence in implementing them. They would be able to write a punchier, shorter, more effective report because it would be addressed to an informed audience.

John prepared the draft report and sent it to Donald. A week or so later he got a phone call from him. 'I'm coming to London', he said. 'Can we get together over a sandwich lunch in your office?'

Donald was his usual forthright self. Pushing the report across the table, he said:

> I'm not having it. You haven't been radical enough. You've created a climate in which much more can take place. Up to now I suppose our critics could say that we were a bit rigid, compartmentalised and blinkered. People tended to be defensive and blamed things on others and on the system. They were overburdened and they didn't have much hope that things would change. Now there's real relief that it's all out in the open. They've raised their expectations about change and their aspirations for the future, even if some of them are apprehensive about what those changes will do to them personally. They're looking beyond their own roles at how the whole system can be made more effective. Don't disappoint them. Have the courage of your convictions. Do more.

John and Philip re-worked the key sections of the report. They sent the new draft to Donald for his opinion – which was to go ahead. A month later Corylus were asked to attend a joint meeting of the Policy Committee and the Education Committee to present their recommendations.

The meeting went through the report thoroughly but positively. In particular, they looked at the sections on organisation structure. 'You're saying', they said, 'that we ought to spend more on management and that the present layer is too thin, so that our people don't have enough time to think strategically. That's not what we expected to come out of this study, and it will cost us more. But we agree.' The report was put to the vote at the end of the meeting. They voted to adopt and implement it.

John kept in touch with Claine while the process of implementing changes went on. During this period Ken Turner, the Chief Education Officer, reached retirement age and his Deputy Michael Anson was appointed to succeed him. A year or so later, Michael wrote to John to say that: 'The structure that you recommended has proved robust and has enabled us to survive the impact of the Education Reform Act.'

Reviewing the assignment, John made a number of points.

> I suppose the most important thing about it is that we were able to help bring about much more change than we or they had expected. We went to Claine primarily as experts in the structure and operation of local authority education services. We became agents of major changes in people's attitudes to their jobs, their employer and what they could and would be allowed to contribute.
>
> There are so many people involved in making changes happen, and you have got to get them together so that they can think about it co-operatively. In doing this, I found that I was using my educational skills more than my straightforward consulting skills. I was quite surprised that the skills I had learned as a teacher were so useful. I had to think about what was going to happen when thirty people got together. What would they be able to do at the end that they couldn't do at the beginning? What did they need in the way of input, structure and chairmanship to make that happen?
>
> Of course, we had to consider whether we were taking too much of a risk in running the workshop, which was the key to the whole thing. We could have had conflicts that ran out of control; we could have had people saying that it was all a waste of time. But you have to have the confidence as well as the ability to work with a group and in a group. You need to have facilitating skills and a sensitivity to people's feelings and how they're reacting. You have to be able to structure information so that people can use it effectively. And you have to be able to see the objectives of a session in terms of what is going to happen to the people who are there.
>
> We have a lot of experience of local government education services. We were ahead of the client there – though sometimes only just. But that wasn't enough for this assignment. We also had to have the ability to procure change.

And if he could turn the clock back? 'I think I would have liked to have appreciated more fully the opportunities for change.'

4.   DEUTZIA MANAGEMENT CONSULTANTS

This case history illustrates the role that consultants have to develop when they discover that, because of a relatively unsophisticated approach to management, the client organisation needs help in making profitable use of the work that the consultants were brought in to do. It also illustrates the role conflicts that arise when it becomes clear that the original client, the executive in the client organisation who commissioned the work, does not have the support of other key members of management.

The organisations and people involved in this assignment were as follows.

Deutzia Management Consultants is a medium-sized consultancy employing over 100 professional staff. It offers a wide range of services but specialises in the human resource and personnel fields. It generates a high percentage of its business through existing clients.

The principal Deutzia consultant in this assignment was Richard Bowes. In his mid-40s, Richard had worked for Deutzia for about 10 years. Prior to this he had held appointments in personnel and in particular had specialised in industrial relations in heavy industry. He was assisted on this job by two other Deutzia consultants, both of whom had had considerable experience in personnel work.

The client organisation was Dillbourne Equipment Hire Limited, a recently acquired division of a major construction group. It owns and hires out equipment to the construction industry generally and has concessions in DIY centres for hiring equipment to the public.

Its annual turnover is in excess of £200 million and it employs about 4000 people. It operates throughout the UK and is organised on a regional basis, the Director of each of the six regions having a large measure of autonomy. It is nicely profitable and the parent group does not interfere much in its affairs. As is often the case in this particular business, most of the employees (including senior management) have been in the industry 'man and boy' and have come up the hard way. The company has few graduates or qualified professionals on its staff.

The Board of Dillbourne consisted of Fergus Dwyer, the Managing Director, the six Regional Directors, the Finance Director and the Sales and Marketing Director.

Soon after the acquisition by the parent group, the Dillbourne Board made a review of the company's operations. They decided to make some changes in order to get more up to date, and one of the areas identified was salary administration. They had no formal reward structure at all. People were paid what their managers thought they were worth and this resulted in anomalies, which were a continual cause for complaints. The Board therefore decided that they needed a Manpower Manager. After advertising the post, they appointed David Threlfall, a man of about 40 who had had a number of personnel jobs in the construction industry. He started with Dillbourne in May 1987.

In the first two months he carried out a basic management audit to assess the kind of talent that the company had. He then persuaded Fergus Dwyer that, in order to effect an immediate overhaul of the reward system, it would be necessary to bring in consultants because he did not have sufficient resources available on his own. He had worked with Deutzia in one of his previous jobs and had liked the professional way they ran things, so he invited them to a meeting with Fergus and himself. Richard went to the meeting with his Director. It was conducted in a friendly, business-like way with Fergus asking most of the questions. Shortly after the meeting, David phoned to say that they had got the job and he'd like them to start the following week.

That suited Richard, because he knew they were going to have to move fast. The task was to develop and install a reward structure for the top 300 Dillbourne people. They had only three months to get it up and running, because the people involved had to be receiving a pay-rise from it by 1 November and there was no documentation, such as job descriptions, on which to work.

Richard and his two assistants therefore prepared a job questionnaire to go out to all those whose jobs would be evaluated. It was sent out with a memo from Fergus explaining the purpose of the study. Though this was the first that they had heard about it, the great majority of recipients co-operated willingly, and as a result it was possible, with some cajoling and hard work, for Deutzia to meet the November deadline.

In the mean time, Richard had held a number of meetings with the Dillbourne Board. He said:

It was at the first of these that I began to get a feel for the kind of problems that the management would have to tackle in the future when the new reward structure was implemented.

We could see fairly quickly that Fergus was not a strong leader: his relationship with the Regional Directors was rather like that of King John and the Barons. He depended a lot on what they thought at any one time, so we knew that we wouldn't be able to rely on him to push through any significant changes.

This was going to be important, because another thing that emerged was the Barons' attitude to the assignment. They obviously thought that what they were buying was a new reward structure in isolation, something that would bring them up to date and wave a magic wand over all the hassle they had been having about low salaries. So at that first meeting we had I talked to them about the need to have an overall policy towards their people's pay and performance, about how our programme fitted into this and why we were doing it, and about what a good reward system is for in the context of better total company performance. I think most of them understood and absorbed this, because the meeting went well. Some of them certainly welcomed it, but there were one or two who stuck in their castles.

By mid-September, the consultants had got enough information to start making a preliminary analysis of how Dillbourne salaries compared with the market rate. It was clear that they were below the median and if, as the Board had indicated, they wanted to match the average of what people could get outside, they were going to have to give some substantial increases in November.

Richard said:

I took this information to the next meeting of the Board. Their reaction, after we had had a number of arguments about individuals, was that if they were going to put money on the table they wanted something in exchange. This led on to a discussion about managing performance in a more professional way, which would involve quite a change in the Dillbourne culture.

The Directors had a lot of difficulty in getting to grips with this and there were a number of reasons behind it. For a start, the Board did not know how to act as a Board. They didn't know how to make decisions as a group – not surprising, perhaps, as they hadn't had many decisions to make together in the past because they could each run their own patch more or less as they wanted. And Fergus couldn't help them very much, partly because it wasn't his style but also – as we discovered at about this time – because he was going to take early retirement and wouldn't be around for much longer to see the whole thing through. That also meant, incidentally, that the Barons were all looking over their shoulders because they knew that one of them was likely to be appointed as his successor. And then there were the problems with David.

His attitude was to rush things along and he was very demanding with everyone in terms of deadlines to be met, sometimes unpleasantly so. In theory this was all very well when we were trying to get the new reward system in place for November, but the trouble was that he wasn't carrying anybody with him. Some of the meetings were fairly tough and there was a lot of flak flying.

David had hung himself on the 1 November deadline and he now knew that it was likely to be pretty unrealistic unless everyone could be persuaded to co-operate fully, so it didn't help when some of the Barons took a 'why should we change?' line. He couldn't handle conflict. His response to the flak was to keep his head down in his trench and leave us to get on with the task of carrying the meeting. On one occasion – when he wasn't there – the Board discussed with me the possibility of firing him, but we saved him from this.

That the new reward structure was in place by November, with people accepting the new salary guidelines, naturally raised Deutzia's standing in the eyes of senior management. All the same, Richard now had a problem. It had come to be accepted – by most, but not by all the Barons – that Dillbourne needed further help from Deutzia in order to get improvements in performance in return for the higher levels of pay that they were now handing out, and the consultancy contract was extended to 1 March to allow for further changes to be made to the reward system and for a review of performance management to be made. But it was not really clear who was in effect the client for this. The Managing Director was not able or willing to push the work through. The original client (David) was losing his credibility. The Board, though not formally divided, were not in unison on what should be done.

'I knew that what was needed was to help them attain a more performance-related culture,' said Richard.

They would have to be much more systematic about telling their people what was expected of them. They had many of the signs of the traditional approach to management that you find in an industry such as this, with managers saying one thing to people's faces and another thing behind their backs. If you talked to a senior manager one day, he would tell you that everyone in his patch was highly competent; a day or so later and he was bemoaning the difficulty of achieving results with the quality of staff that he had. And there were a number of non-jobs and overlaps. For example, all the Regions had someone who was responsible for planning equipment maintenance, but none of them was really expert and up to date with best modern practice and there was nobody in the whole company with the ability and the authority to set and demand high standards. Of course, people knew all this. Somebody said to me: 'Performing well here isn't important.'

The question was how to help effectively, how to handle the politics. I came to the conclusion that the only thing to do was to work with the Regional Directors individually rather than set up a formal company-wide programme. This fitted in with what they wanted, because the ones who had been most receptive of our ideas at the Board meetings naturally wanted us to get things moving on their patch first.

So we began to run a series of workshops in the Baronies. We concentrated on the top thirty or so in each one and we put across the policy and practice of managing performance and effective organisation. I suppose I have to admit that it was tough going. We could only get them to engage on the nuts and bolts. We couldn't get them to address the context, the necessity of changing the whole culture so as to achieve a more effective business. They had worked for a long time in an environment in which adequate results and adequate profits were obtained without taking a hard look at the way people were performing and they didn't see any real reason for change. I'm not saying they weren't efficient. This is the kind of industry where, when you say a piece of major plant has to be on site at 7 a.m. it means 7 a.m. not 6.30 or 7.30, and they were good at doing this. So why should they change? Why should they have to think about moving up to a higher gear and running a business that was more totally effective? After all, the Regional Directors were their own masters. Nobody was taking a look at their jobs; nobody was pushing them and asking whether they could produce better results and threatening to fire them if they didn't. They set their own standards, and that attitude filtered down through the organisation.

Nevertheless, we have had some success, though it has varied from Region to Region. The key factor has of course been the lead given by the Regional Director concerned. In the case of two or three, they've taken significant steps forward and we are currently working with one of them on a much larger scale, looking at the reward system and performance management of their top five hundred staff, for a six-figure fee.

It's possible that the situation in the whole company may change soon. Fergus retired last autumn and the parent company appointed one of the Regional Directors to succeed him. This man has been one of our strongest supporters from the start, so I'm waiting to see, after he has settled into the job, how firm a leadership role he is going to take.

In reviewing the assignment, Richard made the following points.

Our view on what we were expected to do in this assignment changed a lot as it progressed. Initially our impressions were entirely those gained by what we saw through the Manpower Manager's window. So we saw ourselves as a technical resource to him, a sub-contractor for part of his work. Also, we overestimated the client organisation; we didn't really understand or appreciate where they were.

When the full situation began to reveal itself – and when we discovered the hidden agenda item of the succession to Fergus – we saw that it would be an essential part of our responsibility to help the business get more performance oriented and deal with the problem that, because of Fergus's retirement, they were not able to work as a group. This changed our role.

The contribution that we have made came about, first, because we switched on to the Board; second, because we hung in there when it got tough; and third, because we were able to meet the very tight time-scale. If we had not done these things, the assignment would have gone wrong.

With hindsight, we should have been more questioning at the start. Maybe then we should have insisted on a longer time-scale and looked more closely at the culture, which would have revealed earlier the need to bring about a greater emphasis on results and performance. It would also have meant we could work on the problem they had of making collective, committed decisions by the Board.

5. THE ESCALLON CONSULTANCY

This case history is about an assignment in which the client was the UK branch of a bank owned by a Third World country. The assignment began as a straight information technology application but developed into a situation in which the consultants concerned had to give help on a much wider basis, not merely to keep the original brief on track but even to save the bank from possible closure. It also illustrates a problem that frequently confronts consultants: Who in fact is the client?

The organisations and people involved in the case history are as follows.

The Escallon Consultancy specialises in the provision of services in information technology, though it also undertakes other consultancy work. It is closely linked to a well-known organisation in the financial services market. It has been established for over 10 years and employs upward of 800 professional staff. Its client base is predominantly in the UK but it does a lot of work overseas. Many of its clients are in banking, finance and insurance.

The principal Escallon consultant involved in this assignment was Simon Monmouth, a Managing Consultant of about 50. He has had some 20 year experience in consultancy, covering a wide range of activities, and has worked in Third World countries. He has an unusual role within Escallon, which he described as follows.

> The assigments that our firm gets tend to fall into four categories. First, there is the straight process consultancy work: we do a job to defined terms of reference. Second, there's knowledge transfer: we have a very high level of ability in a number of specialist areas – of which treasury management is an example – and our task is to transfer this knowledge to staff on the client's side in a practical way in the course of the assignment. Third, we can help through handholding: we provide the client with a second opinion, undertake a project audit, get a system up and running and so on. Fourth, we do remedial work: clients take on more than they can handle, get into a mess and need assistance in clearing it up. As you'll see, therefore, a lot of what we do calls for specialist knowledge and skills. My role here is to be the non- specialist specialist. When something starts to happen on a job that puts it outside the expertise of the specialists working on it, or when it's fairly clear from the start that there is going to be something unusual coming up, I tend to be called in.

Simon was assisted on this assignment by three or four other Escallon people. Principal among them were Christine Westgard and Sarah Bonetti. Both were in their late 20s and both had had extensive experience of installing and developing computer-based systems in banking operations.

The client in the assignment was the Etavese Farmers Bank (EFB). ('Etavia' conceals the name of a Commonwealth country.) The bank is owned by the Ministry of Finance in Etavia and is one of the half-dozen largest banks in that country. Etavese people began coming to the UK in the 1950s to work and to settle, mostly because the economy of their own country was not good, being dependent on basic agriculture. It was and still is difficult to find jobs there.

By the late 1960s, there were substantial numbers of Etavese living here and the EFB set up a London branch to provide them with banking services of the kind that they – and their fathers – had been used to. The services included the handling of UK–Etavia trading transactions, the usual current account facilities, commercial lending, mortgages and a means of remitting money back to Etavia. As the number of Etavese people here increased, settling in cities outside London, the bank set up additional branches; it now has four or more. It employs about 70 people in the UK, of which over two-thirds work in the main office in London. The current head of UK operations is David Tamana. As will be explained later, he has been appointed since the assignment began and had previously held a senior job in the bank in Etavia. He has two deputies, Paul Oukoh and Luke Firombey. Both have worked in the UK for many years. The events that led to the assignment began in 1986, with an intervention by the Bank of England.

The Bank of England ('the Bank') is responsible for monitoring and controlling standards in all banks that operate in the UK, whether UK-based or foreign-owned (though for the latter only as far as their operations in this country are concerned, of course). It has very considerable powers. For example, it can and does demand regular returns of confidential information about the activities of every bank. Its main controlling strength lies in its power to restrict the activities of, or even close, any bank that it finds to be working to standards that do not come up to its requirements.

For many years, the accounts of the EFB had been audited by a firm of Etavese accountants. In 1986, the Bank became dissatisfied with this arrangement and required the EFB to call in UK account-ants. Following discussions, the EFB selected the organisation with which Escallon is closely linked.

The audit team went in in late 1986. They reported that, though indubitably honest, the EFB was inefficient and not well managed. They considered that its records, its control procedures and its reporting methods were below standard and that one of the things it would have to do was to get automated. The EFB's style of opera-tions in many ways suited its own particular circumstances. It was relatively small and most of its customers' were personally well known to the staff. The procedures followed were similar to those in current use in Etavia. For example, all transactions were cross-checked by hand, and customers accounts were kept in bulky files. There were no computers of any kind in the bank. The only auto-mated process was that used to prepare customers' accounts. It was by now so old that the manufacturer was no longer able to provide spare parts.

The EFB was far from convinced that the recommended changes were necessary. After all, their systems worked, at least to their own satisfaction. In any case, a new computer system would cost money and that was something the bank was short of; it was trading profit-ably, but only just. It was therefore not very surprising that the auditors, recommendations were left for over a year without any action being taken.

During this period the then General Manager of the EFB left for another appointment and David Tamana took over. David was a somewhat tougher manager: bad debts were collected, new business acquired and bank charges were raised. Overall, the bank's financial position was improved. However, no action was taken on the automation recommendation until the Bank of England became gently but firmly insistent.

It strongly suggested to the EFB that it should appoint consultants to advise on the new system and help get it started. As a result of this pressure, Escallon were called in.

Simon took charge of the assignment from the beginning. 'Despite the fact that we were there at the Bank's insistence rather than at the wishes of the EFB,' he said,

> I found it easy to get on with the client and relationships were friendly. We put in two specialists, one on information technology and another on treasury management, because the main things we needed to look at – and we were being prompted by the Bank – were the controls exercised over lending and investment and the computer requirements. Though we knew about the background, it certainly seemed at first that this was a straightforward job, with a strong emphasis on IT.
>
> Then we began to get warning signs. First, the IT consultant told me that she was having difficulties because we were just not talking to computer-literate people. They wanted to run their bank by hand and they didn't trust computer technology. They had store-rooms of files – they had no time-limit for the destruction of files – and that was what they relied on for their records.
>
> Second, the other consultant got off to a bad start. She was looking at their treasury policy, and she found that they would only lend their excess funds to other banks and then only for short periods of time, which meant that they were getting a very low rate of interest on these funds. Now, most banks have carefully worked-out policies on this kind of thing; they increase the risk by a slight margin but they get a better return. When she talked to them about this, she found she was up against a stone wall. They recoiled at the very idea of 'risk' and they said that anyway they had to make sure that the money was available at short call in case they needed it themselves. She couldn't make any headway against this attitude.
>
> The third point was a little more worrying. We found out that the Bank had been receiving anonymous poison-pen letters making allegations of fraudulent behaviour on the part of officers in the EFB. Probably these came from disaffected former employees – David's predecessor had fired some people – but we had to wonder if there was fire beneath the smoke.

Nonetheless, the consultants' work went ahead and in due course the IT consultant put in her report, specifying the requirements of the systems and giving a broad indication of what hardware and software would be needed in order to meet those requirements. At an early stage, Escalon were asked to give an estimate of what it would cost to install the system. This they did – somewhat unwillingly in view of the fact that not all the work necessary to provide a full specification had been completed.

The Bank had meanwhile kept in touch. They called meetings at which progress on the work had to be reported, as they normally do in such cases. The usual practice is for the officers of the relevant bank to attend these meetings unaccompanied, but here Simon was allowed to attend with the people from EFB. David had forwarded to his head office the estimate of cost that Escallon had given, with a request for approval to go ahead. There was a long delay in getting a response. The Bank applied pressure; they said that if the new systems were not implemented by December 1989, the EFB would be closed. Authorisation came in August 1989.

Simon said:

> We completed the specifications and then looked at the various options for the system that would actually be installed. In the end we felt we had to recommend one that would be more expensive than our early estimate. At least we knew it would deliver. We went along to EFB to make a presentation and talked them through what it would consist of and what it could do for them if they used it fully. They were very friendly, but it was still quite a difficult meeting. It was clear that they hadn't realised the full impact of what they were being required to do. Only Luke had any grasp of what the future would be like – he had read a book about computers – and David was obviously worried.
>
> He talked as if they were making an investment in boxes they didn't understand and they were having to do so because the Bank of England had told them they had to so that they could make the returns that the Bank required. He was clearly concerned because he knew it meant throwing out the existing bookkeeping system that they were all familiar with and because the computer was going to be doing things that he couldn't check.
>
> He wanted EFB to work on the implementation alone. But I knew that they couldn't handle it without help; they'd soon be in more trouble and it would turn very sour, particularly if the Bank of England lost patience.

After a further meeting, EFB decided that they would need assistance in the process of implementation. There was, however, some delay in signing the contract for this which meant that the December deadline set by the Bank was fast approaching. A meeting with the Bank secured a postponement until the following March.

Christine continued to work on the assignment full-time and had the help of one other person on a part-time basis. The Escallon consultants began to find a number of problems that caused delays.

It would of course be necessary for the EFB staff to operate the entire system themselves in the future and therefore an operations procedure manual was needed. Arrangements were made for EFB staff to attend computer training courses, but Christine found that they still had difficulty in getting to a point where they could start to use the system, largely because, lacking any previous familiarity with computers, they found the underlying concepts hard to grasp quickly. EFB appointed a new computer manager, but the person concerned had no computer experience and thus had to start from scratch. Christine had to deal with the software and equipment suppliers, not all of whom were as helpful as might be hoped.

The bank's files had to be prepared for computer transcription. It turned out that many of the existing written records – such as the names and addresses of some customers – were out of date or incorrect. This had not mattered before, because the staff in fact knew what the correct information was and had simply not brought the files up to date. But it made the process of preparing the basic data very tedious and time-consuming.

It was soon clear that the March deadline could not be met. Another meeting with the Bank resulted in agreement to a further extension to June but it was made clear that that was it and no more concessions would be forthcoming. If the system was not in operation by June, the EFB would be in severe trouble, and could well be closed.

In late December, a problem of a different kind emerged. The bank staff had, of course, had to continue with all the normal work of the bank during the run-up to computerisation. The additional preparatory work came on top of this and made heavy inroads on their time. Simon said:

> Christine told me that there was considerable discontent about this, and it was made worse by the pay situation. All the people in the EFB, right up to the General Manager, have their salary levels fixed by reference to the comparable rate of pay for the job in Etavia. Salaries there are not high and haven't moved in line with UK inflation, so some of the people here have not had any increases since 1982.

David, realising the vital importance of getting the system working by the date set by the Bank, felt he had to take a tough line. In late

December he issued an order that everyone in the bank would have to work whatever overtime was necessary and that no one was to take any holidays until the computer system was installed. As a result of this, some of the EFB staff got in touch with a trade union. David was told by representatives of the staff that they would go on strike if there were not increases in pay, reductions in the hours having to be worked and more holidays. A strike at this time would of course be crippling to the bank.

[As you will appreciate] said Simon in summarising the position this is still an on-going assignment and my main task at present, apart from trying to keep the Bank of England happy, is to help David deal with the problems he faces, including the potential strike.

It has been a difficult job for us and not at all what we expected when we started. Our staff are all very good people. They are attuned to highly developed ways of working in, for example, the major banks. Here they have had to adapt to what is virtually a different culture. One minute they are explaining to someone what a return key is and the next they are discussing banking policy with a senior officer. They have had to be all-rounders in the widest sense of that word.

There is a very big gap between the culture of the EFB and the environment that we are used to working in – so big that I don't think we fully appreciated it at first. We have not previously had experience of a situation in which there was such a dearth of knowledge about modern computer technology. With hindsight, I would have liked to have had a better understanding of their culture from the beginning. We would then have seen earlier the need for the training-cum-guru role and done something more to help the senior people in the bank come to terms not only with what they were being required to do but also what opportunites there were for them in using modern information technology. As it is, we have become embroiled in things that we don't expect to be involved in. These range from ordering furniture to creating bank policies that are really internal matters. My staff are very good-natured about this but I have pushed them to the limit and I am concerned about the environment they have to work in.

Despite the ups and downs, relationships with the client have been good throughout. David has grumbled occasionally about money – he sometimes talks as if the cost of the project and our fees were some sort of tax he has to pay to continue in business. But I've always made it clear to him that, whatever the problem, I'll give him help – and I think that is appreciated.

At present, close to the Bank's deadline, the computer system is still not operational. Things take two or three times longer to do than our most pessimistic forecasts and every time I tell the EFB staff that they must now stand on their own feet another problem comes along and they ask us to come back again and help them. I cannot walk away from them, yet I cannot run their computer for ever for them either. There is a problem with management expertise in the bank in connection with new technology, and this is allied with an approach to banking that sometimes seems to be that tomorrow is another day. The staff tend to go home at 5 o'clock, whereas in most banks we work with they go when the work is done and not before.

The strike threat has receded. My real worry now is that the bank's staff will not actually succeed in learning how to run the computer, and it concerns me a great deal when I think what the results of this might be. Escallon's prestige is at stake to some extent, and so for that matter is mine. I am beginning to wonder how many more rabbits I can pull out of the hat for this client. If they were not such endearing people, I think we should have taken a much tougher line with them some time ago.

One final point. I must say that this job has made me wonder from time to time who my client really is. On the face of it, the obvious answer is that it's the EFB, but I've given a lot of help to David personally and if he were replaced I doubt that I would get someone better. And yet neither David nor the EFB really wanted us there in the first place. It was the Bank of England who insisted that we should be there and in some ways we have been doing their work for them. It's an interesting thought.

6.   FORSYTHE CONSULTANTS (UK) LTD

In this case history, the assignment began as a short technological study. It quickly developed into a situation in which the client needed, asked for and was given business guidance and on-the-job training of a much broader kind. The case history differs slightly from many of those reported, not because it is less important (it is an excellent and succinct illustration of a situation common in consultancy) but because there were few complications: both client and consultant rapidly realised what was needed.

The organisations and people involved were as follows.

Forsythe Consultants (UK) specialises in information technology. It is the UK consultancy arm of a large multi-national that has interests in a wide range of products and services. Forsythe has been established here for over 10 years and employs about 400 professional staff.

Geoff Armstrong is one of their Principal Consultants and one of the top 20 people in the firm. A chartered metallurgical engineer in his 40s, he began his career in the metal-processing industry. In his mid-20s he joined a firm of consulting engineers and with them worked overseas on the design of two greenfield-site metal-processing plants in Third World countries. A key feature of both these projects was that the consultants concerned had to interact in a sympathetic and subtle way with the clients so as to leave the latter with a sense of having themselves contributed very largely to the ultimate achievement. Following this he had three or four appointments in other companies, both in this country and in Europe, in which there was an increasing emphasis on information technology and on a wider business involvement. He joined Forsythe shortly before this assignment began.

The client was a major division of an organisation then owned by the UK government. It provides services to industry and to the public. It employs several thousand people and has an annual turnover in excess of £500 million. Within the division there is an Information Technology Services Department (ITSD) – an internal consultancy group available to help the division make use of the potential offered by computer applications.

The principal person involved in this assignment on the client's side was Stuart Wakeham, the Division's Director of Sales. In his early 50s, he had worked in this organisation throughout his career.

In 1987, ITSD got in touch with Forsythe. They said that they had a problem they couldn't solve and they wanted Forsythe to do a 'failure study' for them.

A year and a half earlier, they had been commissioned by Stuart Wakeham's office to produce a computer-based customer information system. The requirement was that the system should provide a wide variety of information about all the division's industrial customers – showing for example what each customer's throughput was, what special needs each had, what the nature and terms of the contract were, and so on. ITSD had spent about a million pounds on the project. They had made the necessary investigations, produced a function specfcation (which states in detail what the eventual system will do) and had then endeavoured to programme it. They had failed to do so successfully. They asked for someone to come in for about six weeks to tell them what was wrong.

Geoff was assigned to the job. As he said:

One of the advantages I had was that of bringing a fresh eye to the problem. It didn't take long to find the source of it.

Using technical terms, I can tell you very briefly what was wrong. The people who had produced the function specification had worked on the assumption that it would be programmed on a hierarchical data-base, but the programmers had been told to programme it in DBII which is a relational data-base devised for IBM computers – which is what the Division had. You have to know quite a lot about computers and how they work in order to appreciate the problem and we don't need to go into the technical details here. It's enough to say simply that what they were trying to do was in fact impossible, and it shouldn't have happened, really.

Obviously, part of the problem was communications within ITSD. They were not talking to each other enough. But it went deeper than that, on two counts. First, the people who produced the function specification had made a fundamental error in assuming that a hierarchical data-base would be used. A function specification should be neutral; it's for the people who do the programming to decide exactly how to turn it into something that works on the computer. Second, ITSD didn't have any established project management procedures. So consequently they had no formal project organisation structure in place, no ready reference document setting out defined standards, no clear-cut way of dealing with variations, and so on. It was true that the Project Leader had developed his own procedures, but they hadn't been fully disseminated to every member of the team.

Formal procedures of this kind, set out in manuals to which everyone has access, are essential if a major project is to be successful. Consulting engineers, who have to manage multi-million-pound projects, have been using them for years. I first came across them in the early 1970s. But they are a bit new in information technology; there are even people in IT who think they invented them.

Anyway, what it all meant as far as ITSD were concerned was that they were going to have to start again from square one and do a proper function specification. Stuart Wakeham asked me to stay on and manage the whole project.

During those first few weeks that I was there, we had seen quite a bit of each other and we had got along. He did his job very well but like a lot of people he was confused about IT. He didn't appreciate that you have to separate the information bit and the technology bit, so his view was that what he had asked the ITSD to do was to computerise his customer records. No one had pointed out to him that, to produce what he wanted, it was going to be necessary to look very closely at the way his business actually operated. Every business, or every major part of a business, is a system – call that 'system' spelt with a large S, if you like. The relevant computer system – that's 'system' with a small S – is a reflection or model of it. You have to understand the one before you can produce the other.

When you go into a project of this kind, you can take either a 'hard' approach or a 'soft' approach. In certain cases you can alternatively take a 'failures' approach. The approach you take determines the kind of role you'll have in carrying out the project.

The 'hard' approach assumes that there are people in the organisation who know all about what is going on and who can state, accurately and comprehensively, what the objectives are, how things operate and so on. In other words, they have a pretty good understanding of the total system. Your job then is essentially a rational or mechanistic one. You find these people, take down their knowledge and translate it into a computerised system.

The 'soft' approach makes no such assumption. It takes the line that the reality is a complex one, with many people having different perceptions, opinions and input, all of which have to be brought together in some way so that an accurate model of the whole system can be assembled. The participants will have to learn a lot from each other and reach an acceptable shared view on what is or should be happening. Your role therefore becomes that of counsellor or facilitator, bringing this about.

The 'failures' approach works when something has gone wrong. Your role then becomes that of a diagnostician, using the incidents of failure as your starting points and getting the participants to identify the gaps and inadequacies so as to produce eventually an interpretation that mirrors what they actually want.

When Stuart and I started to talk about what he really wanted, two things soon became clear.

First, he was keen to learn about IT. But he needed the right sort of person to help him understand it, because the specialists he'd come up against tended to be just that – specialists. A lot of very bright people go into careers in information technology; they know about computer hardware and software and how computer systems work, but they often have very little experience of the wider commercial world so they don't have that broader view, that *weltenschauung*. Stuart needed someone who had not only the technical know-how but also the business experience, plus the ability to explain it all. I think that's what I had. Certainly I was different from those he had come across so far, who had led him to believe that it was all a black art.

Second, he was going to have to think a lot about it, because he hadn't got a model of his business. One of the things I would have to do was help him build that model.

In the discussions they had had, Stuart had already made it clear that the hopes and expectations he held for the project would involve getting a lot of data out of the system, so that he would be able to call up virtually anything he liked. No one had warned him that the constraints imposed by the computer technology itself would make this impossible and that he and his senior managers were going to have to make early decisions about the way in which they would actually use the system when it was installed. Geoff had to point this out. His doing so did not go down well with the ITSD, who had tended to give the impression that 'anything is possible' and in any case did not think that it was a good idea to bring senior managers into discussions about technological constraints, because these were solely the province of the specialist.

To get the work done, Geoff was going to have to acquire a real understanding of Stuart's business, to get inside it and find out how he and his senior colleagues really operated it. Only then could he establish what information they needed and thus what functions the computer-based system would have to perform. This extended right down to the detailed level of how they would want the information presented to them on the monitor screens.

'In effect,' said Geoff,

what I did was to run a series of workshops. I started with Stuart, on a one-to-one basis, and then brought in the senior managers. The workshops were intensive, mostly of one or two hours' duration and never more than half a day. They were highly interactive, not just sessions in which I asked questions and noted down the answers. For example, sometimes I would put up a picture of what the system might do for them, and then they'd correct it.

They liked it, but they didn't always find it easy at first. After all, I was getting them to think through, for the first time ever, exactly how their business ran, and they'd been running the business for a long time on an intuitive rather than an analytic basis. But they began to like it, mainly for two reasons. First, they enjoyed the process itself – the process of attaining understanding, which is always satisfying in itself. It was almost like going to business school for them. Second, I think they liked the input that I provided. I was running the sessions not as an information technology specialist but as a fellow businessman – with a fair bit of varied experience – who had a good knowledge of information technology.

The new function specification came out of the workshops and then we got on with writing the programs. We broke it down into modules. Each module covered a major chunk of information; for example, one module covered all the details of the contracts with the largest customers. Then we worked on each module in turn and when it was completed made it available to the users. We didn't go for the 'big bang' approach – you know, when the experts take down the specification, go into hiding and emerge two years later with the whole thing ready to use. We introduced the system module by module.

The project was successfully completed within the year, as agreed.

In reviewing the assignment, Geoff was asked what abilities he felt he needed in order to make it a success. 'First of all', he said,

must come the knowledge of how business and business mechanisms operate. Working with Stuart and his colleagues, I had to be pro-active, not reactive, and that meant being able to suggest to them some of the things that they would want to see in the final result. Second, it was essential to be pragmatic in terms of what could reasonably be achieved for them in the current state of information technology – not forgetting the human interface design. There are dealer rooms in the City where each user has six screens. How do you present the data? Physically, how do they operate the system when they have a telephone in their hands?

Third, a lot of patience and understanding or empathy, because the people on the client's side were having to handle a lot of concepts that were new to them. It's very important to re-emphasise the point that I made earlier, when I was talking about Stuart Wakeham's difficulties in coming to terms with the use of IT. You have to help people realise that IT is about both information *and* technology, and you have to help them comb the two apart if you're going to deliver a solution that will satisfy them in the long run.

And the last point, which doesn't necessarily mean the least, is that you need the ability to get people involved, to ask the right questions, to be diplomatic and not make people feel they're making fools of themselves just because they don't have the kind of specialist knowledge that you have.

7.   GARRYAN AND PARTNERS

This case history is about an information technology assignment for a large research company. The consultants were originally invited to undertake a technological and economic evaluation of the client's computer development proposals but it became necessary, with the client's willing agreement, to look at the way that the IT facilities were being managed and controlled.

The organisations and the key people involved in the case history were as follows.

Garryan and Partners is a medium-sized consultancy that specialises in the information technology field. Established for over 10 years, it employs upward of 100 professional staff and has a wide client base.

Like many of his colleagues in Garryan, Douglas Grange had had considerable mature business experience before joining them in 1983. Now in his early 50s, he had started his career as an electrical engineer and had worked in the engineering industry for several years. He then went to America where he worked in the energy industry and began to specialise in systems engineering. After five years as chief of planning in the customs service (during which time he took a part-time Master's degree and developed a close interest in marketing), he became a consultant in public sector IT applications with another firm. He subsequently returned to the UK and had handled a great variety of projects, and had become a Principal Consultant when this assignment started.

The client organisation was Garamond Laboratories, the research and development division of a major technologically oriented plc. It employs about 2000 people, most of whom are of course professionally qualified. It undertakes all the basic research and product development/testing for the parent company. It spends about £25 million a year directly on IT equipment and related services – around 10 per cent of its annual budget.

The key people in the case history on Garamond's side were Keith Childs, the Finance Director, and Robin Graham, the Information Services (IS) Manager. Keith was a qualified accountant in his 50s. Robin, who reported to Keith and who had a staff of about 100, was in his early 40s – a highly able specialist who had made his career in the scientific applications of computers.

Douglas described how the assignment began.

In 1988 we were invited to meet Keith and Robin. They explained that what they wanted was a strategical review, and the accent would be on money. In particular, they needed to know if they were getting value for money on the very considerable investment they were making, because twenty-five million pounds a year is a lot to spend, even for a large organisation like Garamond. Their MD felt that if they moved all their purchasing to the dominant computer manufacturer in the industry sector and standardised on their equipment, they would get access to a wider range of suitable software packages. They had gone ahead with the installation of the new range but were still left with several key systems running on the old equipment, and little use was being made of standard software packages. A lot of concerns had arisen about the suitability of packages and they needed an outsider to tell them whether these were real or just manifestations of stubbornness. The MD didn't see any pay-offs from the investment in new facilities. He wanted some action.

Keith told me that we were not the only consultants they were talking to – apparently they were in touch with at least one other firm. However, he and I hit it off very well right from the start and we got the job. He said later that it was the maturity of our approach that won it for us, and that would have counted a lot for him because he was new to the company and would naturally have wanted it to go well.

Our offer was to look at who was responsible for IT – who was deciding what to do, how much to spend and whether they had the right applications. It was therefore a fact-finding programme and we set it up accordingly. First, we scheduled interviews with senior managers. Second, we arranged 'focus-groups' with users – structured discussions about how well computing supported their departments. Third, we had focus-group sessions with the people in Robin's IS department. Fourth, we did a questionnaire survey of a twenty per cent sample of users, probing their satisfaction with what they were getting.

When all the information was in, we analysed it. Two major findings came out of this. Point one was that they had no way of knowing if they were getting the best value for money, because the information needed to determine this simply wasn't available within the division. However, we could tell them that it was unlikely that there would be any economic advantage in converting the key systems still running on the old equipment. Point two was about the way the whole thing was being controlled. The users had abdicated to the IS people the decisions about the priorities for applications. The IS department had control – or rather they had been given control – of the IT budget and thus they were in a position to say which applications requests would be implemented and when, and which would be shelved or delayed. All the users had a 'wish-list' and were fighting to get IS assistance. What they got was in IS hands, not their own. In other words, the division was managing supply, not demand, and they needed to reverse this.

We needed to get all this across to the MD and his Board, so we took them away for a day. In the morning we made a full presentation of our findings. Then in the afternoon we settled down to a discussion so that they could talk it through. As you can imagine, we were not sure how it would go, because what we had to tell them went quite a long way beyond what they were expecting.

In the event we needn't have worried, because they leaped at it. They were a very action-oriented group – in the middle of the afternoon the MD asked me if they should fire the IS manager – and so, though we had come largely expecting that our role would be to advocate our recommendations, we found instead that what they wanted to talk about was what they should do next. We had in fact already worked out a number of ideas and the principal one of these was that they should have a programme of looking at applications planning. They needed to find ways of involving the users in decisions about priorities so that bit by bit they would start to take on ownership of IT, and there would be difficulties in putting this into practice because it would involve a shift in attitudes. We could see ways of tackling this and we put our suggestions forward.

By the end of the meeting, they had accepted all our findings, extended our contract for six months and told us to get on with it.

A task force was set up to run an Applications Planning Study. It was headed by one of the Directors and had someone from the IS department as coordinator. Douglas was its technical adviser. It arranged a series of meetings with groups of eight to ten, mostly at manager level. At Douglas's suggestion, the approach taken in the workshops was essentially market-oriented. Participants were first briefed on what was going on and then asked to discuss opportunities – opportunities to progress work in their areas through IT, opportunities to do a better job, the development ideas they had in their minds and so on.

Members of the IS department joined in, to provide costing estimates for the proposals that came forward. The output from the workshops was a series of ideas, difficulties, benefits and priorities. The task force had to report back to the Board in six months. It was not intended – and this was made clear – that this should be a one-off exercise. In future there would be a similar review each year so that a continuous process was set up whereby the users could generate their 'wish-lists' and establish their priorities. The costed results would go to the Board, with recommendations, for a decision to be made about the size of the IT budget.

Changes were made in the management structure, of which the most important was the creation of a new job as IT Manager, reporting directly to Keith and with responsibility for Robin's IS department. (As Douglas said: 'Robin was very good technically, but perhaps he was too technical for what the situation now required.') It was agreed between Garryan and Garamond that there was no suitable internal candidate, so someone from outside was recruited.

The task force completed the Applications Plan in the six months allotted and put in their report to the Board. With the new process now well in the hands of the client, Garryan's assignment came to an end.

In reviewing the assignment, Douglas made the following points.

It was a very interesting assignment because we had to handle problems that were vital to success but were not strictly IT problems. My main difficulty, for example, was whether we could help user management to take on ownership of IT. And, in the first stage, analysing what was needed meant we had to go back to first principles, like the management of supply and demand.

The thing that helped us most was the attitude of the Board. They surprised us at that first meeting, the way they leaped on to what we were saying. Everything moved forward rapidly after that.

With hindsight, I don't think there is very much about the assignment that I would have handled differently. Perhaps I should have liked to have got more involved in the the way decisions were made about prioritisation; I would have probably created a more sophisticated structure.

And his most important contribution? 'I think it was the ability to relate to this group as a fellow scientist. That helped a lot in getting the workshops going.'

8.   HAMMAMEL CONSUTANTS LTD

This case history is about a reliability engineering assignment involving a very large weapons system. It extended over a number of years. Partly because of the size and duration of the project, the consultant concerned found himself having to fulfil a role that was not envisaged at the outset.

The background to the case history is as follows.

Hammamel Consultants Ltd form part of a group that provides a variety of consultancy services, mostly in the engineering field. Hammamel specialises in reliability engineering. It employs over 100 professional staff, has been in existence for over 10 years and operates mostly in UK and continental Europe. For those not familiar with reliability engineering, a brief explanation may be useful.

The object of reliability engineering is to predict and improve the reliability of a total system – a total system that consists of a number of discrete parts or packages that interact together. Some examples of such systems are: a computer installation consisting of a main-frame and ancilliary hardware; a newspaper printing press; a new automobile; or a weapons system. The reliability of the whole system is a function of the reliability of its parts. Each part can be tested to assess the frequency with which it is liable to fail under normal use. Thus the reliability of the whole system can be predicted. From this, action can be taken at the design stage to improve, at lowest poss-ible cost, the reliability of the whole system when in operation. The quality of certain parts can be improved; replacement or mainten-ance schedules can be specified that will ensure that a part is given attention before it is likely to fail; optimum lists of parts to be held in immediate store can be drawn up; and so on. In a way, reliability engineering is thus a child of operations research and quality con-trol. As a technology, it has grown rapidly in the past 20 years. Its use is insisted on by major customers for complex systems, such as defence ministries, for whom predictability of performance com-bined with minimal in-action maintenance costs and spare-part stock-holding is essential.

Hammamel's consultant for this assignment was Bill Hannar. Now in his mid-30s, he took a degree in mathematics and then began his career working in telecommunications. After a number of years there, he moved on to a large and well-known defence industry con-tractor, where he began to specialise in reliability engineering and in course of time became their Principal Reliability Engineer. In 1985 he was head-hunted for Hammamel specifically for the key role in this project. He had from childhood spoken the European language in which business on this project was conducted. The client in the assignment was High-Space Incorporated. This name conceals the identity of one of the largest European manufacturers of military systems. In 1984, High-Space won a contract from the Defence Ministry of a NATO country to develop and produce a complex, advanced and very expensive weapons system, to be mounted on a mobile platform. Their role was that of prime con-tractor. They or their subsidiary companies would develop a large part of the system, but other defence companies would also be involved as sub-contractors. The Defence Ministry insisted that the highest possible standards of reliability engineering should be applied to the project and required High-Space to employ specialist consultants for this. As a result, Hammamel and another firm were appointed. The other firm worked mostly on the theoretical aspects. Hammamel's job was to manage all the reliability engineering.

Bill explained:

The essence of our task was to look at and predict the availability, reliability and maintainability of the system under action conditions. The system, being mounted on a mobile platform, would be away from base when it was used and the defence people therefore needed to know how often it would break down, what effort would be needed to put it right, what on-board spares would be needed and what the availability of spares would be. We would have to simulate what would happen and produce numerical performance targets for every part of the system.

Each sub-contractor was responsible for the reliability of his own part of the system, so we had to control what they did in this respect. As we were working for the prime contractor, High-Space, we produced a reliability plan for the total system but we also produced a specification of what the sub-contractors should do and on this they based their own reliability plans. These plans had to be approved by us and then became part of the relevant contract document. Officially, of course, the plans were approved by the Quality Manager of High-Space but he was working on our advice.

I had a couple of other Hammamel people working with me on the project and during the first two years we spent most of our time producing or reviewing documents and going to meetings with the prime contractor and the sub-contractors for discussions. We had extra work put on us when the other firm of consultants had their contract ended because High-Space weren't satisfied with their performance.

One or two problems began to surface early on, and they involved the sub-contractors. Some of them were in fact High-Space subsidiary companies and they were able to bring internal pressure to bear so that the targets they were set were not as tough as those given to outsiders. Also, which made it more difficult on our side, it turned out that the contracts with them were actually no more than internal orders, not legally enforceable contracts that referenced the overall reliability plan we had set up. Among the sub-contractors who were not owned by High-Space, there was one in particular with whom we had problems. They were a division of another major manufacturer of defence systems. We considered that the reliability plans they produced were deficient and we kept turning them down because they weren't good enough.

After Bill had been working on the project for about two years, two significant changes were made.

Until then, there had been no upper limit set to the total development cost of the project. High-Space billed the Defence Ministry on an agreed basis for all the work that was done. The Defence Ministry now began to get fidgety about the mounting costs and wanted to move to a fixed-price basis for completion of the project. After a lot of negotiation, High-Space reached agreement on this – an agreement which of course included fixed prices for the completion of the work of the sub-contractors. However, the sub-contractor with whom Bill had been having particular difficulty would not agree a price that High-Space thought reasonable unless the reliability plans that they had already submitted were accepted. They therefore continued to work on the previous cost-plus basis.

Shortly after this, High-Space decided to take on responsibility for the reliability activities themselves. There was no implied criticism of Hammamel in this; it was simply that they wanted to work in a different way. They appointed a senior member of their own staff with the title of Reliability Consultant, reporting to the Quality Manager and taking on the coordinating and approving roles. Hammamel's contract was continued but they worked in an advisory capacity to the Consultant.

'At first,' said Bill,

everything went well. But after a time we began to notice that the quality of in-puts from the sub-contractors started to fall. We would hear indirectly that documentation was being approved over our heads and contrary to our recommendations. This came at an important stage when equipment was starting to be produced by the sub-contractors and assembled by the prime contractor. Obviously, one of the main questions we had to address on the whole project was whether all the different equipment parts and packages would work together, and with the actual equipment available we needed to assess the real – not the theoretical – reliability of the system as it would exist.

The Consultant had other responsibilities within High-Space, and he was absent for significant amounts of time. This had two effects. First, we lost a certain amount of fundamental data that would enable us to assess the real reliability. Second, our job became that of coordinating most of the documentation and offering advice to the Quality Manager direct. We were left with all the responsibility we had had before for the success of the project but we didn't have the authority that we had formerly had.

Not long after this, the Quality Manager left High-Space and a lot of his staff went at the same time. The Consultant was promoted in his place, but we continued to lose most of the vital data that we needed to assess real reliability. Then the Consultant himself left.

We were asked to pick up the pieces. The new man appointed as Quality Manager knew a lot about quality management but he didn't really understand reliability. However, he was a very bright bloke and quick on the up-take, so he was a very easy person to work for. All the same, what it meant was that our role had become even more political. We were the lynch-pins because, after all, we had been working on the project longer than anyone else. We had worked closely not only with High-Space but also with the sub-contractors, whom we had been advising on a friendly and unofficial basis for a long time – with the prime contractor's approval of course. If there was anyone who could pull the whole thing together and give the Defence Ministry a system with a known reliability, it was us. And that in fact was what happened. We found our way through the politics of the new situation, and helped High-Space to deliver it satisfactorily.

Looking back on the assignment, Bill made the following points.

When I came into the High-Space job, our role had been effectively defined as a purely technological one. But it became, of course, a highly political one. We had expected that we would have the normal powers in a situation of this kind, the power to say what should and what should not go forward. It turned out that, if people didn't want to take my advice, I couldn't make them – though they did, once they had confidence in my ability.

I found there were three essential ingredients for success. First, technological competence; second, making it an invariable practice always to offer true and honest advice, however complicated the political background became; and third, to take a friendly approach with everyone, no matter how I felt about the way things were. Just to illustrate that last point. I can remember an occasion when one of the sub-contractors was in financial difficulty and on top of that their submissions were not very good. I had to go over and see them. I went through my own letter with them, telling them which points they should concentrate on and where they could soft-pedal. It wasn't that bad – the bloke was very friendly.

A lot of things could have gone wrong on this project. There could have been constant confrontations with everything getting bogged down in a series of quarrels. If we had not been patient, if we had not worked hard to get people thinking that something we wanted was their own idea, this might have happened.

And his most important contribution?

'Well, quite simply the reliability plan would have fallen apart without us.'

9. ILEX CONSULTANTS LTD

This case history is about an information technology assignment for an insurance company. It illustrates the difficulties that consultants have to face when there are management and interpersonal communications problems within the client organisation.

The organisations and key people involved were as follows.

The Ilex Consultancy specialises in information technology. It employs over 400 professional staff. It has three main divisions, each of which is largely autonomous. One of them – which is the focus of this case history – provides consultancy services over a broad range of IT activities. The two other divisions specialise in services to the financial market and to government departments respectively. The company has been operating for 20 years or more.

Jenny Irving is a Managing Consultant in her early 40s. After taking a degree in mathematics, she started her career in technical programming. She moved up through a number of appointments in software houses and consultancies, and joined Ilex as a consultancy line manager in the late 1980s. She was assisted in this assignment by two of Ilex's staff: Ian Galcombe, a consultant in his early 30s who specialised in data communications, and John Brydon, another mathematician who had held a broad range of jobs in the computer industry.

Ivybridge Insurance plc is a medium-sized, second-tier insurance company. It employs about 2000 people. It has its headquarters in a large provincial city and operates through a chain of 70 or so branch offices located throughout England and Wales. These branches service the insurance brokers and independent financial advisers who are the main source of initial contact with its policyholders. The company, which has an image of traditional worth, does not advertise widely and is therefore heavily dependent on these people to provide its premium income.

The principal Ivybridge people involved were Ashley Warwick, the IT Director, Helen Markham, who was a project manager in the IT Department, and Tony Berne, the Marketing Director.

Jenny explained how the assignment began.

In early 1989, we got a letter from Ivybridge, written by Helen. It invited us to tender for a study to review the architecture of a proposed local area network for their branches. It was a pretty brief letter and didn't give a lot of detail, so I rang her up to find out a bit more about the situation before we decided whether or not to bid. It was soon clear that they wanted help quickly so, once I had got her talking, she was happy to give me an off-the-record story of the background.

She mentioned two IT projects that her department were handling. One they called IBIS, which stood for Interactive Branch Information System. The other was a long-term system plan for the development of their mainframe systems which they referred to as LSP. Both, she said, were very important for the future of their business. Compared to their competitors their IT was behindhand and this was inhibiting their ability to trade effectively. They couldn't provide a fast enough service in, for example, quotations to their agents; they were slow on administration; and people who took out policies had unacceptably long delays in getting them in writing.

The insurance industry today is highly competitive, so a good service to the agents and other front-line people is essential. Insurance companies are able to launch new products – types of policies – very quickly. It takes only three months from conception to marketing; product life-cycles, which used to be long, are now much shorter, averaging around two years. But there's not much point in developing a product if you don't have the computer systems to support it – to register the insurees, arrange premium payments, administer claims and so on. Insurance marketing people are prone to claim that it is the IT in their companies that is holding them back, and this isn't surprising.

Helen, who was the project manager for IBIS, told me that this was what was happening with them and she didn't hide the fact that their system was overloaded. They had taken a lot of business as a result of the introduction of personal pension schemes, and this was the main cause. There were administrative inefficiencies within the system that her department, the IT department, were working to get rid of. It sounded as if there might be good long-term business for us in all this, but what she wanted immediately was someone with a good background in communications technology to review the LAN (local area network) architecture that had been developed as part of her IBIS. She needed to know if it would support the right security, the right level of capacity for the expected traffic and the right functions. She wanted the job done in a month, and we were coming up to the Easter holiday.

It happened that I knew we had Ian available, and his experience would make him an ideal man for the job, so I told Helen that we would put in a bid. She said that they were fairly certain that at least one other firm would be bidding, so when I wrote the letter of offer I made the fee pretty tight. And of course I agreed to be the Project Director for the assignment.

We got the job, and Ian went down to the company's headquarters to do it. Because of other commitments that I had at the time, it was a couple of weeks before I caught up with him and when I did the news was not good. He said that the project was in difficulty and that he was extremely pushed – but, as he added, 'life's like that in consultancy'.

Now Ian is a very nice guy. He is able, hard-working and always does a first-class job, even if the price doesn't warrant it. But people do tend to take advantage of him. So I asked him what was going on, and what he was reviewing. 'There's nothing to review,' he said. 'What are you doing then?' 'Well, I'm trying to sort it out for them.' 'Sort what out?' 'IBIS – you see, they don't know what they want it to do. I'm trying to find out and make some guesses so that I can tell them if the LAN architecture will support it.'

From what he told me, it was all an incredible muddle. IBIS was no way at the stage of development that I had been led to believe when I talked to Helen over the phone. There was no real architecture at all. They had simply decided that they didn't want a system based on mini-computers – they had had them in the past but they got so old they had to get rid of them – and that what they would have in the future would be a PC-based network, i.e. interacting clusters of personal computers in the branches linked to a mainframe at headquarters. But they hadn't worked out what these PCs would actually do – what functions they would perform. This information was essential if Ian was to carry out the assignment.

So he had been trying to fill in the gaps for them. He wasn't allowed to talk to any of the eventual users, but he had found out that some of the people in the IT department had interviewed a sample of users about a year previously and he had talked to them. On this basis, he had written a list of the applications that IBIS could undertake. He had then found out from Helen how many people there were in the branches, so that he could calculate how many PCs there were likely be when the system was set up. From this he had worked out roughly what might be the volume of traffic on the LAN. He was planning to complete all this in the following week or so, tidy up the numbers and then put in his report. Given the situation as he found it, he had done his usual first-class job and he had worked evenings and weekends to get it done. But it was all based on assumptions and hypotheses. At least it covered everything in the letter that I'd written, so we had done our best for the client.

Ian completed his research and, over the Easter holiday, wrote up his report. It was submitted to Helen in draft form a few days later. Having read it, she called Ian to a meeting, at which she said she was unhappy with it. She didn't discuss any of the difficulties he had had but concentrated on the validity of some of the assumptions he had made. Among other things, she told him that the staff numbers for the branches were wrong – even though she had given him these numbers herself. She asked for additional work to be done without further charge in order to correct some of the 'inaccurate assumptions', as she referred to them.

Jenny said:

Ian telephoned me after the meeting and I went down to see him. I spoke to Helen and we agreed that a small extra charge should be made. Given all the unbooked hours that Ian had put in on the assignment, we would just come out of it showing a small profit so in the circumstances it was clear that the best thing we could do was go along with what Helen had asked for.

However, as you can imagine, I was not happy with the situation. For one thing, we were reporting at too low a level in the client organisation – Helen was three levels below the IT Director – and this didn't help our chances of getting further work out of Ivybridge. I thought of the possibility of presenting the final report myself, getting some of the more senior people to come along to it, but for various internal reasons this was not a good idea so I left it to Ian to finish off the final report for me to check and then present it to Helen himself.

I knew that Ivybridge had recently appointed a Marketing Director, so I decided to make an approach to him. I rang him up, got an appointment and went along to see him with one of our sales staff. The main area that I wanted to talk to him about was competitor analysis, but it wasn't long before he began to pour out his troubles.

There had been no marketing director before him and he'd been brought in by the Managing Director personally in a 'white knight' role to get Ivybridge on a better business basis. He'd found himself in a very political situation with a lot of in-fighting and internal bickering and general all-round suspicion. At the root of it lay the problems with the company's IT.

The IT Director, Ashley Warwick, was clearly no friend of his. He described him as very aggressive and as having made many mistakes and enemies. There had been a lot of trouble with IBIS; LSP, the long-term system plan, was far behind the schedule that had been promised. He himself was never given any chance to contribute information or requirements to the IT development programme. Listening to everything he said, it was all too obvious that here was a man who was privately despondent about his company's ability to do the things that were necessary for survival in a competitive world.

He asked what we thought should be done, so we discussed with him different ways of viewing IT and in particular analysing the activities of competitors to get a lead from that – which is something you can do by researching information that has been published in the technical press and elsewhere. He was interested in this as a possible and politically acceptable route, and he said that he wanted to arrange for us to meet the IT Director to discuss it in greater detail. This was fine with me, so we closed the meeting at this point.

Incidentally, in the course of it he mentioned that Ivybridge had had some contact with another division of my own company. Later, I found out that they had asked for a quote for producing some special software. Our people felt that the specification was inadequate and had tried to talk to Ashley Warwick about it. He wouldn't make himself available for discussion so they had tried to talk to the MD instead because he was somehow involved. He wasn't there, so they had left a message with his secretary to say they thought it was all a mistake and asked him to phone back. The MD didn't, but Ashley did. He was absolutely furious, so they had decided not to bid.

A few days after this meeting, Jenny got a call from another member of the IT department, the Telecoms Manager. He said that they had more work for Ilex; they wanted them to review the wide area network that would connect the branches to the mainframe at headquarters. With the IBIS experience in mind, she asked him what exactly it was that they had for review and was told that it was a diagram. She replied that Ilex would be happy to look at a diagram but they would need to discuss how far they could take it before giving any commitment. She therefore arranged for another of her staff, John Brydon, to go there for a couple of days.

On his return, John reported back. It was, he said, a fairly simple diagram, one that they intended to give to the suppliers of the mainframe for guidance. It wasn't going to get them very far, and he explained why. He had also found out that part of the problem at Ivybridge was that the people in charge of IBIS, of the LSP and of the wide area network (all of which were highly interdependent in the design of the new systems) were not talking to each other. It was a very difficult political situation and would need decisions higher up the line before anyone could determine whether the diagram had any real validity or not. Jenny wrote a carefully worded letter to the Telecoms Manager advising him that there would be a major risk if he were to decide to specify anything for the WAN (the wide area network) on the basis of what he had shown John.

A week or so later, Jenny got a call from Ashley Warwick's secretary asking her to go to a meeting with him. She went down there a few days later. She said:

I don't think that I have ever been to a meeting like it in my life. He was in a towering rage and I had to put up with a stream of abuse, personal and otherwise. He started out on the software incident, for which he seemed to want to blame me. He went on and on about unprofessional conduct, about consultants themselves being disorganised and more of that kind of thing.

Then he shouted at me: 'Why have you been talking to the Marketing Director?' I had kept calm throughout all the blustering, and I told him quietly about the discussion of competitor analysis and explained how it could be useful to his company. Gradually I calmed him down until, from being enraged, he was merely brusque.

'Anyway,' he said suddenly, 'the reason that I've brought you down here is because I want you to do some more work for us, because you're quite right in what you told my Telecoms Manager.' He had apparently seen the letter that I'd written and had recognised from it the level of interaction between IBIS, the LSP and the WAN. He now wanted us to do a study of the WAN. I tried to convince him that it was in fact necessary to look at the whole system, but I could make no headway. He said he had had other consultants in the previous August and their study had been 'useless'. At least he agreed that the WAN was central and that because the requirements of the system were changing, it might be necessary to look at them again. So I sketched out for him what we could do, and the meeting ended.

When I got back here I began work with John on writing a proposal, which we worded with considerable delicacy. It focused on the WAN of course but it gave us access to a lot more things, including access to the users, and in order to choose the WAN we made it clear that we would have to look at the requirements of

IBIS and the LSP. We also included provision for workshops with the IT staff; this would be our means of getting them talking to each other. The only problem we had was in the reporting relationship. Ashley insisted that this should be to the Telecoms Manager. We got over that one by having a steering committee with Ashley on it.

The project was scheduled to have a four-month duration and involved two Ilex people (including John as Project Manager) and two from the IT department. The care put into the wording of the proposal paid dividends. The project team were able to assess the requirements not only of the WAN but also of the other parts of the system. John was able to get round the branches, the junior levels of the marketing department and other potential users. (Jenny was still talking to the Marketing Director, but unofficially.)

Jenny continued:

I kept a close eye on the project and in the course of it we learned much more about the client. The three interconnected projects had been going for some time before they made the initial contact with us, and both John and I had been rather puzzled as to why they had never got anywhere. We discovered that the managers immediately reporting to Ashley were scared of him and were unwilling to make decisions in case they proved to be wrong. So, when faced with a technical decision, a manager would find some technical issue – usually spurious – that needed investigating first and thereby pass the ball to another manager's court. John and I agreed that the best way he could help the client was to act as a 'ball-boy'. He picked up the issues and dealt with them, leaving the way clear to make real decisions.

Ilex completed their assignment successfully, with a great deal of progress made. They took Ivybridge through to the point where the LAN architecture and the network were fully agreed and a prototype branch system was up and running. By the end of their involvement in the project, the people responsible for IBIS and the WAN were talking to each other, though those on the LSP were still at loggerheads with their colleagues. The project report was sent, as Jenny put it, 'to all and sundry'. The post-project feedback was good.

In reviewing the assignment, Jenny made the following points.

I think our most important contribution was our ability to see and understand the real problem, in spite of all the obfuscation and fuss, and persuade people to allow us to address it. We had to change our relationship with them so that we could help them more, and we succeeded in doing this.

If the clock could be turned back? I think I might have taken more risk and gone to see the IT Director at a much earlier stage in the proceedings. I don't think there was any need to change the team I had, but the guy who put in all the hard work now knows that he should have drawn the attention of his Project Director to it sooner than he did.

10. JUNIPER CONSULTANCY

This case history is about a large construction project in a Third World country, and is specifically concerned with project management. The consultants were called in when the project began to go awry. In order to get it back on track, they had to adopt a very flexible approach and they therefore entered the assignment knowing only that they might be required to take any of a range of roles to achieve final success.

The organisations and people involved were as follows.

Juniper is a large multi-disciplinary consultancy offering a wide range of services in engineering, information technology, management consultancy and project management. Established for over 30 years, it has upward of 1000 professional staff.

Peter Jensen is one of the three Directors of Juniper's project management group. In his early 50s when this assignment started, he is a chartered mechanical engineer. Prior to joining them in 1975, he had held a number of senior appointments in manufacturing industry including that of managing director in a metallurgical industry company. He had run a number of Juniper's major project management assignments, in some of which the capital spend had exceeded £1 billion. Working with him on the assignment was John Asher, a Principal Consultant in his early 40s who specialised in project planning techniques.

The client in the assignment was Jeharna Industries ('Jeharna' conceals the name of a Third World country), the state-owned organisation responsible for the operation of all base industries in the country. These included petrol refineries, chemical plants, steelworks and electricity generation. The assignment was concerned with one of the largest plants, which manufactured products that were vital to the Jeharnian economy. The Chairman of this sector of Jeharna Industries was Emillo Crestino, a very experienced and able industrialist in his 50s. He had a Board of about 10 members, and ran the sector effectively as Chief Executive.

Peter described how the assignment started.

It was early in 1980, and I had just returned from running a very large project management job for one of the oil companies. I went along to see my Board Director to bring him up to date on the conclusion of the project. He told me that he had had a phone call overnight from Emillo, whom he knew quite well. Emillo was calling from Washington where he was in negotiations with the World Bank. Apparently he had a project in hand that was being funded with World Bank money, and it was in trouble. He needed some support in the round of negotiations and wanted someone with the right background to get on a plane straight away.

As you know, the World Bank supports a lot of projects in Third World countries. They watch them carefully and there's a very good reason for this, apart from simple prudence. People tend to think, when they hear about such-and-such a project being World Bank funded, that the Bank is putting up all the money. That's not so. Nearly always they put up only a small part of the capital – about five per cent or so. The rest is put up by other lending organisations. But because the Bank have a reputation for vetting all their projects extremely carefully, it isn't hard to find these other lenders. In this way, the Bank makes its available funds go much further.

But if one of the projects goes wrong, the Bank will lose its good reputation in this respect, and that would make it difficult to raise loans on future projects. So the Bank is a very watchful lender.

Peter got the plane to Washington that day. With him he took something that he had recently developed as a result of his experience on the last few projects that he had been working on – a Project Audit Questionnaire. This was an analytical method for surveying the health of any large construction project. It went into every detail of every single aspect of a project – technical, financial and managerial, asking questions that would reveal where and how a project was going awry.

In Washington, he held separate meetings with Emillo and with World Bank officials. He learned that the concern of the latter had arisen because the Jeharna project was falling behind. Money wasn't being spent and the project had virtually ground to a halt. He found that he got on very well with Emillo. He was approachable and reasonable. He had only recently taken on the job of Chairman and he was as interested as anyone to discover what was going wrong.

Peter knew that in situations of this kind there is always a balance to be struck between courage and foolhardiness, and he decided that in this case it would be possible to move things along quickly. He therefore arranged a special meeting between Emillo and the Bank officials, with himself sitting on Emillo's side, at which he proposed that the Bank should ease its pressure for a time, during which he and John Asher would go out to Jeharna and make a survey of the current state of the project using the method developed in his Project Audit Questionnaire. The overall intention was that, as a result, Emillo would put forward proposals for bringing the project back on line. The Bank agreed to think about this, and Peter came home.

Two weeks later he got a phone call from Emillo. The proposal had been agreed and he wanted Peter and John to get out to Jeharna as quickly as possible in order to negotiate a contract for providing the relevant consultancy services. As Peter said:

> We were on the next plane that we could get, with our suitcases and a box of biscuits that John's wife had made. In two weeks, with the help of a local lawyer, we had drawn up the contract and got it signed. We were to be there for the next four years.
>
> The contract was to review the whole management structure and the project itself, and make it all work – through the client. What we were going to find could have been anything – lack of adequate project management control techniques, bureaucracy, local politics, internal strife within the client organisation or whatever. So we had no idea of what kind of roles we would have to take, except that we knew we would be agents of change.

They planned for three stages in the assignment. First there would be an investigation stage, in which they would look in detail at where the project stood at that time, covering the technology, the financing, the cost management, the management of the teams at head office and on site and the resources available. This they expected to take about six months, at the end of which time they would report their findings to the Board and have them checked for accuracy. In the second stage, they would generate proposals on how to effect change. This stage would take a further three to four months. In the final stage they would assist in implementation and monitor progress to see that it went according to plan.

'Early on', said Peter,

> we found that we were not the first consultants to have been there. The place was full of reports that had been written by other consultants, gathering dust. They had one thing in common: they had all tried – and had failed – to impose their own systems on the project. So we realised how right we had been to insist that

our approach would be to help the Jeharnians to get it right in their own way, with our guidance.

The project itself was, in essence, to introduce very large modifications into the existing production capacity. You can get some idea of the size of the thing if I tell you that in today's terms the total capital cost of the modifications was around five hundred million pounds. We found that in engineering terms the project was reasonably well defined. The programme, however, was hopelessly optimistic. But some of the real troubles started to emerge when we looked at the cost management, which was excessively complex and restrictive.

Cost management, which in very simple terms is the controlling and recording of the amounts paid to contractors and subcontractors for work carried out, is one of the ways by which you measure the progress of a project. (The other, of course, is in terms of hardware on site actually completed.) The Jeharnians had enormous problems here. In addition to the World Bank finance, they had loans from two hundred other lenders covering eight different currencies. That meant eight different rates of exchange and eight different rates of inflation. So how do you report expenditure: in terms of dollars yesterday, or yen last week, or what? Add to this the fact that the accountancy was being done by two different methods – inflation accounting for Jeharnian purposes and historical accounting for the World Bank. It was all very complicated indeed.

However, it was when we looked at the management structure that we realised we had got to the source of the delay and the under-spending that had given the Bank cause for concern.

To explain what the problem was, I'll need to explain briefly the three basic options that you have when you set up the form of organisation for a project.

First, there's the functional form. The Project Manager sits on top of a series of watertight boxes, separate departments each dealing with a different discipline – engineers, the contracts department, planning, site work – and he manages the interface between them. This kind of organisation is successful for small projects but is disastrous for dealing with major projects because the decision-taking is far too centralised.

Second, there's the task form. In this the project is broken down into a number of different sub-projects. In a power station, for example, you might have the boiler house, the turbine room, the fuel storage area, the cooling towers and so on. Each task force is a mini-project of its own with all the functions it needs –

the engineers, the planners, the site people and everyone else – and it reports formally to the Project Manager.

Third, there's the matrix form, which is really a combination of the two previous types. As in the second form, you split the whole project into a series of sub-projects and you have a Project Manager in charge of each. But they don't have their own self-contained resources to get the job done. They call up the resources they need as and when they need them from a series of departments – engineers, contracts, planning, etc. – that are headed by Department Managers whose job it is to maintain high professional standards and to find ways of optimising resouce utilisation. The Project Managers and the Department Heads both report to the Project Director. This form has its complications – for example, it depends heavily on high standards of communications – but it can be very effective when used well on a large project.

In Jeharna we found an organisation with four characteristics. First of all, the individuals involved from the Chairman down were all very competent people. Second, the project organisation was functional and all matters were referred through the complete management hierarchy for decision. Third, the Project Director was completely overwhelmed because he found himself in a position where all decisions, even minor ones, were referred to him. He had a very large office, which was mostly occupied by tables, and every table was stacked with piles of documents about two to three feet high, all of them waiting for his attention and decision. Fourth, the project team was very large. There were in excess of a thousand staff, and the necessary bureaucracy was obscuring the project objectives and causing severe delay. Procurement, for example, was a big bottleneck, with insufficient people to handle it.

Our brief thus became to sort all this out.

The report that we made to the Board at the end of the first stage focused on two things. First, we proposed that the project organisation needed to be reviewed. Second, we proposed that the key to getting the project back on track lay in giving people practical help in specific areas, working alongside them and assisting them to get their own systems running effectively. We selected treasury and finance, cost management, procurement, and the overall planning of the project as being the areas that would benefit most from this approach. The Board accepted the report and so we went forward to the second stage.

On the management side, it was a question of getting agreement by both the Board and by the senior managers on a suitable structure to go to. The way we approached this was by working first with the Board. We ran a series of seminars for them, in which we concentrated on getting agreement on what it would look like at the end when the changes had been implemented. In the seminars, we gave them some input on the general theory of project management, on levels and methods of control and so on, and we stimulated and joined in discussion.

We had formed the view – but it needed checking out – that at that time in Jeharna the concept of the matrix organisation would be quite alien to the industrial culture of the country. Each individual needed to have one boss. In fact, I believe that there are a lot of countries where the matrix form is just not possible, where an individual finds it extremely difficult to report to two bosses. We can do this in the UK fairly successfully, and probably in North America, but perhaps in few other countries. In the course of the seminars with the Board, we found that they shared our view, and their inclination was to go for the task form of organisation.

But it would not be enough simply to get a Board decision to this effect. The views of the senior managers also needed to be taken into account – and here we are talking about the top ten or so key people on the project. We therefore ran a five-day seminar for them. We started by presenting papers that set out the different options available, with an analysis of the pluses and minuses of each. We then asked them to respond by saying what they thought should happen. The Chairman and the full Board were at the seminar and everyone joined in the discussion. The outcome was a recommendation for a change of management structure into a task force system.

However, it wasn't enough to stop there. The Jeharnians are a very democratic people, and they won't do things willingly and effectively just because someone tells them to. They need to get involved before they give real commitment. So we arranged for all the senior managers to hold their own seminars with their subordinates at all levels down to senior supervisor – about a hundred and fifty all told. There was a lot of talking and lobbying throughout this process. Finally, we had one single large meeting with everyone, all one thousand plus of them, at which the representatives of the hundred and fifty middle managers put their views on what should happen. In the end, we had won the day. There was general agreement which would lead to successful implementation.

The details of the new structure were then worked out. The organisation was redefined and split into a number of small groups based on separate individual areas of construction. Each area or sub-project was made as autonomous as possible and control was maintained by defining the area task quite formally. They were expected to control their sub-projects within certain limits of authority and had to report regularly and formally on their progress.

It was now time for Peter to strengthen his team in order to provide the practical help that had been agreed, with consultant staff working alongside certain senior managers and helping them to get their systems running effectively. More Juniper people therefore came out to Jeharna, bringing the team up to about half a dozen.

They were very carefully briefed on arrival. Each one was an expert in his own field and had been used to operating in an executive role in previous Juniper projects on which he had worked – though some had had experience on overseas projects in which the task had been analagous to this one. Peter emphasised to each that all the decisions on the project would be taken by Jeharnian staff. Their role was to sit alongside their assigned executives and help them to make good decisions. They learned the techniques of mentoring – of asking questions, of quietly challenging assumptions, of using the occasions of regular progress reports as learning vehicles, of helping them to talk through problems and find solutions. It is probably true that some of them found it all somewhat strange to start with, but they took to it readily. 'It was', said one, 'rather like teaching at first – a throw-back to my days at university and the tutorial relationship.'

The careful initial briefing, combined with the skills that the Juniper staff developed, proved to be very necessary. It would have been a great mistake to assume, simply because of the successful seminars that had been held, that everyone on the Jeharnian side was, and would continue to be, fully committed to change as events unrolled, especially in these unusual circumstances and in the context of a project of this magnitude, where so much was at stake and where so many things could go wrong.

'As is usual', said Peter,

there was in fact great opposition to change by some. It was not at all easy and we all expended a great deal of nervous energy, without respite, over those four years.

We were constantly on edge to drive our points home and not lose the battle – and the fact that our contract was subject to review every six months by Emillo and his Board didn't make things easier. We were always welcome, but at the same time we were also very conscious that we were interlopers. This meant that we had to be constantly watchful of our words. On the one hand, there was the fear of going too fast; on the other, the missed opportunity of not going fast enough. We had to restrain the enthusiasts and encourage the laggards, learn to recognise our friends and beware of those who, openly or privately, were against us.

There was, for example, one particular senior manager who we knew had never been in favour of the changes that we brought about, and he made no secret of the fact. At least he was straight about it and didn't work against us deviously. We concentrated a lot of effort on him, tried to help him along and advise him, but I have to admit that despite everything we were not successful. In the end, he fell out with Emillo and some of the key members of the Board, and he moved on. I always regretted that we were not able to bring him round.

We had to work extremely hard and diligently to keep the sentiment running in our favour, day by single day, because if the climate of opinion had begun to go against us it could all have gone horribly wrong. The consequences of even one small mistake could have been very destructive, and we were all of us always aware of this. As leader of the Juniper team, the main brunt of the responsibilty for the success of our work naturally fell on me. There were three things in particular that I concentrated on. First, helping and encouraging the individual members of the team. I can't emphasise too strongly that what we were doing was not only very difficult and delicate but also it was quite new to most of us, so it follows that everyone needed guidance and sympathy in getting through the hardest and most frustrating patches that inevitably occurred. The second thing was making sure that communications flowed well within the team and that no one got isolated, so that we all knew what was going on, what were likely to be the main problems that were coming up and what we would do about them. Third, I had to keep our objectives under constant review. Throughout the project, we succeeded in keeping the great majority of the Jeharnian staff on our side, but we never ever took this for granted.

It took time, and additional difficulties crept in because of a deterioration in the Jeharnian economy as a whole. The World Bank, however, became satisfied with the progress that was made and the pressure on Emillo and his Board was eventually eased. Finally, after four years, the project was successfully completed.

In reviewing the assignment, Peter made the following points.

In any job, the main difficulty that you have to expect is whether the client will accept what you're going to have to do. This one was no exception, but the complication here was that we had no idea what to expect when we began. We therefore had to keep a very open mind and be prepared to do or to obtain whatever was needed. This meant that we had to have our antennae out to find out what in fact it was that was needed. We had to review our own objectives every six months, redefine our scope, go to the Board with proposals and get their agreement.

Of a whole range of skills, knowledge and understanding that we had to have, I would rate first an understanding of how people relate to each other, especially people who are not of the same nationality. Of course, we needed top-class knowledge of project management techniques. And in this project there were some very difficult financial problems that only high level expertise could have sorted out. But behind all this I found that a lot of broad business experience was absolutely vital.

Looking back, I don't think there is very much I would change about the way we handled things or the Juniper staff we brought in. They all responded excellently to the unusual challenge we gave them.

One last point. We were very lucky to have in Emillo an outstanding Chairman. It was his commitment throughout that made it possible to achieve the success we did. But probably we wouldn't have got the job in the first place without a man of his ability being there.

11.   KERRIAN AND PARTNERS

This case history is about an assignment for a steel producer. It began as an assessment of a major capital investment decision but developed into a situation in which the consultants had to recommend a significant change in the client's business. It illustrates the problems consultants face in the highly charged emotional environment that often results in such cases.

The organisations and key people involved were as follows.

Roger Kerrian and Partners is a comparatively small, up-market consultancy that specialises in strategic planning services to top management. It was founded by the present Chairman about 20 years ago. It is based in the UK and has a small number of office locations, some of which are overseas. It employs up to 100 professional staff, most of whom tend to be younger people of very high calibre.

Michael Kington is one of the Partners. Now in his mid-30s, he began his career in law but soon moved into consultancy. He joined

Kerrian about 10 years ago and since then has worked on a wide variety of assignments. As a Partner, he usually takes the leading role in the assignments that he handles. He was assisted in this assignment by six of Kerrian's staff.

The Konig Steel Corporation is a medium-sized steel company and is based in a NATO country. Brought together as a result of mergers in the past three or four decades, it has a turnover running into ten figures. It is reasonably profitable but has a high level of debt. It has three plants, located within a radius of 200 kilometres. It employs upward of 10 000 people.

Its Chief Executive was Robert ('Bob') Pentall. Aged about 55, he had worked in the steel industry all his life and had come up through the commercial side. He had been running Konig for several years. The Production Director was Karl Bouckard. Then in his mid-40s, he too had worked only in the steel industry. He had for many years been in charge of Konig's Plant A.

Michael explained how the assignment began.

We had first worked with Konig in the early 1980s – in fact it was one of the first jobs that I was involved in when I joined Kerrian. We stayed in touch with them after that, both informally with Bob and Karl in particular, and by giving a seminar for the Board once a year in which we summarised current developments in the steel industry. We knew that they faced increasing problems, partly because of over-capacity in the industry generally and partly because of their own individual circumstances.

Of their three plants, they had invested well in continually modernising two of them. Plant A, however, had been somewhat starved of investment, and this was something that we had discussed with them from time to time. They knew, of course, that sooner or later they were going to have to make a decision as to whether to invest heavily in Plant A or whether they would have to close it down. But it was a very difficult decision for them to make and they put it off for as long as they could.

For various reasons to do with the company's history, this plant had special significance for a lot of people in Konig. So whatever decision they eventually reached about it was going to be a watershed for them. If they decided to invest heavily in it, they were effectively deciding that Konig would continue to strive to maintain its traditional place in the market – and there were strong feelings around that they should do so, even though that market was highly competitive. If on the other hand they decided to close it down, it would be tantamount to announcing to their staff and to the world that Konig were withdrawing in part at least from their position as one of the leading steel producers. They had had to shrink little by little in recent years because of the over-capacity in the market, so a decision of this kind would have a pretty devastating effect on morale. On top of this, with their high level of debt, it was unlikely that the other two plants would on their own be able to sustain the overheads that the company had round its neck, and this would mean that the whole structure would have to be reshifted.

Obviously, therefore, it was going to be an extremely emotive decision, and not one that they were likely to approach with cold rationality.

Karl's own position in all this added to the problem. As you know, he had been closely associated with Plant A for a long time. When the first pressure had begun to be felt, several years ago, that it might be necessary at some time to close Plant A, he had managed to achieve some very worthwhile cost reductions. What he had done was to develop certain modifications to the steel-making process – modifications that none of Konig's competitors had been able to copy – that resulted in significant energy savings on a wide range of products made in Plant A. Konig were able to produce them at five per cent less than the competition – and a five per cent saving in tight market conditions is an enormous advantage.

He was therefore the champion of investment. He felt that if he could get substantial capital put into new technology for Plant A, the additional savings this would bring, combined with the savings that arose from his own special process, would give Konig the opportunity to continue to compete successfully in a price-sensitive market. However, Karl himself was not a very good protagonist of causes. He was basically a production man, not very articulate when compared to some of his colleagues on the Board, and he didn't think that his arguments were getting all the attention they merited.

That, anyway, was the general background to the assignment. After we had been knocking on Konig's door for quite a long time, I finally got a phone call from Bob in early 1988. He told me that the Board had discussed the Plant A investment decision the previous week, and that the general feeling was they should go ahead with it. However he himself felt uncomfortable with it because, he thought, it hadn't been looked at carefully enough. It had finally come to the top of the agenda when time was running out – if they didn't make the decision very soon, it wouldn't be viable – and this had vitiated the quality of the decision. He wanted the decision checked, so he asked us to go over and advise the Board on whether or not they should invest in Plant A, and if so at what level and in what kind of plant.

I was able to put together a team of half a dozen with the right kind of specialist knowledge and we were on our way, with no more than six months to get the job done.

Plant A was a flat-rolling mill. Without going into unnecessary detail, it had been designed to produce high-graded steel of the kind used in the manufacture of, for example, automobiles and domestic 'white goods' hardware. Output quality has to be maintained at high levels in order to meet the increasingly tight specifications on which the industrial customers insist – and are able to obtain because of the competitive nature of the market. There are, of course, other separate sectors of the market for steel products. These include the small-tonnage, high-value sector for special steels, the market for wire products, and the market for lower grade steels as used in, for example, the construction industry.

Each sector of the market requires a type or grade of steel that is particular to it. (That is a slight over- simplification, but only a slight one.) Each type or grade of steel requires a process method that is particular to it. (Again, a slight over-simplification.) For every process method, there are usually a number of options: for example, it is possible to produce certain types of steel by either a batch method or a continuous casting method. What this all means effectively is that once a decision is made about the production method to be installed in any new plant, there is little flexibility in the type of market the plant will be able to serve during its working life. Investments in plant involve very large sums of money (a large greenfield site can cost over £5 billion before the start button is pressed) and therefore the early decisions are critical.

Michael explained how this affected the study that they were being asked to carry out.

Konig had a leading place in the market for high-graded flat-rolled steel products. This was what they were known for, and they had fought hard to win it and retain it. It obviously made sense to Bob and his Board, therefore, that they should continue to serve it. But if they were going to do so successfully, there were a lot of questions that needed to be answered that would determine the viability of Plant A in the future. What was going to be the level of demand for these products to the year 2000? What technical and material developments were likely that would lead to the substitution of other materials for steel in the automobile industry? What would be the level of foreign penetration of the market? Was the market base strong or weak?

The more we looked at these questions, the more we found that they were virtually impossible to answer. We and the Konig people who were working with us on the study held meetings with the company's customers and with others who could give us a feel for the future of the market and the technological changes that could be expected. We began to realise that looking at these questions wouldn't help, because there simply was no reliable information available. I began to feel uncomfortable about the assignment because we had no real traction on the problem. We simply couldn't find an analytical approach that would lead us to a solution.

The atmosphere in Konig itself didn't help. There was a great deal of emotion around. On the one hand there were those who were convinced that it was insane to invest in steel production anyway at this time, and on the other there were those who thought it was imperative for Konig to invest in order to stay in business. Karl was going through a very difficult patch, too. I got different numbers from him all the time about the existing steel plant, and it became necesary to go to their engineers in order to get accurate information. It was only by talking to them, incidentally, that we found out they had already had a design job done for them by another firm of consultants, from which some very expensive plant proposals had resulted that would have been totally unviable and would have made insufficient use of the cost-saving technical development that Karl had invented.

It was, however, this discovery that gave us our fundamental conceptual breakthrough. It led us to realise that there was an unarticulated but important segmentation emerging in the flat-rolled business. It had nothing to do with the macro-economics that we had been looking at: it was technologically driven. Basically, the industry was in the process of a gradual but continuing bifurcation into two parts, which we'll call Segment I and Segment II.

We began looking much harder at the state of the competition in both of these emerging segments. Looking at everyone else's announced production plans for the future, we found that more companies were investing in plant that would service Segment I. Going by what was published alone, it meant that in all but a boom year Konig would have enough capacity from the B and C Plants to serve the likely anticipated market, as far as we could estimate it. But if you looked at Segment II, things were different. Hardly anyone had announced plans that would indicate that they were going into it, and furthermore, because of the production methods used for this segment by the existing capacity, output costs per tonne were relatively high and were likely to get higher as the plant aged – and no amount of investment in modifications would reverse this. So there was going to be a business opportunity in Segment II that no one else had seen, because it was contrary to the culture of Konig and all the competition to aim for this segment, although it is in fact larger and more stable.

We started testing this out. We had a meeting with Karl and laid it out to him. To start with, he bought the concept, but he couldn't stay with it. His problem was that he found it difficult to define what Segment II was – remember that we were talking about a future segmentation of the market, not one that was already recognised, and he came up with some sophisticated arguments as to why Konig should stay where it was, firmly entrenched in Segment I.

We told Bob about it. He found the logic very compelling and he liked the concept, but his line was: 'If you can sell the idea through the organisation, I'll support it. You haven't proved it yet. There isn't enough on our order books for steel products in Segment II at present to justify major investment and we'd have to walk away from some very hard-won business.' So it was clear that, even if he could see the opportunity, he wasn't going to give a strong lead in exploiting it.

Thus there began a period in which Michael and his team found that they were undertaking a role that was quite different from the one envisaged when the assignment started. They had gone to check out the company's own plan for investment in Plant A. They now not only had to evaluate a different investment opportunity; if the evaluation proved positive, they would have to lead the organisation through the process of a strategic change in its business.

Michael said:

The first thing we had to do was to define in much clearer technical terms what steel for Segment II was, which meant looking at a whole range of variables such as carbon content and surface quality. Making use of the five per cent advantage that Konig's special process yielded, what kinds of steel could be produced? We worked closely with the engineers on this, but we were expected to come up with a lot of the technical answers ourselves. When we had got most of the solutions here, we had to check the order books and the market to assess the levels of demand. Then we had to analyse their cost capability against the competition. Everything looked okay, provided that we could sell sixty per cent of the total capacity within a range of about two hundred kilometres of the plant, and the market predictions were at least as good as this, which gave us further price advantages.

Our investigations took three or four months. During this time we held seminars for Bob and the top management and told them things as we progressed. These were open sessions, with questions and some hard arguments coming at us. It was important to keep them in close touch with us, to get them involved in what was coming out even if we were doing all the work, because in the end it was going to be their decision.

At the end of the period, we got all the facts and numbers as far as we could get them, and we put them in front of them at a half-day session. They got to the point of agreeing the full logic, but there was still no real commitment because they were not sure that they wanted to be in Segment II anyway. So a lot of discussion came up about, for example, the level of technology that was appropriate and whether they should use the Plant A site or abandon it and go for a greenfield site. There were strongly put arguments for and against each view. Both at the seminar and behind the scenes afterwards, they were saying to us that they wanted us to tell them what to do. We responded, as we had to, that they must decide, because it was their business, not ours, and while we could get and had got all the obtainable information on which the decision rested, they would have to live with the consequences.

They didn't reach a decision, and they pressed us further to make the choice for them. We agonised a lot about this: could we make a recommendation? Should we? Were we bound to do so even though we felt strongly that we shouldn't? What was the best way of helping them to deal with a situation that they found extremely difficult and emotive? In the end, we found a method.

We held a final seminar with them. There were in effect three main options from which they had to choose. I and two of my colleagues each took one of these and advocated it singly and wholeheartedly. Then we recommended a process. We suggested that they appoint three middle managers whom we named and ask them to assemble a full case. These three were people who had come to our attention because they were exceptionally able and intelligent, and they each had a strong personal long-term commitment to the company. Their task would be to use all the information we had collected and synthesise all the assumptions we had made, and come up with a recommendation.

This was agreed. The three worked on their own, without any further input from us, and came to their own recommendation. It was that Konig should pursue our business idea, use the Plant A site and make use of low-cost technology. Bob and the Board accepted the recommendation and went ahead.

In summarising the assignment, Michael made the following points.

This was a difficult assignment, but it was also one in which our level of achievement was high. It was difficult because of the unexpected: the unexpected intractibility of the problem we were first presented with; the unexpected option – totally counter-intuitive – that we came up with; the unexpected difficulties of dealing with an organisation that was suffering from decision-making paralysis; the unexpected roles of pushing the banner forward and of leading a technological process with engineers who were far better qualified than we were plus.

The decision that Konig had to make was critical for their survival in the future. They were betting the company, and it's fair to say that without us they would have bet on the wrong thing. There is no way they would have seen the emerging bifurcation in their markets if we had not been there, let alone make a decision to go for it. We redefined their business for them, and on top of that we saved them two hundred and fifty million pounds plus.

What could have gone wrong? Well, we, like them, could have found ourselves vacillating in the face of a hard, emotionally loaded decision. Instead, we were used as a forcing function, and our achievement lies in the way we were able to take up that role and see it through. So, looking back, I don't think there is very much I would change about what we did or how we did it, even with hindsight. We met the unexpected, and we succeeded.

12.   LAURUS PROJECT MANAGEMENT SERVICES

Laurus, a project management consultancy, was approached and asked to submit a fee proposal and schedule of works for managing a project for a new warehouse which was needed in a short time period. Laurus had previously managed the building of an extension to one of the existing warehouses for this particular company.

The firm was successful in its bid and Peter Baines, a Project Manager in his mid-30s, was assigned to the project.

The client company, Raxham, was a food manufacturer – a subsidiary of an American corporation. The contact in the client company was John Cooke, European Facilities Director with responsibility for all construction work undertaken for the company in Europe. This project involved mainly a one-to-one relationship between Peter Baines and John Cooke. Peter always went through John if he needed access to any other person, although this was a rare occurrence.

Once appointed, Peter, in agreement with the client, decided to opt for a design-and-build project (where the contractor not only builds but finishes the design using his own design team) rather than the more traditional method of the constructor only building to a pre-specified design.

He selected, on behalf of the client, a firm for each of the professional areas which were required for the project: quantity surveyors, architects, structural engineers and service engineers. The selection of the consultants was quite quick because Peter had obtained tight fee bids in response to his specifically worded requirements. The consultants would be involved in the design of the building to the stage when the design-and-build contractor would take over responsibility for the design and construction. At that point the role of the client's consultants changed to technical advisers to Peter on the contractor's interpretation of the contract.

Whilst Peter was selecting consultants he was also obtaining a brief from John which would be the basis for the design work. The architect, in coordination and in tandem with the engineers, used the client's brief and took the design of the warehouse to the concept stage.

During this period there were two or three occasions when Peter made presentations back to the client to show how the design team were interpreting the brief and to ensure that the project was unfolding in a way that John wanted. The presentations took the form of written specifications which the client signed off as having been agreed or else he'd write comments for consideration by the team.

An interesting feature of this project was that half of the warehouse was to be fully automated. For the company, this meant a total change in the concept of distribution: centralisation of their distribution and automation of operations. Building this warehouse was the largest project that Raxham had undertaken in the UK. Peter also had the task of coordinating the selection of consultants and contractors to produce the design of the automated system.

The client's consultants reached a stage when the design was sufficiently advanced and agreed by the client such that the project could be put out for tender by design-and-build contractors. A number submitted proposals in response to the tender, all submitting a price, a programme of work and written specification and drawings detailing what they'd construct for the price. Peter chose two and, after a period of negotiation, reached agreement with Notingly

Contractors. This contractor's price was the lowest and the proposals seemed compatible with the client's requirements.

Before making the decision on which contractor to appoint, Peter obtained as much background information as possible. He asked that when the contractors submitted their tender, they provide full information on key individuals to be involved in the project: the site agent, the contracts manager and the director in charge.

As part of the procedure the contractors presented their team to the Project Manager and the client's consultants for interview. Later, a visit was arranged to the site where the agent was currently working. In some projects Laurus would try to get a recommendation from the last client and even speak to the architect involved. On this particular project they didn't get a reference because they had worked with the contractor before; but, as described, they did go and visit the agent's last site.

At the start of this project, Peter thought there were two areas in which problems might arise. Firstly, getting the brief right, but this difficulty did not prove to be the case, since the client was unusually clear as to his requirements. Secondly, that a second sub-contractor was required on site to install the automated warehouse system as this was specialised and never intended as part of Notingly Contractors's works. Because of the tight programme it was necessary to have the two contractors on site at the same time and this is always potentially problematic. As it transpired the contractors did not interfere with each other's progress.

A site located near to a motorway (all of the products of Raxham were transported by road) had already been chosen before Laurus was appointed. The contractor set up on site and there was about a six-week delay before starting actual building work, whilst the contractor produced detailed designs for the foundations. The project was timed for twelve months from start to completion date.

With a design-and-build project the design work is always going on for later trades not needed on site at that stage. Once the design for the foundations had been produced, and whilst they were being built, the design for the frame was under way, and so on. Having this overlap is another way of keeping the programme tight.

Throughout the course of the project there were monthly site meetings between Peter and the contractor and monthly programme meetings on a two-week time lag from these.

On a quarterly basis there were meetings between Peter and John, although Peter provided a monthly brief written report of progress. Lots of other individual meetings took place between Peter and the client's consultant design team, between Peter and the solicitor, building control people, planners, etc.

From Peter's point of view, the project went well for the first nine months. It then became evident that the contractor was not going to meet the end date and indeed that the cost was more than the fee agreed to date by the client's quantity surveyor. A third aspect was that the quality of the work was deteriorating rapidly. (This often happens when a contractor is rushing to get the job done.)

Peter put the contractor under more and more pressure to get the work done. This was achieved by reiterating in writing what the contract entitlement was and that the contract allowed for damages to be deducted if the work was not completed on time. Peter saw his role of controlling the project as increasing in scope. Where something is not going right, within the powers that Project Managers have, Peter thought he could take action and this heralds the broadening of his role. Corrective action was needed to put the project back on track.

During the course of the project, as described earlier, Peter kept John up to date at monthly intervals. At month nine he did not alert John to the problem although he would probably have been aware that Peter's reports were getting a little more pessimistic. But it suddenly came to everyone's attention at month nine that something was afoot.

Assessing progress was essentially Peter's responsibility, but not exclusively. In discharging that responsibility he obviously got as much assistance as he could. The main assistance that the consultants could give him on that matter was probably less than on the technical side.

It was initially thought that in response to the pressure, the contractor, in agreement with Peter, would complete the project about one month late. Peter informed the client of that fact, and he reluctantly agreed to accept the building one month late and to waive any damages he might have deducted. So the project continued for a month or so on that basis. But it then became apparent that even this extension was not going to be sufficient.

In the end the contract was completed three months later than planned. The additional two months took in Christmas, so the two weeks or so around Christmas were worked at half pace which did not help.

During the last months of the project, Peter held difficult meetings with the contractor. A typical site meeting after month nine would be on the following basis. The contractor would have put forward at the beginning of the meeting his report. This report would indicate the progress he was making, usually better progress than Peter's information would suggest. So they would have an, often heated, discussion about that. The second part of the contractor's report would go on to describe the sub-contractors that were coming on site, *when* they were coming on site and the delivery dates of the materials.

Once again Peter would challenge him to ensure the sub-contractors were coming on site in a coordinated fashion and when required. Often there would be a disagreement about that. Peter would then pick up with the contractor on various comments regarding the quality of work where it was felt to be below acceptable standard and then the latter would argue that he thought he was providing a satisfactory standard of work. Any discussions on costs were not brought into site meetings. Matters of cost were dealt with outside the site meetings by the quantity surveyor.

There were therefore two views on quality, Peter's and the contractor's.

The specification set a standard of work and it was a matter of interpreting what the specification said.

Specifications can never be 100 per cent clear and on a project which is going well the Project Manager and contractor can reach agreement reasonably quickly as to what that interpretation should be. But where the contractor realises that costs are going up, that it is getting tighter and tighter in terms of time, then he's actually making a very strict interpretation of what the specifications say. Meanwhile, in protecting his client, Peter was also making a strict interpretation, but in the opposite direction. In some respects they were moving further apart which led to the uncomfortable site meetings that were held.

Eventually on a majority of cases agreement would be reached, but that agreement might take a number of meetings and a number of items of correspondence rather than it being agreed verbally the first time it was raised, which is often the case.

When the building was complete and acceptable for the client to occupy, Peter had to produce a list of minor defects together with some more major items. He produced quite a large document of defects which was sent to the contractor to make good.

However, on completion of the project the actual cost of the project was not agreed. Legally the agreement is between the client and the contractor but Peter, acting on behalf of the client, agrees the costs with the contractor. It has taken a further fifteen months to reach an agreement – the law and arbitration were not involved. This has meant a lot of meetings and correspondence.

Now the project is finally over, Peter and the firm have asked themselves what can be learned from this experience. The first thing that had to be done was to interpret the client's requirements. That was done successfully because at the end of the day the client is very satisfied with the final product.

A lot of time was spent in disagreement with the contractor regarding the interpretation of two or three contractual clauses. In future Peter would ensure that those contractual clauses were drafted differently, and that in drafting they were checked by a solicitor.

There is a standard form of contract that is used in the building industry which has been in use since 1981, but the actual clauses over which there was disagreement did not have much in the way of case law attached to them.

Another thing that Peter would probably change is the procedure for monitoring the contractor's performance on site, especially in relation to progress, such that there would be more advanced warning of likely delays which might be accruing. He would probably institute a more detailed reporting procedure.

From the financial point of view, it is the quantity surveyors' responsibility to advise the client about the anticipated final building costs of the project and Peter thought that the quantity surveyor would agree that the client should have been notified earlier than he eventually was that the building cost of the project was escalating.

Of course, this is all very well in retrospect, but at the time, with the monthly programme meetings and the quantity surveyor signing the monthly cost reports, everyone thought that all was well and that the reporting procedures and the monitoring were sufficient. It turned out not to be. Yet on another project additional procedures could be instigated and they might not turn out to be necessary.

Normally a project would not have the severe problems that this one has done. Those problems required various actions on Peter's part which normally would not have been necessary. Peter felt that this project has called upon all the skills which he, as a Project Manager, would be required to use. There were a number of very testing aspects.

Subsequent to completion, the contractor put in a claim for what he thought was the right amount of money that he should be paid and he backed that up by reference to the contract.

Meetings have taken place with the contractor where he can more fully describe his argument to back up his report. Peter has spent a lot of time looking at the contract and looking at the specification to put together his arguments. He has been referring back to the client's consultant design team for technical back-up. Where he agreed with the contractor on a particular item the quantity surveyor has determined the amount of money due.

The other aspect since completion was the rectification of the defects. These are niggling things, not affecting the client's occupation of the building, but Peter still does not believe the client has got what he paid for until they are corrected.

That has called upon his skills to negotiate and communicate and put over his point of view verbally, in writing and through use of the telephone, as well as in correspondence.

Peter pointed out that with project management the activity involves actually managing a particular project. It is not like an ongoing management consultancy: here the project manager is always addressing the project, and that project takes place in a specific context. In construction, with the exception of house building, each project is different. Although the project manager goes through the same procedures when undertaking a design-and-build project, the problems are different, yet the managerial expertise that is required should be transferrable across projects.

In conversation with the quantity surveyor, several other skills and abilities required of a successful project manager were identified.

For example, because of the nature of the role it was very helpful if a project manager had experience of working for both a client (as a consultant) and for a contractor (in an advisory capacity) so as to be aware of both aspects of a project. It was felt that a specialised professional, such as an acoustics manager, was unlikely to be a successful project manager because his specialism meant he never saw a project as a whole.

A project manager often has to work with conflicting advice. Since different disciplines have a different focus, he needs a sufficiently broad technical knowledge to appreciate what is being advised and why. Then he needs to be able to make his own decision based on that information. Very often these decisions have to be made at meetings, when a number of options are presented at the same time and one has to be chosen.

The Project Manager needs a broad understanding of a diverse range of issues: what the client wants; the project's development; financing of projects; the structure and politics of the client's organisation.

Finally, as a leader of a team, the Project Manager has to be able to give advice clearly, to convey instructions and to give clear directions.

13.   NEANTHIS MANAGEMENT CONSULTANTS

This case history is about an assignment that involved extensive process consultancy. It is an excellent illustration of the role of the consultant as a change agent, carefully and successfully helping the client organisation to move on to a higher level of achievement.

The organisations and key people involved were as follows.

Neanthis Management Consultants specialise in human resource management (HRM) consulting services. Established many years ago, they have grown successfully and now employ over 300 professional staff. They are well known for their expertise in organisation development (OD), and they are good at helping clients make profitable use of newly developed approaches in HRM and related productivity management.

Peter Nairn is one of three or four people at the top of their OD group. A chartered psychologist and now in his mid-30s, he began his career in the Civil Service. He worked for several years as an internal consultant in a large information technology/systems organisation, handling a wide variety of HRM and OD projects. He joined Neanthis about three years ago.

The client in this assignment has the pseudonym of the National Corporation. It conceals the identity of a quasi-governmental organisation. Briefly, National provides services directly to the public and in doing so competes with some private sector companies. It employs several thousand people and operates throughout the UK. In recent years, it has been given much greater autonomy (and with that, accountability) than it had previously.

The key person on National's side in the assignment was John Newton, the Chief Executive. In his mid-50s, he has worked within National for most of his career.

Some time before the assignment began, the man who is effectively John Newton's Chairman called a special meeting of all those who reported to him. Broadly, the purpose of the meeting was to ask them to begin a review of the effectiveness of the operations that they controlled. There was, however, a specific request. The Chairman said:

> I should like you, please, to take a close look at total quality management (TQM) as a way of getting better results. Without in any way telling you what you should do or how you should do it, I would ask you to find opportunities for making significant use of TQM to attain major business improvements.

TQM is, in essence, a management technique that originated in manufacturing industry. Through the development of new working and management practices (especially involving changes of attitudes toward quality among all employees), its aim is to evolve new production systems and methods that result in zero-defect products. The principles of TQM can be applied to service industries, but it is not always easy to do so. For example, in the production of consumer goods a defective product can be rejected before it reaches the consumer. But in, let us say, a service company such as a building society, an important aspect of the total 'product' is the quality of the reception that a potential investor or borrower visiting a branch gets from the staff. An isolated slip-up (or quality defect) in the way one customer is handled on a wet Monday morning is for ever beyond recall.

John Newton had heard about TQM but, like the majority of those who run service industries, he knew little about how it could be applied in his kind of business. He had had a long-standing friendly relationship with one or two of the senior people in Neanthis so, when he got the request from his Chairman, he turned to them initially for advice.

Peter Nairn takes up the story.

We have a group of people who specialise in TQM, so it was naturally with them that John started his discussions. However, because we have learned that TQM applications nearly always lead directly to the heart of how an organisation is run, I was involved at a very early stage.

We talked to him and explained the background and philosophy of TQM, and we were able to introduce him to companies that were doing it so that he could see it in operation. The important thing that we emphasised to him is that TQM is not, as some people think, a business strategy in itself; it's how you implement your strategy. So you must have a strategy first, and that in turn means that you have to know where you want to go. In other words, if you're going to apply TQM successfully, you first have to sort out what business you are in and where you want to be – that is, your mission – and what strategy you'll adopt to achieve that mission. You also have to think about where you want to be in the future – your vision and how you'll get there, because you need strategies for that as well.

John came to us because he needed to learn what TQM was all about, see for himself whether, and if so how, it could work in his business and get a clear picture of what the pay-off would be. We helped him in that process, and we suggested to him that his immediate short-term aim should be to find out if he felt committed to the idea of applying it in National. If he found that he was, then his next step would obviously be that he would want to talk to his colleagues on National's Board, so we suggested that he think in terms of making a presentation to them.

Over a period of about four or five months we had a number of meetings with him and showed him round. At the end of it, he felt certain that he did want to go ahead. We recommended that he take his Board away to a hotel where they could concentrate on this and nothing else. On Day One, he would make his presentation and then give them full rein to discuss his proposals. They needed to do this on their own, so we would not be involved on Day One. If they decided that they wanted to go ahead, we would be available to help on Day Two.

John agreed with this, and the meeting was arranged. At the end of the first day, the Board decided that they wanted to go ahead. Peter and a colleague from Neanthis's TQM group joined them on the second day.

They provided more information and answered a lot of questions but, more important, they said that there were two essential tasks that had to be undertaken. Task A was that the Board should sort out and decide the organisation's mission and vision. Task B was a diagnosis of National: a research project on the attitudes, feelings and perceptions of its staff, its clients and its customers. The outcome of Task A would be a clear statement, to which all the Board would be committed, of what business they were in, where they wanted to stand in that business, and where they were going in the future. Task B would reveal the factors that would help and hinder them in achieving the goals set in Task A. Together the accomplishing of the two tasks would enable them to identify a strategy, in which TQM would play a key part, for getting where they wanted to be.

The Board agreed. Neanthis were subsequently asked to help with both tasks. Peter headed the team of four that dealt with Task B and worked with one other colleague on Task A. He said:

We often find that it is quite easy to get an agreed statement of mission, but that wasn't the case here. We asked ten different people and got eleven different answers. John was very surprised at the diverse views we got.

Part of the problem was that they had not really learned to talk to each other. So, at an early stage, we put in some team-building sessions which helped them to work together effectively. It took three difficult months to reach agreement on putting the existing business together and come up with a statement of mission that they could all comfortably and fully agree on.

Then on to the vision – which became quite contentious. It took a long time to help them realise the opportunities that were available. For one thing, they tended to think that their masters exercised controls that didn't in fact exist. Several times I heard people say: 'We can't do that because we wouldn't be allowed to', which just wasn't true. For another, they hadn't had much experience of creative business thinking. They hadn't, for example, heard of brainstorming or de Bono's six thinking-hats technique, so we introduced them to both.

We structured the agenda for their meetings and managed the process. We determined the way that time was used – in syndicate work, plenary meetings, brainstorming sessions and so on. We also set the rules. One of the rules, for example, was that meetings could only take place if everyone was there, with no exceptions. On one occasion one of them failed to turn up at the last moment. It was at a hotel and everyone else had got there the night before and was ready to go. We kept to the rule that had been agreed and wouldn't let the meeting happen.

But what we did not do – and this is very important – was lead them in what they should think or decide. They came up with all the ideas, moulded them and evaluated them. It was essential that we created in them the ownership of everything that was decided.

They had to get it right, because they wouldn't have a second chance. They were producing their own tablets of stone. And the tablets would be wrong if there was someone in their midst who didn't buy it.

At the end of six months, they had what they'd been working for. A single piece of paper with about a hundred and twenty words on it. But it was a clear statement of their mission and their vision, and they were all behind it.

In the meantime, Task B had gone ahead and had been completed. Using questionnaires and interviews, the Neanthis team had obtained the relevant information from samples of National's staff, clients and customers. Peter and his colleagues kept the findings to themselves until Task A was through.

About a month after the Board had completed the statement of mission and vision, Neanthis arranged a one-day feedback seminar for them on the research findings. Again setting the agenda, they agreed with the Board that this particular day would be spent on feedback only. Discussion would come better later, when they had had a chance to digest the findings.

Peter said,

What we gave them was a snapshot of the views of the people who mattered in their business. For obvious reasons related to confidentiality, I can't tell you what the research showed, but I can tell you that it caused several sharp intakes of breath. Some of the findings showed that people's wants and attitudes were very different from what the Board had expected. The feelings of the staff on certain factors, for example, were much more favourable than they had thought they would be, and the factors that the customers considered important caused a lot of surprise.

A week after this we arranged a three-day meeting for them. On the first day, we gave a full opportunity to talk about and play with the facts from the research study – like 'em or hate 'em. On the second day we focused on the interaction of the Task A mission-and-vision statement and the Task B diagnosis. We helped them to get out a list of the things they needed to do in order to achieve their vision in three to five years' time. A lot of the emphasis in the items on that list was on the quality of the services they provided.

On the third day we started by reminding them of what TQM is. We took them back to the earlier seminar when John had made his presentation and we'd followed it up. We went through with them all the implications of applying TQM; we had thought through a lot of this for them and we backed it up with documentation. After that, and part way through the day, we left the meeting, telling them they now had to decide whether they wanted to go ahead with TQM. John ran the rest of the session. At the end of the day, they decided that they did want to go ahead.

What was the nitty-gritty? Achieving quality at the front end was not the key issue. That was only an outcome of the key issue. The key issue was the way they recruited, trained and managed people. The main focus and attention therefore had to be on management – how their managers treated people, and the sort of role models they were. It was not about smile campaigns. It was about management and about recognising that change had to come from the top.

That was the end of the assignment as originally contracted. Subsequently, National asked Neanthis for additional help – on implementing TQM, on setting up projects (with National project leaders) to tackle the list of tasks that had emerged from the second day of the final meeting, in guiding them to ensure that they preached and practised the same things at the same time, in piloting the cascade process through chosen parts of the organisation, and in putting together training materials.

In reviewing the assignment, Peter made the following points.

The key behaviour was that of John Newton, who wanted to take things on board and change himself. Usually when you talk to a Chief Executive about his management style and suggest, for instance, that he should make himself more available, he tends to go round talking about it and saying: 'My door's open.' John's not like that. He'll do it, and then when someone says: 'I see your door's open a lot more these days,' he'll just nod and say that, yes, he thinks it is. His willingness to adapt and his quiet strength made a lot of difference, especially in an organisation that still had to explore how much power and independence it had.

Looking at our own contribution, I would say that in the wider sense it was our abilities in process consultancy that counted. I've had some experience elsewhere of not putting enough effort into the process side and being left with a feeling that things were incomplete, that there was incomplete ownership of the change programmes that had been decided on. You learn from that, and things were different here. We needed, and had, good process skills with a good kit-bag. And at the detailed level, we had a stock of 'war-stories' – similar cases that we had handled elsewhere; and we were able to say: 'No, you're not ready to do that yet.'

Things might, of course, have gone wrong. We could have become time-scale or event driven, and then we should not have got the level of commitment that was achieved. We had to be very wary of a mis-reading by us of any 'yes' that was not real.

If the clock could be turned back? Well, I sometimes wished that I had more in-depth knowledge of TQM. But no, there's nothing significant about the assignment that I'd want to change. I'm happy with it as it is.

14.   THE OLEARIAN CONSULTANCY

This case history is about a computer systems assignment for a large quasi-government organisation in a West European country. It illustrates the problems that consultants face when they are called in to put right a major project that has gone sour – in this case because of inadequate performance and personality clashes.

The Olearian Consultancy specialises in information technology (IT). It has upward of 400 professional staff and offers a wide range of services in computer systems design, software production and so on. It was founded in the late 1970s, has been growing steadily since and has an up-market image.

Bill Orwell is one of Olearian's Principal Consultants. Now in his mid-30s, he took a degree in electronic engineering and worked in telecommunications for a few years, during which time he took a part-time Master's degree in digital systems. For the next seven years he worked for a number of companies in the computer industry as systems engineer, analyst, team-leader and eventually project manager. He joined Olearian three or four years ago.

In the organisation that became the client in this case history, we shall be concerned with two of its many divisions. First, there was the Procurement Division, which as its name implies was responsible for procuring all goods and services that the organisation required. Second, there was the particular operating division that was involved, which we shall call the User Division, which was to become the eventual customer of the computer-based system that is the focus of this study. And, since Olearian were not the suppliers of the system, we shall also be concerned with the people who were – a large and well-known software house whom we shall refer to as the Prime Contractor.

The Procurement Division had commissioned from the Prime Contractor a multi-million-pound system that was intended to assist the User Division in, broadly speaking, its office automation and training activities. (The exact function of the system is not relevant to this study.) It was being supplied on a fixed-price contract. It included the provision of some standard hardware and software, but the major part of the cost was to go on the production of some specially written software.

Olearian became involved in early 1988 when they were invited to tender for an audit of the project. It had then been running for 18 months and was 9 months behind. They offered a heavyweight team and won the job.

Bill had other commitments at this time so he was not part of the audit team, but he heard what was going on. He said,

It was all text-book stuff. They were doing most of the wrong things. There was no adequate planning, no milestones by which to measure progress, no unequivocal statements of requirements and no agreed mechanism for acceptance of the final product. Added to this there seemed to be poor discipline and some clashes of personality, mostly because a very senior member of the User Division was getting in on the act as the self-appointed project manager. Some of the hardware had been delivered but, because of the delays, the machines originally specified were no longer available and the new machines were not performing adequately.

Our audit team took six weeks to do their job, and they then presented their report. Briefly, what they said was that if the client was not going to cancel the project, there were a number of problems that would have to be addressed. High up on the list were the needs to prepare a full specification, lay down a proper time-table and specify a series of progress milestones. They also said that it was necessary to take out the man in the User Division who had been throwing his weight around and replace him with his deputy and change the Project Manager in the Prime Contractor.

The Procurement Division accepted all this, and then asked us if we would manage the project because they didn't want to cancel. There was, however, some sort of price to be paid by us for having recommended the staff changes. They wanted a different Project Manager on our side, and that's how I became involved. We negotiated an open-ended time-and-expenses contract in which our task was to put the project back on track.

As part of our audit report we had recommended that the missing base-line documentation was developed quickly. By the time I arrived an agreement on the specification had been reached. However, no plan or acceptance mechanism had been agreed. These took much longer to establish than originally planned. One of the difficulties I had was that the User Division and the Prime Contractor were not talking to each other. As a result the meetings had to be held on a one-to-one basis.

There were two other things that I did over that summer. First, I set out to convince everyone that we would need an independent acceptance team to test the separate parts of the system as they were commissioned. This was going to be essential if we were to avoid perpetual wrangling about whether the different parts were or were not doing what they were supposed to do. The team would have to carry out two kinds of test – functional and performance. Let me use an analogy to explain that. In a car, you may have a functional specification that it will have e.g. an engine of, say, 1600 cc and a carburettor of such-and-such a design. Your functional test is then to examine or measure to check if this is so. You may then have a performance specification that the car will do nought to sixty in ten seconds, and you can only test this by trying it out. We had the specifications in the document that was negotiated and we needed a team to do the testing.

The second thing I had to do was ease the tense political situation. I began to build bridges with the senior man in the User Division and with the Director and Project Manager in the Prime Contractor, and I also set out to satisfy the top man in the Procurement Division that we were doing a good job. In addition, I tackled the organisational side. I reactivated a steering committee of representatives of both users and procurers, with myself as Deputy Chairman, to which I reported as Project Manager; the project people from the Prime Contractor and the User Division then reported to me. This was in place by the end of the summer and by the early autumn I'd got agreement on the acceptance team. It was headed by one of our own people and he too reported to me.

We now needed to complete the planning, upgrade the hardware and get the system-acceptance criteria agreed. Producing a base-line plan was very difficult to do, because the user was making use of the hardware as it was installed for other purposes and this reduced the time that it was available. As to the acceptance criteria, no one knew how to do this, who would do what or when. There were lots and lots of meetings – still one-to-one because they still weren't talking to each other and there was a great deal of mucking about. It was all patient negotiation and slowly building up credibility at several different levels. But at least a plan of sorts began to develop and the Prime Contractor started to use some reasonable planning tools. However, the plan was not 'signed up to' by both sides.

One key political event occurred in the autumn. We were reaching one of the milestones, which was to test a modification on one of the packages. If the test went through, the Prime Contractor would get a stage payment. Now there were in fact two related tests to be done, and it was the first that would determine the payment. I knew, however, that they weren't ready for this one but they were ready for the second, which was due to come later. I decided to reverse the order of the tests in the plan.

Now you'll remember that when we did the audit we had recommended that the man in the User Division – let's call him George – who had been throwing his weight about should be removed and that his deputy – and let's call him Allan – should be appointed in his place. Well, George had by no means let go of the project and he used his status and his organisational relationship as Allan's boss to stay in touch.

After I had made the decision about the tests, I got a very curt summons from George's office to go and see him. He had with him one of his subordinates, and he proceeded to tell me that I couldn't do what I had done. I told him that I could and I had. We argued this for a time, and then he said we'd go and see his boss – who was really very high up in the user hierarchy. The three of us went along straight away. After he had heard it all, this man didn't mince his words with George. 'It's Bill's responsibility,' he said, 'and if he wants to do it in that way, it's his decision.' And he went on to tell George, with the subordinate still there, that it was none of his business and that he should stop interfering.

The effect of this was threefold. It established my credibility with the Prime Contractor, it showed the users who was boss and it reassured the procurers, because we had met a milestone. But it also meant that I would have to work to get the users' co-operation back.

By the end of the autumn I had got the users and the contractor talking to each other, at least some of the time. I had set up some sub-committees in which they had to work together –

though Allan put his foot in it on one occasion by attempting to negate a package of work that the contractors had done, which raised all the old animosities again. I now had to deal with the way that the Prime Contractor was working.

One of my difficulties was that I had no transparency into his organisation. I had to accept his outputs as and when they were produced, without any real knowledge of why delays were occurring and what future delays there would be. We had, as I say, developed a plan of sorts but it wasn't good enough – he said he was too busy to plan – and consequently we still had no contractually binding end date.

Through the steering committee, I made sure that the procurers knew about this, and as a result they asked for a progress audit. This was a three-day job, and it was undertaken by one of our Directors. He obviously consulted me, but I didn't tell him what to write. His report criticised the users for intransigence and said that, while the contractors were making progress, they needed a proper plan. The steering committee then told me to go off with the contractors and put one together. We did so. Minor problems caused the project duration to go out two months beyond people's expectations, which didn't go down well, but at least we had an end date.

It then got a lot easier. I was seeing into the contractor's organisation, monitoring what was going on. I could look at the float on the plan and the progress that was being made by the different parts of their team. When the float of one of the sub-teams went right down, I could draw it to the attention of their project manager, prove that they had a problem and get them to put extra resources in to bring things back into line.

Things improved with the users, too, where there was a complete change of staff. George and Allan moved away altogether and some new faces appeared instead. I had to brief them – not forgetting that they had almost certainly talked to their predecessors – and we were soon working together without any problems.

By March 1989 we had hit two important milestones. The users now had to start thinking about how to take the project on board when it was completed. This provided the background for the last hitch we had.

The specification called for the system to be able to handle a peak load of a hundred and twenty people all using it simultaneously when it was in operation. Obviously, therefore, the final performance test involved putting a hundred and twenty bums on seats. The problem was where to get them. The users said they didn't have them and the contractors said the same. We could have provided them but we'd have wanted to charge for them, and the procurers didn't fancy adding anything more to the costs. As part of the acceptance criteria we had suggested equal responsibility for providing staff. This proved the key to reaching agreement. The Prime Contractor committed to develop automated means of generating the load, the user to developing the data for the trial and the necessary logistics (such as organising terminal lay-outs). All this was planned and coordinated at another meeting at a much more informal level – perhaps the most effective of the project.

I was getting along well with George's successor. Before each meeting of the steering committee, we would brief the Chairman together. The procurers were happy with the way things were going and were leaving the project alone. This allowed me some flexibility in formulating some recovery plans for minor slips. The Steering Committee almost accepted my recommendations without question – again building my credibility with the Prime Contractor. In the end, we hit the revised project plan with a week or two to spare.

Looking back at it now, I'd say there were a number of really difficult things about the project. The first was to keep your own confidence going. It was necessary, but hard, to 'helicopter' and know whether you were doing the right things and picking the right priorities – I was entirely on my own. Keeping patience with people who were behaving like children was not easy, nor was finding the right balance between being the dictatorial Project Manager and the wilco engineer; I could have screwed it up by being too hard. Other difficulties were in building relationships with some of the players, in both the users and the contractors, in having no real power but only influence, and in knowing when to be pragmatic and if so how much.

Things could have gone wrong – and we were responsible for accepting the final system. There was a big risk in that for me and my company, especially as there was significant technical complexity needed to produce it. So perhaps our most important contribution was to get the people who could in fact do the job to work together.

If the clock could be turned back? I think I would have stuck out earlier for a proper project plan. I was too soft on this, and it caused me a lot of problems. Which brings me to the biggest lesson that I've learned from the project. In a situation like this, you have more power and influence than you realise at the time, particularly towards the end of a project. How to capitalise on it remains the difficult question.

15.   ROMNEY AND ASSOCIATES

This case history is about an office relocation assignment. It illustrates the problems that consultants face when the decision-making on the client's side is diffuse and when a third party is introduced between consultant and client.

Paul Romney and Associates is a firm of architects who have a specialist division that assists clients who have to relocate their offices. The practice has offices in London and in two other cities in the UK. It employs over 100 professional staff, of whom about a fifth are in the specialist division. The practice was established by Paul Romney in the mid-1970s.

Chris Read is one of two Associates in the specialist division. Now in his 50s, he has been with Romney's for the past five years. He began his career in the army and on leaving became the partnership secretary for a firm of accountants. In that appointment he had useful experience of office relocation. Seeking a mid-career change, he contacted Romney's and was offered a job as a Project Manager. He has handled a number of assignments in which the clients were professional firms headed by autonomous partners.

The clients in this assignment were Reynolds, Richter and Romfold, a leading firm of solicitors in a major city in the northwest. The firm has around 20 partners and employs upward of 200 people. It is a long- established, traditional firm with a wide range of commercial and private clients. Like many successful solicitors, it has expanded considerably in the past 10 years. Its Senior Partner was Malcolm Romfold and its Head of Administration was Peter Syme. The assignment began when Malcolm Romfold phoned Romney's. He said that his firm were going to move into new offices, that they wanted some assistance and that he had been referred to Romney's by one of his firm's clients. He asked for a meeting to talk about the move.

Chris said:

We found that they were already fairly far down the road. Ideally, we like to get involved before our clients have selected a building, but when we met Malcolm, Peter and their letting agent Andrew Simpson, they told us that they had already decided on the new offices that they would move into.

Their existing offices were in a number of houses, some interconnecting, in what had once been a residential street near the city centre. The new offices belonged to one of their major clients and were about half a mile away. They hadn't at that stage signed a contract for the lease, but the close nature of the relationship virtually made it a foregone conclusion. As a result, we were not going to be able to work in the way that we like to – and it turned out that that would not be the only departure from our usual practice.

Normally, we make a presentation to a prospective client and if we are selected follow this up with a proposal. We then establish the requirements, taking into account plans for growth, help the client select from the available choice of locations, do the space planning for the identified building, do the interior design and detailed lay-out and manage the whole project. In this case, Malcolm wanted Andrew Simpson to do the project management, leaving us to do the space planning and design. Having Andrew as Project Manager divorced us from the client somewhat, but we would of course have access to them for interview purposes. We would have preferred it otherwise, but decided to accept the assignment.

We did the interviews and compared the information we got from them to the opportunities offered by the new building. We didn't like what we found. First, it wasn't big enough for their intended rate of growth, but also the character of the building simply wasn't suited to their requirements.

It was a listed building, a fine piece of Victorian architecture. You could say that it had prestige and that the siting of it was good, but it would not divide up easily into the units that they wanted because of its large rooms and high ceilings. Solicitors need accommodation in which every partner and associate can have his or her own private space. Therefore we had to go back to Malcolm and Peter and tell them that the building wasn't right for them and it would be extremely difficult to fit them in. They listened to what we said but told us that they wanted to go ahead anyway. They were, they considered, already too committed by the negotiations that had taken place and they did not want to change their plans, because of the close relationship with the landlords. They asked us to do the best we could in the circumstances. They were an important client and they would need the high level of expertise that we can provide, so we got on with the job.

Our immediate task was to produce a lay-out for the building, showing where the offices and meeting rooms would be. There were a lot of difficulties in doing this because we couldn't get accurate information about details of the building. It was part of a phased development and the landlords had employed a firm of architects to handle it. A lot of work was having to be done on the site as found – a great deal of *ad-hoc* work – and there were problems in making the drawings available. Even those that did become available were not always accurate; on one floor, for example, they showed one window less than there actually was.

This meant that we had to do a lot of checking and this in itself was a problem because the whole place was effectively a building site and access was limited. If we had had full control of the project and had been able to talk directly to the client about what was happening, things would have been easier, but everything had to go through Andrew. He was in no way unhelpful but he had many other commitments to look after besides this, which meant that communications were stretched.

We managed somehow to produce a lay-out by the date we said we would and we put it forward, via Andrew. With it, we submitted an estimate of the cost, at about one and a half million pounds. We got approval of the lay-out but were asked to reduce the costs to one million pounds by cutting down on the design standards – not good news for us as our fees on this particular job were to be fixed as a percentage of the final costs.

It was by now the beginning of June. According to the programme, we would have possession of the building by the end of August. There would then be an eighteen-week period of fitting out and the client would move into the new offices at the beginning of January. We took on board an additional quantity surveyor to handle the extra work and they nominated a firm of M & E (mechanical and electrical) consultants to undertake the necessary specialist work. The M & E consultants would normally have been under our control but, because of the unusual management arrangements on this job, they regarded themselves as reporting to Andrew.

The first serious slippage in the programme occurred in late June, when the client asked for a significant part of the agreed layout to be changed. There are always difficulties in dealing with any organisation in which there is a group of autonomous people at the top, any of whom can veto a decision made by one of the others if it affects them. It's very different from a situation in which there is a clear chief executive who can reach a decision and make it stick. Apparently something of this kind must have happened here. And, because we were at one remove from the client, we couldn't help them in the way we normally do in such circumstances.

The changes they wanted meant that we had to re-design the lay-out of the two main floors. This caused two problems. First, it put the programme back. Second, we had to negotiate payment of fees for the aborted work that we had done, and we had to do it indirectly through Andrew – all complicated by the fact that the client underestimated the effect of the change and the additional work that it caused.

By the end of July it became clear that the contractors who were working for the developer were falling behind. To make it worse, we began to find an increasing number of errors in the information that we were being supplied about what they were doing – for example, a drawing of the floor trunking system that they were putting in was one metre out with reality. We had to return to the building on a number of different occasions to check and re-survey. A lot of time and value was spent on this, and it was difficult to get the client to appreciate what the implications were.

After a lot of to-ing and fro-ing, the developer eventually said that he would give us the building by mid-October, six weeks late. He did so, but when we got in there we found that a considerable amount of his work still had to be done. There were so many defects to be rectified that we told the client that he should refuse to take possession until we had given it approval; we provided chapter and verse as to why they should do this. Unfortunately, it turned out that the terms of their lease did not give them any right to reject the building so they in effect said to us: 'You've got to go in there and get the job done.'

They simply didn't realise what they were asking. We spent two weeks in drawing up, with the contractor's clerk of works, a consolidated list of all the snags. Some of these were minor, such as scratches on doors, but others were more serious. We had by now appointed our own contractors for the work we were to carry out and they were unable to go ahead with their own programme. Let me give you two examples from many. The screed on some of the flooring was defective, so while this was being rectified our contractor was unable to work in the area. Some of the electric wiring was not up to safety standards and had to be renewed, which again prevented any other work being done in the vicinity. Our contractors had to operate on an *ad hoc* basis, not knowing from one day to the next where work could be done. A proper programme isn't possible under these circumstances.

As far as we ourselves were concerned, the repercussions were that I and my principal assistant were having to spend a lot of time on negotiations, meetings, arguing and chasing, mostly having to go round via Andrew. Everything took a long time. It reached the point where we had to tell the client that it would be necessary for our contractors to rectify anything that was causing a serious hold-up and that they would have to claim the extra costs of this from the developer. Andrew agreed to this, but the client had no guarantee that that the developer would pay and I have since heard that this is a matter of dispute.

The delays caused the final completion of the project to be put back further, and it was early March before we were able to get them in. Even so, there was another twist to the tale. In order to counter the rising costs, the client began looking for ways of making reductions. They decided that they would use their existing furniture as far as possible in the new location instead of buying new according to our designs. We then had to make an inventory of all that they had and recommend what should go where.

There are a number of things that have come out of this assignment. The major element is the problems that arose because we were forced into taking over a building before it was ready. This reflects not only the client's relationship with the landlord but also the way in which the project was managed. In view of what happened, it is now easy to see with hindsight that I needed direct access to Peter and to Malcolm. With no reflection on Andrew's ability, I don't think the client was best served by insisting on the arrangement as it was. We are used to dealing with partnerships, and this job has been different because we could not manage the whole thing. Part of the fault here is ours: perhaps we were more concerned about losing the job than we should have been. Where we have imposed our standards – and this is where we have made our most important contribution – the client got a well-designed building that will do the job, within the constraints that the building itself set.

16.   SPATIUS MANAGEMENT CONSULTANCY LTD

This case history is about a human resources management (HRM) consultancy assignment for a hospital. It illustrates the problems that consultants experience in situations where there is unwillingness or unreadiness in the client organisation to make changes to meet changed circumstances. It is an excellent example of the divide between the consultancy roles of expert (on the one hand) and change agent (on the other), and of the grey areas in between.

The organisations and key people involved were as follows.

Spatius Management Consultancy Ltd is based in London and has been operating for about 10 years. It is owned by a large parent company. It employs about 50 professional staff and specialises in HRM assignments.

Donald Shore is one of its senior consultants. Now aged about 30, he began his career in personnel in heavy industry and then took an MBA. He joined Spatius five years ago and has handled a wide variety of HRM assignments. On this job, he worked in a team with three colleagues. One of them, a man with considerable management experience in the National Health Service (NHS), had been recruited by Spatius to head up their consultancy services to the health sector market.

The client in the assignment was the Scotwood Hospital. Located in a major city in southern England, it employs upward of 2000 people. It had decided to apply to operate as an independent Trust. Some brief notes about this will be useful here. Under the provisions of the National Health Service and Community Care Act 1990, hospitals may if they wish apply to the Secretary of State to become independent Trusts within the NHS. If this is agreed, they then have considerable autonomy and responsibility for running their own affairs. In order to achieve this status, they have to make a detailed formal Trust application, which requires them, among other things, to submit a complete business plan. Just part of the stipulation is that they have to state how they will manage their human resources – and show that they are capable of doing so effectively. (They also, of course, have to show that they are capable of managing a great many other aspects of their affairs.)

Scotwood, having decided to apply for independent Trust status, considered that they needed expert assistance in certain areas in order to prepare a submission that was likely to succeed. One of these areas was HRM. They therefore set up an internal committee which invited bids from consultancy firms for the relevant work. The committee included the General Manager of the NHS District in which the hospital was located, the Unit Manager of the hospital, the Director of Nursing and the District Personnel Manager. The briefing document called for a review of Scotwood's HRM policies and procedures together with recommendations for changes, so that the hospital would be able to complete their application with the best chance of success. Spatius put in an offer and won the job – largely, they later learned, because they were able to show themselves as experts in HRM.

Donald said:

One of our first impressions when we started the assignment was that the personnel function at Scotwood was not strong on the policy-making side. They were very competent at handling day-to-day matters such as grievances and recruitment, but it was just that they had never had policy freedom. Policy matters in the NHS are very largely determined centrally. This leaves the personnel people in the hospitals around the country with the procedural task of carrying out the details of what, in policy terms, has already been decided.

There has been a powerful tradition in the NHS for the different categories of staff – that is, the doctors, the nurses, clerical/

administration staff, the technical staff and the hospital management – to be regarded and managed as separate but interacting groups. The loyalties and feelings of affiliation of the individuals concerned tend to be towards their own group more than towards the particular hospital in which they are working at any one time. Their pay and conditions are decided centrally and their career progression is seen as being within the NHS nationally rather than locally. Of course there are quite a few exceptions to this, but that is the general picture. So it was against this background that we set up our study.

The Spatius team began their investigation using a fairly basic HRM policy model, focusing on four interdependent areas that would have to be managed: employee relations, employee resourcing issues, reward systems, and information and control systems. They concentrated on the first three of these, and considered the character and structure of the HRM function needed to support progress in each one. They left the information and control systems to be looked at in greater detail at a later date.

Having got agreement that the committee that hired them would be a steering group for their study, they set out to collect the data that they would need for their analysis. They did this, first, by interviewing all the people at senior management level and, second, by arranging a number of focus groups of up to a dozen people each from the levels just below this.

The objectives were to assess what Scotwood were doing about HRM at the moment, to define in broad outline what they needed to do, to clarify what policies they would need to develop, and to specify what steps they would have to take in order to deliver these policies.

Donald continued:

I think it's fair to say that as the information-collecting stage gathered pace, all the members of our team began to feel that they were dealing with a culture that was very different to what they had expected. We had assumed that the attitudes and involvement of the people we were talking to would be more typical of, say, private sector industry than they turned out to be – they had, after all, decided together that they were going to go it alone. Also, we couldn't help but be surprised at the extent to which the different occupational groups saw themselves as separate. There was no feeling of: 'We're all in this now. What do we need to do to make it work?'

I'm not saying – I'm certainly not saying – that the people from the different groups couldn't or wouldn't work together. There was a very high feeling of client involvement, a strong orientation towards patient care, and this resulted in outstanding teamwork in the working situation. But when we got them talking about HRM matters, there was no feeling of common ground. Nurses' pay, for example, was a matter for the nursing people, and so was nurses' training, recruitment, employee relations and all the rest. Nothing to do with the doctors, the administration people or the support staff. No feeling that there might be policies on, say, staff communications that would apply to everyone in the hospital. There was certainly no concept that HRM should be an integral part of the general management process in the hospital. Everything to do with HRM policies was decided centrally, so people had got used to accepting what was handed down to them without querying whether their own hospital might do it differently.

In a vast organisation like the NHS, with policies and procedures being laid down from above, there was inevitably a great deal of bureaucracy. I remember on one occasion asking one of the personnel people what courses were available for staff to take, and being shown a pile of papers six inches high. Yet there was no link-up of any of the courses with the identification of training needs or any type of evaluation system.

Everyone we talked to had spent the whole of their working lives in this kind of environment, so it was maybe asking a lot of them that they should now make the change to deciding their own destinies, determining their own policies and integrating them into their day-to-day management practice.

Perhaps their feelings at this stage were best summed up by something that the Nursing Director said when I interviewed her. She was very clued up on nurses' pay and the employee relations policies set down by the Royal College of Nursing, and she was dedicated to her own area. She said: 'I set the objectives for my own people. My job is to see that the nursing side here is run as well as possible, not to deal with what is going on in the hospital as a whole or what it is trying to achieve.'

We were holding regular meetings with the steering group, who represented top management, and we began to find parallel feelings and attitudes there. At an early stage, we set out to get them thinking about strategic policy decions in HRM. It was going to be a vital area for them if and when they got their Trust approval. They were going to have to make major decisions that would essentially set the culture of the way people were managed. And they had to look at the financial side of personnel in a new way. For example, if they signed a fixed contract with their local health authority and their wages went up too much, they could find themselves making a loss.

They didn't have the concept of sitting down to discuss the organisational climate or the way people were managed. They weren't used to meetings like that, to thinking like that or to making policy decisions like that. Why? Because what makes sense for an NHS of hundreds of thousands of people doesn't make sense for an independent body of two thousand or so. And because the things they had had to discuss in their meetings previously had related to their place in the NHS structure – very different from the things that an independent body needs to discuss.

This affected our role in the assignment. Of course, at the beginning of the job, we recognised that we didn't have a full understanding of how their organisation worked. We didn't know what to expect, because we were on such different ground. But we weren't ready for the absence of any policy-level control in HRM or for their apparent inability or unwillingness to get more out of us than they'd expected. We had thought that they would want to achieve a high level of managing HRM and that they would be critically examining the recommendations that we made in each area. This didn't happen.

Soon, therefore, we began to build into the interviews and the focus groups questions like: What do you think the trust's stance should be on such-and-such? What should be its policies on this? How should its procedures on that be evolved? What if you guarantee that there will be no changes in that? In other words, as well as being information-collecting sessions, they became tutorials and ways of assessing the people and the situation.

Donald said that quite a lot that was beneficial came out of this but a lack of any real sense of involvement was still there in what people said. The enormity of what the hospital was going to do had begun to come over, yet they were still dedicated each to their own areas and not to the objectives of the hospital as an independent entity.

At the end of the three-month period – which the team regarded as phase one of what needed to be done – Spatius put in their report.

It began by emphasising the underlying principles of the review. That HRM should become an integral part of the general management process. That the work of personnel specialists was needed to support and facilitate the achievement of general management goals. That developing a more sophisticated approach to HRM would be an incremental process, tackled as part of management's strategy for handling change. That the development of HRM policies needed to be integrated across all the four main HR areas. And that factors such as staff attitudes needed to be constantly reviewed because they would determine the pace of change.

It then went on to recommend, against a background of Scotwood's existing HRM being at an early stage in its development, the short-term action that was needed in the key policy areas. Donald gave some examples: training and developing line managers so that they could deal quickly and effectively with any industrial relations problems; clarifying local consultation arrangements; moving towards a managed approach to pay so as to provide internal equity and external competitiveness; and upgrading the employee-resourcing systems. It also recommended the appointment of a new Board-level Director of Human Resources.

Very soon after the report was submitted, Scotwood telephoned to say that they were delighted with the report. They incorporated virtually all of it into their Trust submission. Some time later they phoned again to say that they had just heard that the application had succeeded.

Donald said:

We went to see them to talk about future developments – because, after all, as we had emphasised to them, the report was only a first phase, the starting point for evolutionary change. We gave them an overview of the tasks that now had to be tackled.

The response we got was not an eager one. It was almost as if, in submitting the report that had helped them to achieve their goal of Trust status, we had done all that they required of us. They just sat on the report, happy to have dealt with the intellectual side of assessing what was needed but more than happy now to sit back and leave action until later. There was absolutely no feeling of urgency – in fact quite the reverse.

After quite a lot of pushing by us, they agreed to extend the assignment and asked us to begin some detailed planning and policy development. We went into a further round of meetings, interviews and group discussions. Our team worked extremely hard. We identified a dozen or more policy areas in which action was needed and we drew up short, medium and long-term plans for every one of them. We set everything down on paper and went through it with them.

They agreed politely with almost all we said. But action? Well, that was another matter. We could not get them round a table to agree on what their approach to industrial relations would be. We could not get them to set down their organisation chart on paper or begin developing a real salary structure. We could not get them to make headway on the appointment of the HR Director. In short, we could not get them to knuckle down and start purposefully on the many tasks that had to be accomplished.

Slowly, we managed to change this state of affairs. In a way, you could say that it was done more by attrition on our side than by enthusiasm on theirs. But on the reverse of the coin, we learned that it was as much our presentation style as their lack of experience in a new situation. For instance, I found that I could get them to consider policy issues by using carefully selected real-life examples. Instead of saying: 'You need an industrial relations strategy with an agreed bargaining mechanism, defined negotiation/consultation/unilateral issues, etc.', I put a number of situations to them such as: 'Your largest trade union comes to you and asks for a meeting to negotiate a single union deal for the new trust. How do you react?' Their response indicated the policy direction they want to take, and we could then clarify, refine and determine it.

Keeping the momentum going took patience and persistence, but they have now accomplished quite a lot. This includes making a study of communications, which involved groups of staff totalling two hundred, and re-designing the performance appraisal system. They have recruited two new HRM specialists and will soon be appointing the HR Director. I'm happy to say that things are really starting to move.

In reviewing the assignment, Donald made the following points.

The assignment has for us been different to most of the others that we undertake. With previous clients, for example, we have not had such difficulty in getting the information we wanted. This wasn't because Scotwood were unwilling to answer our questions or that they were in any way defensive, but because the questions we needed to ask covered ground that was unfamiliar to them, so they found it difficult to give us digestible answers. No one previously in our experience had had these kind of difficulties.

I believe that if you asked them what our most important contribution was, they would say it was our report – because that is what helped them considerably to get Trust status. But if you ask me, I would say that it was our ability in the end to help them put strategy into terms of day-to-day action.

If the clock could be turned back? I think there are three things I would have liked to have had. First, more time to be able to devote exclusively to this assignment. Second, more experience in the role of change agent so that we could have helped them to move on more quickly. And third, a greater ability to make sense of a lot of diverse information so that we could have got to the heart of the problem sooner.

17. TAMARISK CONSULTANCY

This case history is about an assignment in the insurance industry. It illustrates the problems that consultants have to deal with when they find, unexpectedly, that they have to take on the role of change agent or process consultant. It is also a good example of the problem of establishing who the client is.

The principal organisations and people involved were as follows.

The Tamarisk Consultancy is part of an organisation that provides a range of services in the financial sector. The organisation's headquarters are in Toronto and it operates through offices in Canada, USA, Europe and the Pacific basin. Tamarisk is based in London and offers general management consultancy services. It employs about 20 professional staff, most of whom are under 40 and have an MBA or other postgraduate qualification.

Hannah Tay is one of their senior consultants. Now in her early 30s, she has a first degree in economics. She worked for five years in personnel and then took an MBA. She joined Tamarisk about four years ago, since when she has worked on a wide variety of consultancy assignments. Tamarisk's team on this job also included Ken Grant and David Simmons.

The client in the assignment was the Torworth Insurance Company. Torworth is American-owned, and the result of a merger that took place in the late 1980s between Torworth's own UK insurance division and a (then) UK-owned insurance company. Torworth's own company had operated entirely by direct sales; that is, it employed a field force of sales consultants who made direct approaches to prospective policy-holders. The UK company had operated through a network of a dozen or so offices located in cities in England and Wales. It had sold its policies exclusively via intermediaries such as insurance brokers.

The key people involved on Torworth's side were: Allen Charlwood who, based in New York, was the worldwide Operations Director; Bob Farrell, the Managing Director of the UK company; and Nick Layton, the UK Finance Director. Bob and Nick had been Directors of the UK company prior to the Torworth acquisition, as had their colleague, the Marketing Director. The UK Operations Director had previously worked for Torworth.

Hannah described how the assignment began.

A year or so ago, two of the senior Directors of our parent company were on a business trip to New York and called in on Allen. He told them that he had problems with his UK operations, which he looked on as an investment. The acquisition was not working out well, and in particular it wasn't producing the 15 per cent return on capital that had been expected. This was bad news for him, especially as he had been instrumental in arranging the acquisition. Our Directors persuaded him to give Tamarisk three months to look at the problem, with a mandate to reduce costs by about a quarter.

He agreed, and contacted Bob to let him know what was going to happen. On our side, we were handed the job and told to get in touch with Torworth here. Ken, David and I went along to see them with one of our London Directors. We gave them a presentation of what we proposed to do and how we would work. In the course of this, we became aware that Bob had handed over to Nick the responsibility for interacting with us. Because of the way the job had been sold, we began the assignment with only the broadest outline of what we were going to do. Initially, therefore, we had a lot of information to get. We needed a detailed breakdown of costs, of course, but we also had to get an understanding of their business so that we could achieve a perception of why things weren't going well and what ought to be done.

Fairly soon it became clear that we were dealing with two different cultures – the direct sales side and the intermediary side. Effectively the merger had never really taken place. The two sides tended to look down on each other and continued to operate separately, so systems were duplicated and this resulted in probable over-staffing. This was especially true on the intermediary side, which was very traditionallly run. Part of the complication here was that a lot of the senior management of the direct sales side – that's Torworth's own side – had left since the merger, so really it was the people who had been acquired, not the acquirers, who had taken over the running of the business.

We spent the first two weeks in getting out a lot of numbers, in looking at organisation charts and in interviewing people at different levels to find out what they thought the problems were. We could see that it wasn't very efficient but our real difficulty lay in the fact that there was no vision of where the company was going. They had a Board of twelve or so Directors which held monthly meetings but this served as a political forum, not as a business strategy group making business decisions. It had had our involvement imposed by New York and didn't really want a lot to do with us except Nick, who could see there were problems.

We knew we'd have to do something about this if we were to get anywhere. Ken got to work on Bob and Nick and persuaded them that a strategic study was necessary, because neither they nor we would be able to sort things out unless they knew where they were going and what market they were in. It would take us much deeper into their business than we had imagined when we started out, but it had to be done.

Our proposal was agreed, though with the proviso that it had to be handled very delicately. Only the 'inner six' of the Directors knew about it, and Ken and I had to undertake it ourselves in parallel with the original study on productivity and cost reduction – though we did get some help from two or three junior Tamarisk staff. All the same, it caused a few problems because people started to tell us that we were not doing what we had said we'd be doing.

Over the next two months we looked in detail at their business and where they stood *vis-à-vis* the competition. We built up a complete model of their cost structure. We had regular meetings with the inner six and at the end of this part of our work we put together a document for them.

Essentially it was a discussion document, challenging them to think through where they wanted to be. It set out the facts, and the alternatives on which they would have to decide. The difficult thing about it was that it had begun to become clear through our work that the only place they could make the kind of money that the parent company demanded was on the direct sales side. The intermediary side just would not yield the level of revenue required.

Now as you'll remember, Bob was an intermediary man and so was his Marketing Director. So too for that matter was Nick. They found it very difficult to accept the logic of our findings. They couldn't disagree with the facts but they couldn't bring themselves to accept the consequences either. It was going to become a question of whether they would act on what we had put forward or whether they would try somehow to shelve it and get by.

Concurrently we had been working on the productivity review. Looking at the company area by area, and by getting rid of certain kinds of business and certain geographical areas, we found we could produce savings for them well in excess of 25 per cent of their costs without any significant harm to their total revenue. We presented these findings to Bob and Nick. Then within days we took each individual sector to the relevant director.

Bob was inclined to push this aside also, but Nick was determined to fight the fight. He made certain that Allen, in the USA, got a copy of our reports. He asked us to help him plan implementation primarily of the productivity study but also of the strategic study too. We said that we would help with implementation but that we could not be the implementers. This was partly because some of the things that it would be most difficult to do directly affected the top management. For example, they needed to reduce the number of Directors they had on the Board and tighten up the content and frequency of Board meetings.

The decisions on what was going to happen were effectively made by Nick and the Americans. Bob got instructions from New York to go ahead and implement, but he couldn't bring himself to do so and it wasn't long before he left Torworth. A new MD came in from the USA with a brief to work with Nick on implementation. They got down to doing all the immediate things. We helped them with this stage and they have since extended our consultancy assignments with them.

In reviewing the assignment, Hannah made the following points.

Everything we achieved in this job had to be sold on personal relationships. Right from the start, we weren't there at their bidding. They didn't like what we were doing but they respected our professionalism. So it was important for us to find out who our clients were and who our friends were. We had to gain their trust and confidence.

There were times when I felt vulnerable. I was working in an industry of which I had previously had little direct experience and therefore no long-term in-depth understanding. I was aware that I was sometimes only one step ahead of the client, and I was often out on my own without managerial support.

What we were doing was process consultancy. The skills needed in this are really quite different from the skills needed in the assignment as it originated. I never would have believed that we should have to get so involved in order to get them to accept our recommendations. We produced a lot of bound volumes, but that wasn't what they paid us for. Because we're talking about empowering people in the client organisation to change their own situation. I was doing much more counselling with Torworth's people than I had expected, asking questions like 'Why?' and 'What can you do?'

If the clock could be turned back? I think I should have liked to have had from the start a much clearer understanding and definition of consultancy roles in the whole of our team.

10 Conclusions

We have nearly completed the task we set for ourselves. It only remains to draw together the arguments we have put forward for achieving superior consultant performance in a competitive environment, and to make some comments about the future.

WHAT ARE WE TRYING TO SAY?

We define consultancy as a process in which a consultant provides a service to a client (i.e. an organisation or an individual acting on behalf of an organisation or a unit within that organisation) for the purpose of meeting that client's need; the service is based on the expertise of the consultant. As part of this process the consultant will find that he or she will have to fulfil certain roles. Effectiveness in these roles will depend upon individuals having mastered the competences or skills underlying each of the roles, and their professional judgement and expertise in adopting the right roles according to situational needs (e.g. as generated by the client, the client system, and the goals of the assignment).

The 1+7 model is a vehicle for learning the key roles consultants may find themselves called upon to adopt.

WHY ARE THESE THINGS WORTH SAYING?

There are three reasons. First, similar models in the literature have flaws which limit their generalisability, their scientific credibility, and therefore their value for training purposes. Second, while many consultants are trained to a high standard in their field of expertise by virtue of being members of related professional bodies, this does not necessarily mean that they have been trained in the generic competences which are drawn upon in the consultancy process. Moreover, the growing activities of management consultants are not yet monitored and controlled by a recognised professional body, although developments are moving in that direction. A sounder scientifically based body of knowledge relating to the process of consultancy will facilitate these developments.

Third, the growth of this industry and its economic importance to many countries does increase the pressure for enhancing the competitiveness of consultancy firms. Competitiveness is achieved through a multitude of methods, but an important avenue is through the quality of service. In most service industry it is now taken for granted that quality of service means meeting, if not exceeding, the needs of the client or customer in such a way that the client is satisfied. A significant difference between consultancy and certain other service industries is that sayings such as 'the customer is sovereign' and 'the customer is always right' may often be quite inappropriate. The client is paying a consultancy fee because he or she requires expert help. It is the professional responsiblity of the consultant to provide this expertise even though it may ultimately result in the client being proved wrong. Just as the medical doctor has to advise a patient within a broader and unique context of factors (family circumstances, seriousness of a disease, ethical code, etc.), so a consultant has to deliver his or her expertise within a broader and unique context.

A client-oriented approach in the consultancy industry is a great deal more complex than in many other service industries. The 1+7 model recognises this, and gives more substance to the concept by incorporating the following features: giving centre stage to the role of expert; recognising that so-called process skills are not a voluntary option in delivering expertise but an essential element; providing a user-friendly framework for representing the key roles which consultants may be called upon to play in the course of meeting client needs; emphasising the importance of being able to perform successfully in all the identified roles because of the unpredictable nature of client needs once an assignment has commenced.

HOW CAN THE 1+7 MODEL BE USED IN THE TRAINING AND DEVELOPMENT OF CONSULTANTS?

The client-oriented approach characterised by the 1+7 model is not likely to emerge through trial-and-error learning; nor can its practical value be immediately realised once the theoretical knowledge has been learned. For a consultant to be consistently effective on a range of assignments requires both theoretical knowledge (which can be learned through off-the-job methods, including private reading and reflection), and professional judgement and expertise (which requires on-the-job experience for its development, supplemented if possible by more controlled off-the-job simulated experiences). It is this professional judgement and expertise (in our terminology, practical as opposed to theoretical knowledge) which is most likely to differentiate the experienced consultant from the novice. This is most apparent when consultants are required to display an amalgam of roles to meet the changing situational needs of an assignment.

By incorporating the 1+7 model in a training programme for relatively inexperienced participants, they will become more aware of the complexities of the consultancy process and their implications for the roles they will have to learn to play. The model creates a strong conceptual framework around which to hang their experiences, and so speed up the process of meta-cognitive learning. For more experienced participants, the model can be used in a developmental programme to facilitate a critical review of the existing cognitive models influencing their behaviour and performance. Such off-the-job learning opportunities will enable consultants to change or to re-fit their mental models, taking into account their personal experiences and new theoretical knowledge.

WHAT MORE NEEDS TO BE SAID?

Knowledge is a dynamic commodity. The 1+7 model of consultancy roles is sufficiently abstract to accommodate foreseeable changes. Knowledge advances are more likely to occur with respect to the detailed competences underlying the eight roles and it is here that further refinements will be required. Research on the validity of the model continues; this is essential, given the qualitative nature of the empirical work so far carried out. This book is intended as a contribution to the development of a sound scientific base and a practical theoretical framework for the understanding of the consultancy process. If it succeeds in stimulating further research, as well as proving of practical value to consultants and their trainers, then the effort of writing it has been well worth while.

Knowledge is also a powerful competitive tool – if used sensibly. But the sensible use of the 1+7 model of consultancy roles does mean that readers must recognise that it deals with just one aspect of consultancy – albeit a very important one! This book does not touch on the more managerial and commercial aspects of consultancy such as organising a consultancy firm, managing its resources, marketing its services and so on. These are essential, but without consultants skilled in providing the client-oriented services of the kind we have been discussing, such firms will not survive for long.

Bibliography

Abbott, A. (1988) *The System of Professions – an Essay on the Division of Expert Labour,* Chicago, University of Chicago Press.

Allen, J. and Davis, D. (1993) 'Assessing some determinant effects of ethical consulting behaviour: the case of personal and professional values', *Journal of Business Ethics,* vol.12, no.6, 449–58.

American Institute of Certified Public Accountants (1991) *Statement on Standards for Consulting Services, Definitions and Standards.*

Argyris, C. (1970) *Intervention Theory and Method,* Reading, MA, Addison-Wesley.

Argyris, C. and Schön, D. (1974) *Theory in Practice: Increasing Professional Effectiveness,* San Francisco, Jossey-Bass.

Ausubel, D.P. Novak, J.D. and Hanesian, H. (1978) *Educational Psychology – A Cognitive View,* 2nd edn, NY, Holt, Rinehart and Winston.

Baldwin, T. and Ford, J.K. (1988) 'Transfer of training: a review and directions for future research', *Personnel Psychology,* vol.41, 63–105.

Bandura, A (1986) *Social Foundations of Thought and Action,* Englewood Cliffs, NJ, Prentice-Hall.

Bartlett, F.C. (1932) *Remembering,* Cambridge University Press.

Bartol, K.M. and Martin, D.C. (1991) *Management,* New York, McGraw-Hill.

Belbin, R.M. (1981) *Management Teams: Why They Succeed and Fail,* London, Heinemann.

Bennis, W.G. (1973) *The Leaning Ivory Tower,* New York, Jossey-Bass.

Bines. H. and Watson, D. (1992) *Developing Professional Education,* Milton Keynes, Buckinghamshire, Open University Press and SRHE.

Blake, R. and Mouton, J. (1972) *The Diagnosis and Development Matrix,* Houston, TX, Scientific Methods.

Blake, R. and Mouton, J. (1976) *Consultation,* Reading, MA, Addison-Wesley.

Block, P. (1981) *Flawless Consulting: A Guide to Getting your Expertise Used,* San Diego, CA, University Associates.

Bloom, B.S. and Krathwohl, D.R. (1956) *A Taxonomy of Educational Objectives,* NY, Mackay (reprinted in 1972 by Longman).

Boekaerts, M. (1992) 'The adaptable learning process: initiating and maintaining behavioural change', *Applied Psychology: An International Review,* vol.41, no.4, 377–97.

Bosworth, D. with Baker, M. and Owen, D.W. (1992) *Review of the Economy and Employment,* Occupational Studies: Part 1, Institute for Employment Research, University of Warwick.

Boud, D. and Griffin, V. (eds) (1987) *Appreciating Adults Learning: From the Learners' Perspective,* London, Kogan Page.

British Invisibles (1993) *Annual Report and Accounts 1992.*

Brown, J.S., Collins, A. and Duguid, P. (1989) 'Situated cognition and the culture of learning', *Educational Researcher,* vol.17, pp.32–41.

Bruner, J.S. (1966) *Toward a Theory of Instruction,* Cambridge, MA, Harvard University Press.

Bruner, J.S., Goodnow, J.J. and Austin, G.A. (1956) *A Study of Thinking,* London, John Wiley.

Bryman, A. (1989) *Research Methods and Organisation Studies,* London, Unwin Hyman.

Buchanan, D. and Boddy, D. (1992) *The Expertise of the Change Agent: Public Performance and Backstage Activity*, Hemel Hempstead, Prentice-Hall.

Champion, D.P. *et al.* (1985) model referenced in Champion *et al.* (1990)

Champion, D.P., Kiel, D.H. and McLendon, J.A. (1990) 'Choosing a consulting role', *Training and Development Journal*, vol.44, part 2, 66–9.

Chickillo, G.P. and Kleiner, B.H. (1990) 'Skills and roles of consultants: training implications', *Journal of European Industrial Training*, vol.14, no.1, 26–30.

Cole, M (1985) 'Zone of proximal development? Where culture and cognition create each other', in *Culture, Communication and Cognition – Vygotskian Perspectives*, ed. J.V. Wertsch, London, Cambridge University Press.

Cole, M. and Scriber, S.O. (eds)(1978) 'Introduction' in *Mind in Society – The Development of Higher Psychological Processes* (Vygotsky, L.S. – translated from the Russian) Cambridge, MA, Harvard University Press.

Commission of European Communities (1992) *Panorama of EC Industry*, Brussels, Commission of European Communities.

Cunningham, I. (1988) 'Openness and learning to learn', ch. 4 in *Beyond Distance Teaching, Towards Open Learning*, ed. V. Hodgson Milton Keynes, Open University Press and SRHE.

Decker, P.J. (1980) 'Effects of symbolic coding and rehearsal in behaviour-modeling training', *Journal of Applied Psychology*, vol.65, 627–34.

Dewey, J. (1966) *Selected Educational Writings*, London, Heinemann.

Downs, S. (1992) 'Learning to learn', ch. 4 in *Handbook of Training and Development*, ed. S. Truelove, Oxford, Blackwell.

Dreyfus, H.L. and Dreyfus, S.E. (1986) *Mind over Machine: The Power of Human Intuition and Expertise in the Era of the Computer*, Oxford, Basil Blackwell.

Dryden, W., Edwards, D.C. and Woolfe, R. (eds) (1989) *Handbook of Counselling in Britain*, London, Tavistock/Routledge/BAC.

Dyer, W.G. (1987) *Team Building : Issues and Alternatives*, 2nd edn, Reading, MA, Addison-Wesley.

Egan, G. (1990) *Exercises in Helping Skills*, 4th edn, London, Brooks/Cole, Chapman and Hall.

French, W.L. and Bell, C.H. (1984) *Organisational Development: behavioural science interventions for organisational improvement*, 3rd edn, Englewood Cliffs, NJ, Prentice-Hall.

Fullerton, J. and West, M. (1993) *Management Consultancy: Dimensions of Client–Consultant Relationships*, Centre for Economic Performance, Discussion Paper no.99, London School of Economics.

Gist, M., Stevens, C.K. and Bavetta A.G. (1991) 'Effects of self-efficacy and post-training intervention on the acqusition and maintenance of complex interpersonal skills', *Personnel Psychology*, vol.44, 837–61.

Glaser, R. and Bassok, M. (1989) 'Learning theory and the study of instruction', *Annual Review of Psychology*, vol.40, 631–66.

Goldstein, I.L. and Gilliam, P. (1990) 'Training system issues in the year 2000', *American Psychologist*, February, 134–43.

Golembiewski, R.T. (1992) (ed.) *Handbook of Organisational Consultation*, New York, Marcel Dekker.

Greiner, L.E. and Schein, V.E. (1988) *Power and Organisation Development: Mobilising Power to Implement Change*, Reading, MA, Addison-Wesley.

Hamm, R.M. (1988) 'Clinical intuition and clinical analysis: expertise and the cognitive continuum' in *Professional judgement: A Reader in Clinical Decision Making*, ed. J. Dowie and A. Elstein, Cambridge University Press.

Harvey, D.F. and Brown, D.R. (1988) *An Experiential Approach to Organisation Development*, 3rd edn, Englewood Cliffs, NJ, Prentice-Hall.
Hellriegel D. and Slocum, J.W. (1992) *Management*, 6th edn, Reading, MA, Addison-Wesley.
Heron, J. (1990) *Helping the Client*, London, Sage.
Honey, P. and Mumford, A. (1986) *Manual of Learning Styles*, 2nd edn, Maidenhead, Peter Honey.
Huczynski, A. and Buchanan, D.A. (1991) *Organisational Behaviour – An Introductory Text*, London, Prentice-Hall.
IMC (Institute of Management Consultants) (1993) *The Practice of Management Consultancy : Training Modules for Consultants*, London, IMC.
Kanter, R.M. (1983) *The Change Masters: Corporate Entrepreneurs at Work*, London, Allen and Unwin.
Katz, D. and Kahn, R.L. (1978) *The Social Psychology of Organisations*, New York, Wiley.
Katzenbach, J.R. and Smith, D.K. (1993) *The Wisdom of Teams – Creating the High-Performance Organisation*, Boston, MA, Harvard Business School.
Keeble, D., Bryson, J. and Wood, P. (1991) *Entrepreneurship and Flexibility in Business Services: The Rise of Small Management Consultancy and Market Research Firms in the UK*, Working Paper no.13, Small Business Research Centre, University of Cambridge.
Knowles, M.S. (1975) *Self-Directed Learning*, London, Association Press, Follet Publications.
Knowles, M.S. *et al* (1984) *Andragogy in Action: Applying Modern Principles of Adult Learning*, San Francisco, Jossey-Bass.
Köhler, W. (1929) *Gestalt Psychology*, NY, Liveright.
Kolb, D.A. (1983) 'Problem management: learning from experience,' in S. Srivastava (ed.) *The Executive Mind*, San Francisco, Jossey-Bass.
Kolb, D.A. (1984) *Experiential Learning: Experience as the Source of Learning and Development*, Englewood Cliffs, NJ, Prentice-Hall.
Kubr, M. (1986) *Management Consulting*, 2nd edn, Geneva, International Labour Office.
Lawrence, P.R. and Lorsch, J.W. (1969) *Developing Organizations*, Reading, MA, Addison-Wesley.
Lewin, K. (1935) *A Dynamic Theory of Personality – Selected Papers*, London, McGraw-Hill.
Lewin, K. (1951) *Field Theory in Social Science*, New York, Harper and Row.
Lippitt, G.L. (1969) *Organisational Research*, Englewood Cliffs, NJ, Prentice-Hall.
Lippitt, G. and Lippitt, R. (1978) *The Consulting Process in Action*, La Jolla, CA, University Associates.
Lippitt, G. and Lippitt, R. (1986) *The Consulting Process in Action*, 2nd edn, La Jolla, CA, University Associates.
Lippitt, R., Watson, J. and Westley, B. (1958) *Planned Change: A Comparative Study of Principles and Techniques*, NY, Harcourt, Brace and World.
McLean, A.J. Sims, D.B., Mangham, I.L. and Tuffield, D. (1982) *Organisation Development in Transition – Evidence of an Evolving Profession*, Chichester, Wiley.
Maister, D. (1984) 'Job assignments set the pace in professional service firms', *Journal of Management Consulting*, vol.1, no.1, 32–7.
Male, S. (1990) 'Professional authority, powers and emerging forms of "profession" in quantity surveying', *Construction Management and Economics*, vol.8, no.2., 191–204.
Margerison, C. (1988) *Managerial Consulting Skills*, Aldershot, Gower.

Margulies, N. (1978) *Conceptual Foundations of Organisational Development*, London, McGraw-Hill.

Markham, C. (1991) *Practical Management Consultancy*, London, Institute of Chartered Accountants.

Markham, C. (1993) *The Top Consultant*, London, Kogan Page.

Marton, F., Hounsell, D. and Entwistle, N. (1984) *The Experience of Learning*, Edinburgh, Scottish Academic Press.

MCA (Management Consultancies Association) (1993) *President's Statement and Annual Report*, London, MCA.

Metzger, R. (1989) *Profitable Consulting: Guiding America's Managers into the Next Century*, Reading, MA, Addison-Wesley.

Mintzberg, H. (1973) *The Nature of Managerial Work*, New York, Harper and Row.

Mumford, A. (1991) 'Learning in action', *Personnel Management*, July, 34–7.

Munro, A., Manthei, B. and Small, J. (1989) *Counselling – The Skills of Problem-Solving*, London, Routledge.

Muns, R.E., Roussey, R.S. and Whitmer, W.E. (1991) 'Practical definitions of six consulting functions', *Journal of Accountancy*, vol.172, no.5, 43–5.

Nees, D.B. and Greiner, L.E. (1985) 'Seeing behind the look-alike management consultants', *Organisational Dynamics*, Winter.

Neisser, U. (1967) *Cognitive Psychology*, NY, Appleton-Century-Crofts.

Nevis, E.C. (1987) *Organisational Consulting: A Gestalt Approach*, NY, Gardner.

Pavlov, I.P. (1927) *Conditioned Reflexes*, London, Clarendon Press.

Payne, A. (1987) 'A European view of management consulting', *European Management Journal*, vol.5, no.3, pp.154–62.

Pedler, M. (ed.) (1991) *Action Learning in Practice*, Aldershot, Gower.

Pettigrew, A.M. (1985) *The Awakening Giant: Continuity and Change in ICI*, Oxford, Blackwell.

Pettigrew, A.M. (1987) 'Context and action in the transformation of the firm', *Journal of Management Studies*, vol. 24, no.6, 649–70.

Piaget, J. (1971) *Science of Education and the Psychology of the Child*, Harlow, Longman.

Porras, J. and Silvers, R.C. (1991) 'Organisational development and transformation', *Annual Review of Psychology*, vol.42, 51–78.

PRS (Property Research Services) (1987) *The architect in a competitive market*, Report on behalf of the City of London and Westminster Society of Architects and RIBA, PRS, London.

Quinn, J.B. (1992) *Intelligent Enterprise*, New York, Free Press.

Revans, R.W. (1980) *Action learning: New Techniques for Management*, London, Blond and Briggs.

Revans, R.W. (1982) *The Origins and Growth of Action Learning*, Bromley, Chartwell-Bratt.

RICS (Royal Institution of Chartered Surveyors) (1984) *A Study of Quantity Surveying Practice and Client Demand*, London, RICS.

Robertson, I.T. (1990) 'Behaviour modelling: its record and potential in training and development', *British Journal of Management*, vol.1, 117–25.

Rogers, C.R. (1951) *Client Centred Therapy*, Boston, Houghton Mifflin.

Schein, E. (1969) *Process Consultation*, Reading, MA, Addison-Wesley.

Schein, E. (1987) *Process Consultation: Volume 2: Lessons for Managers and Consultants*, Reading, MA, Addison-Wesley.

Schlegelmich, B., Diamantopoulos, A. and Moore, S.A. (1992) 'The market for management consulting in Britain: an analysis of supply and demand', *Management Decision*, vol.30, no.2, pp.46–54.

Schmidt, W. and Johnston, A. (1969) *Continuum of Consultancy Styles*, Occasional Paper of the University of Southern California Business Administration Department.

Schön, D.A. (1983) *The Reflective Practitioner: How Professionals Think in Action*, London, Maurice Temple Smith.

Schön, D.A. (1987) *Educating the Reflective Practitioner*, San Francisco, Jossey-Bass.

Schroder, H.M. (1989) *Managerial Competence: The Key to Excellence*, Iowa, Kendall/ Hunt.

Skinner, B.F. (1953) *Science and Human Behaviour*, New York, Macmillan.

Snell, R. (1991) 'Experiential learning at work: why can't it be painless?' *Personnel Review*, vol.21, no.4, 12–26.

Snow, R.E. and Swanson, J. (1992) 'Instructional psychology: aptitude, adaptation and assessment', *Annual Review of Psychology*, vol.43, 583–626.

Steele, F. (1975) *Consulting for Organisational Change*, Amherts, MA, University of Massachusetts Press.

Steele, F. (1982) *The Role of the Internal Consultant: Effective Role Shaping for Staff Positions*, Boston, CBI Publishing.

Stewart, R. (1982) *Choices for the Manager: A Guide to Managerial Work and Behaviour*, London, McGraw-Hill.

Strang, A. (1987) 'The hidden barriers', Ch. 3 in *Beyond Distance Teaching towards Open Learning*, ed. V. Hodgson, S. Mann and R. Snell, Open University Press and SRHE.

Stryker, S. (1982) *Principles and Practices of Professional Consulting*, Boston, MA, The Consultant's Library.

Summers, E.L. and Knight, K.E. (1975) 'The AICPA studies MAS in CPA firms', *Journal of Accountancy*, vol.139, no.3, 56–64.

Svenson, L. (1990) 'Knowledge as a professional resource: case studies of architects and psychologists at work', in *The Formation of the Professions: Knowledge, State and Strategy*, ed. R. Torstendahl and M. Burrage, London, Sage.

Szilagyi, A.D. and Wallace, M.J. (1990) *Organisational Behaviour and Performance*, 5th edn, London, Scott-Foresman.

Tannenbaum, S.I. and Yukl, G. (1992) 'Training and development in work organizations', *Annual Review of Psychology*, vol.43, 399–411.

Tolman, E.C. (1932) *Purposive Behaviour in Animals and Men*, NY, Appleton-Century-Crofts.

Torstendahl, R. (1990) 'Promotion and strategies of knowledge-based groups' in *The Formation of the Professions – Knowledge, State and Strategy*, ed. R. Torstendahl and M. Burrage, London, Sage.

Training Commission (1988) *Classifying the Components of Management Competences*, Sheffield, Training Commission.

Turner, A.N. (1982) 'Consulting is more than giving advice', *Harvard Business Review*, vol.60, part 5, 120–9.

Vosniadou, S. (1992) 'Knowledge acquisition and conceptual change', *Applied Psychology*, an International Review, vol.41, no.4, 347–57.

Vygotsky, L.S. (1978) *Mind in Society* (ed. by M. Cole and S. Scriber and translated from the Russian), Cambridge, MA, Harvard University Press.

Walton, R.E. (1969) *Interpersonal Peacemaking: Confrontations and Third Party Consultation*, Reading, MA, Addison-Wesley.

Weick, K.E. (1979) *The social psychology of organising*, 2nd edn, Reading, MA, Addison-Wesley.

Weinstein, C.E. and Underwood, V.L. (1985) 'Learning strategies: the how of learning' in *Thinking and Learning Skills: Relating Instruction to Basic Research*, ed. J.W. Segal, S.F. Chipman and R. Glaser, vol.1, Hillsdale, NJ, Erlbaum.

Weinstein, C. E., Goetz, E.T., and Alexander, P.A. (1988) (eds) *Learning and Study Strategies*, San Diego, CA, Academic Press.
Weiss, H.M. (1990) 'Learning theory and industrial and organisational psychology', ch. 4 in *Handbook of Industrial and Organisational Psychology*, ed. M.D. Dunnette and L.M. Hough, 2nd edn, vol.1, Palo Alto, CA, Consulting Psychologists Press.
Williams, A.P.O. (1987) 'A client–consultant organisational learning model', *Personnel Review*, vol.16, no.4, 10–17.
Williams, A.P.O., Dobson, P. and Walters, M. (1993) *Changing Culture: New Organisational Approaches*, 2nd edn, Wimbledon, Institute of Personnel Management.
Wooten, K.C. and White, L.P. (1989) 'Toward a Theory of Change Role Efficacy', *Human Relations*, vol.42, no.8, 651–69.
Zitelli, J. and Tucker, M. (1991) 'Management Advisory Services', *Journal of Accountancy*, vol.139, no.3, 56–64.

Index